BEFORE AND AFTER THE TUTORIAL

Writing Centers
and Institutional Relationships

Research and Teaching in Rhetoric and Composition
Michael M. Williamson, series editor

BEFORE AND AFTER THE TUTORIAL

Writing Centers and Institutional Relationships

edited by

Nicholas Mauriello
University of North Alabama

William J. Macauley, Jr.
College of Wooster

Robert T. Koch, Jr.
University of North Alabama

HAMPTON PRESS, INC.
NEW YORK, NEW YORK

Library of Congress Cataloging-in-Publication Data

Mauriello, Nicholas.
  Before and after the tutorial : writing centers and institutional relationships / Nicholas Mauriello, William J. Macauley, Robert T. Koch.
     p. cm. -- (Research and teaching in rhetoric and composition)
  Includes bibliographical references and index.
  ISBN 978-1-57273-996-3 -- ISBN 978-1-57273-997-0 (paperbound)
  1. English language--Rhetoric--Study and teaching. 2. Writing centers. 3. Report writing--Study and teaching (Higher) 4. Resource programs (Education)--Management. 5. Tutors and tutoring. I. Macauley, William J. II. Koch, Robert T. III. Title.
  PE1404.M374 2011
  808'.042071'1--dc22
                                        2010051806

Hampton Press, Inc.
307 Seventh Avenue
New York, NY 10001

For
Dr. A. Priscilla Holland,
whose dedication to teaching, collaboration,
and institutional relationships continues to inspire

CONTENTS

FOREWORD

Leaping (Cautiously) Into the Future of Writing Centers

Muriel Harris

One of the great strengths of writing centers is our flexibility—our ability to leap into the unknown to see what is out there and to think about how we can expand our work in more directions to meet changing conditions and new needs. Flexibility is not only a strength when shaping a writing center's work, it is also a characteristic mirrored in the daily work of tutoring. Flexibility in the tutorial allows us similarly to change course when we find our conversation with the writer is not headed in productive directions and perceive a more fruitful or appropriate path to take. Thus, flexibility is a foundational principle that guides the collaborative interaction of our work. Tutors do not and should not plunge into a tutorial with an agenda of their own or a mental syllabus to follow. That denies the very collaboration of tutor and student to set an agenda before starting to talk, a quality that makes the interaction so effective. Clearly, the direction that the tutor and student go on, like the writing center itself, is open to switching directions. And so it is with services our writing centers offer: We are open to switching directions as well as exploring new ones.

But therein lies a challenge because, to continue this metaphor of traveling, we need to think through the implications of an old Ladino saying that echoes one used in recent auto commercials and social reform mottos: "Not all roads are straight." We can take that to mean not all roads are the same or are clearly marked, that we have to bend and curve a bit to stay on course, that we might not wind up where we thought we wanted to be, that there may not be a direct way to get there, or that there are destinations we hadn't planned on but are excellent places to wind up in (or maybe even all of the above). John W. Collis, author of *The Seven Fatal Management Sins* (1998), similarly invokes the metaphor of roads when planning the future of a company. He reminds executives that "there are curves and hills" and they need sharp vision to "implement or help others properly implement the plans" (p. 153). Collins quotes the Danish physicist and Nobel Laureate

Niels Bohr, who was known for his realistic assessments of the world: "It is very hard to predict, especially the future."

This uncertainty in forecasting the future is a perspective from which to consider what happens when writing centers reach out to build relationships. A plan or perceived need (or recognized one) starts that journey into the future. It takes courage, time, and a great deal of determination to make these new relationships work, especially as Collins had noted, because it involves interacting with others who will be part of implementing the plan. Our characteristic flexibility and collaboration, principles that define our modus operandi, will mean that plans are likely to shift, take new directions, and perhaps wind up as something not exactly envisioned from the start. But before we contemplate plans for building relationships beyond the writing center, we have to confront the question of "why?" Why add to our work? Why should we try to respond to newly perceived projects, challenges, or services? The most prosaic reason might be that, as we become more involved with other programs on our campus or in the community, we become more integrated into the foundation of our institution. We aren't going to be perceived as hanging out on some margin if our centers are built into structures and programs that are integral to the institution's structure. From a perspective of literacy enhancement as to why we seek new relationships, writing centers contribute to a culture of writing on campus, and we cannot turn away from that important goal by ignoring involvement that furthers this vital goal. Perhaps the most compelling reason for reaching out to build relationships is that our writing centers are ideally suited to become partners in literacy relationships, something we engage in every time a student walks in the door looking for help with writing—any writing for any course. And another reason to seek partnerships on campus is that we grow internally by what we learn and do as part of those relationships. We learn more about how writing accompanies learning in other fields; we stumble on new questions to research. Tutors who accompany Writing Across the Curriculum (WAC) courses learn about writing in other areas; writing center personnel who collaborate with library personnel learn how to assist with students' research processes; and writing centers that create websites, online tutoring opportunities, Facebook pages, Second Life sites, blogs, or Twitter accounts offer tutors opportunities to create and work within new environments that technology offers. In summary, the relationships we develop enrich us, our tutors, our writing centers, our campuses, and our communities in ways we are beginning to describe and document.

When we understand why we seek to grow along with our partners in these new relationships, we then have other questions to confront. How, for example, do we decide among the growing number and diversity of directions in which writing centers are moving? Consider some of the many ways that writing centers are reaching out, finding new paths, new technologies, new relationships, and new constituencies. We can build stronger connections to the larger world of rhetoric and composition through the research results we produce and the other scholarship that adds to a general understanding of how to assist writers to develop their skills. Such knowledge contributes directly to the whole field of composition's understanding of teaching writing. By training grad students for Writing Program Administration (WPA) work and training peer tutors who will be teaching at the secondary level, we contribute to the further development of the teaching of writing as well as prepare its future teachers. We work with admissions offices to enhance the institution's attraction to potential students and attract funding from development offices with our contributions to the institution's educational mission. (Think of all the named writing centers that continue to be created.) College-level writing centers are contributing to the community through outreach to high schools; high school writing centers are building strong constituencies with other teachers who include writing in their classes; writing centers are connecting to libraries—and collaborating with them—and to residence halls through satellite centers; and writing centers are providing resources for faculty by offering materials online, holding classroom workshops, assisting instructors as they develop their writing assignments, sending tutors to their classes, holding writing workshops for faculty in the writing center, and working to build a culture of writing on campus through these connections as well as offering poetry slams, open mic nights, and writing contests, and producing newsletters. We are joining with other faculty as we create faculty advisory boards to support and assist with our work. We are creating social networking sites for tutors and students in Second Life, Facebook, blogs, and Twitter. We are developing YouTube videos, podcasts, and other online tutoring environments in cyberspace and creating spaces for working with distance learners. We are establishing community writing centers and working with students engaged in service learning. We are melding with learning centers, working within larger centers for writing excellence, and supporting WAC movements on campus. We are adding assistance with other forms of communication, such as spoken communication and electronic communication, as well as reading help. We are reaching out to grow effective working relationships with comp teachers by integrating our work with that of these instructors who teach writing or include writing in their courses. We help them understand what a writing center does and what it offers their students.

Because there are so many doors we can open or are considering opening, we have to resist jumping on our horses and riding off in all directions. So, some cautionary advice can be helpful. It's important to keep in mind Stephen North's (1994) "Revisiting 'The Idea of a Writing Center' " because, in that article, he articulates how our idealistic visions of our work can mislead us into a false understanding of our work. North takes a critical look back at what he created with his "idea of a writing center" and predicts neg-

ative side effects of continued growth in directions that look appropriate. As
he notes:

> [B]ringing center and classroom, teaching and tutoring, into . . . [a]
> tighter orbit would surely generate as many new tensions as new oppor-
> tunities, and I foresee plenty of stormy politics and raised voices.
> (North, 1994, p. 16)

North also cautions us not spread ourselves too thin, not to add to our
workload so that it exceeds our resources or that it wears us out. Moreover,
he concludes, we cannot be the righter of all literacy wrongs on campus:

> I do not believe it is finally a good thing for a writing center to be seen
> as taking upon its shoulders the whole institution's (real or imagined)
> sins of illiteracy, either: to serve as conscience, savior, or sacrificial vic-
> tim. (p. 17)

Stretched too thin or in directions that are not appropriate to what we are
committed to poses an additional danger of losing our foundational principles of collaboration or active learning or interaction with students one to
one. (Consider the very real concern that asynchronous tutoring might look
a lot like offering teacher comments, especially when the communication
comes to a halt after the tutor returns a paper she has commented on, never
to hear from that writer again.) And as many of us have already found, when
our workload increases and increases, new responsibilities are folded into
our job description, usually at a time when additional resources are difficult
to come by. Moreover, we often have to expend additional time and energy
to educate administrators as to where and how we are expanding and why
we need to go there. We have to decide between that route of obtaining necessary resources first or starting out on our own, building services, and then
seeking administrative support when we can show success. Without sufficient investigation, we may also inadvertently be planning to engage in projects that may be considered possible invasions of the academic terrain of
others (turf battles we didn't realize were turfs already staked out by others). For example, might offering workshops for faculty about adding writing to classes be viewed as stepping into what a WPA or WAC director consider their responsibility? And other efforts misfire because there really isn't
a need yet. Some services we are somewhat hesitant to build turn out to meet
major needs that no one realized were absent. But despite the reality of
uncertain outcomes and overloads and lack of resources and potential political skirmishes, expansion can create strong relationships with colleagues
outside our center, invigorate a center (and us), open up new areas of
research, and model writing and responding strategies that move composition teaching along.

So we come back to the question of where and how we decide which relationships to build with others on our campus, given the variety of ways that new relationships are being built by writing centers, given the current lack of additional resources (if needed), and given the danger of moving into inappropriate or unproductive areas. Because writing centers respond to local needs and are shaped by local contexts, there aren't models for everyone to follow. Maybe models will be developed. Or maybe not. Maybe we will continue to share descriptions of our programs and research as suggestions for each other to consider. Here we run into the problem of where each of us leans on the spectrum of deciding whether writing centers are all too locally constructed to be able to theorize about at a more general level of models or whether we incline toward the opposite view that writing centers all share larger theoretical guiding principles such as collaboration and student-centered learning. For those of us who tend toward the end of the continuum that sees all writing centers as structured by local settings, this book has much to offer in the way of specific suggestions for outreach and relationship creation that we can think about, modify to suit local contexts, and engage in our own further expansion. The chapters outline programs and note steps that work, that were defeated for various purposes, and that have to have certain institutional conditions present in order to even be considered. For those of us who agree that larger and more universal theories of the writing center have been, can be, and are being constructed, we can see in the chapters of this book the common principle of looking outward and building relationships as enactment of collaboration. From this perspective, building relationships is a contribution to making writing centers central to an institution's commitment to developing writers' abilities to compose effectively, thus banishing the notion of marginality. Webs of connections across campus, out into communities, and into cyberspace ensure our place in academic instruction. In other words, this collection has something to offer every reader who works in and thinks about writing centers. Moreover, in writing these chapters, the authors have engaged in collaboration with other writing center people and with their academic communities, encouraging us by the very successes these authors have had to continue to expand, develop, build, and reach into spaces and relationships yet to be developed.

REFERENCES

Collis, J. (1998). *The seven fatal management sins: Understanding and avoiding managerial malpractice.* Boca Raton, FL: St. Lucie Press.

North, S. M. (1994). Revisiting "The Idea of a Writing Center." *Writing Center Journal, 15*(1), 7–19.

ACKNOWLEDGMENTS

This book is informed, in large part, by our beliefs, principles, and experiences as writing center directors and administrators. It is therefore fitting to thank those members of both the University of North Alabama (UNA) and College of Wooster communities who have contributed to our centers' success. First, we would like to thank UNA President William G. Cale, Jr., and College of Wooster President Grant Cornwell for bringing to their respective campuses the idea that leadership is about opening doors; that idea permeates this collection. In addition, we would like to thank our colleagues in our respective departments, our writing consultants, our students, and all the contributors to this collection.

This book is informed, in large part, by our beliefs, principles, and experiences as writing center directors and administrators. It is therefore fitting to thank those members of both the University of North Alabama (UNA) and College of Wooster communities who have contributed to our centers' success. First, we would like to thank UNA President William G. Cale, Jr., and College of Wooster President Grant Cornwell for bringing to their respective campuses the idea that leadership is about opening doors; that idea permeates this collection. In addition, we would like to thank our colleagues in our respective departments, our writing consultants, our students, and all the contributors to this collection.

Individually, the editors have many people to thank. Nick would like to thank Mrs. Laura M. Harrison, whose generous support of the Laura M. Harrison Distinguished Professorship of English at UNA allowed him the time to work on this collection. He would also like to thank our undergraduate student interns from UNA's program in Professional Writing, Sandy L. Morris and Jillian Tomberlin, who worked on this project. Bill would like to thank his wife, Debi, for her patience, encouragement, and support . . . especially her patience. Rob would like to thank retired Assistant Vice President for Academic Support Services, A. Priscilla Holland, for her unwavering support. He would also like to thank his partner, Jonathan Simms, who demonstrates endless patience and always listens.

In closing, we would like to thank Series Editor Michael M. Williamson, copy editor Heather Jefferson, our reviewers, Publisher Barbara Bernstein, and her staff at Hampton Press for their support.

INTRODUCTION

THE LOCAL AS A MEANS RATHER THAN AN END: WRITING CENTERS AND INSTITUTIONAL RELATIONSHIPS

Nicholas Mauriello
William J. Macauley, Jr.
Robert T. Koch, Jr.

> [T]o think well as individuals we must learn to think well collectively—that is, we must learn to converse well. The first steps to learning better, therefore, are learning to converse better and learning to establish and maintain the sorts of social context, the sorts of community life, that foster the sorts of conversation members of the community value.
>
> —Kenneth Bruffee (1984, p. 640)

What are writing centers responsible for? And who are they responsible to? These are seemingly simple questions but questions whose answers vary from institution to institution, highlighting the local nature of the center itself. As Muriel Harris (2007) acknowledges, writing center work is "so complex and varied—and individualized—that *we* have yet been able to come up with sound bytes that illuminate what *we* do" (p. 75; italics added). As writing center personnel, we may interpret this lack of a sound byte as a positive aspect of our work, one that keeps us connected to the campus at large. Yet for many others on campus—faculty, students, staff, and administrators—there *is* often a sound byte associated with writing centers: They tutor! And this is often expanded to include *for the English department*, clearly showing us that those around us, those most responsible for our sustainability, believe *they* have an accurate answer to at least one of our opening questions.

This apparent disconnect in audience and purpose may be rooted in the nature of the university itself, where the term *local* is often defined as disciplinary. Each department carves out its territory, digs a moat, and displays its coat of arms. Bill Readings (1996) underscores this isolationist mentality when he states, "In the University, thought goes on alongside other thoughts, we think besides each other. But do we think together? (p. 191). For writing center directors, Readings' question might elicit an initial emphatic, *Of course WE do!* But are our tutorials, the core of our institutional identity, nothing more than second-hand reactions to disciplinary demands? Does the fact that we tutor students in a variety of disciplines make us collaborators with those disciplines or passive responders? How do we, as Bruffee (1984) demands, learn to "converse better" and "establish and maintain the sorts of social context, the sorts of community life, that foster the sorts of conversation" needed to create meaningful institutional relationships?

Michele Eodice (2003) had it right that we have to think about what we can export to other parts of the campus community. But she may have underestimated where we need to go, what we need to do, and what it will take to do it. It is not solely collaboration that we must export; it is the same practices and mentalities that we have been developing within our centers for years, particularly those interpersonal skills that make our tutorials successful. By exporting our existing strengths to the campus at large, we can then start to build the types of campus collaborations that have a chance to change disciplinary boundaries.

Take, for example, where a successful tutorial begins and what defines that success. We meet students where they are. We ask questions about what they are working to accomplish, what their goals are, and what their concerns might be. These same local questions are the exact ones that we must ask our potential collaborators from across the university if, as Bruffee (1984) writes, we wish to "think well collectively." We simply cannot be a resource for them if we never make ourselves available to their needs and concerns.

In a successful tutorial, we proceed by balancing what we have to offer with what students want by working between our interests and theirs. We cannot work from our own perspective—that is not tutoring but directing, and that is not what we do. In order for us to work with campus constituents effectively, we must never direct, and we must make sure that our practices encourage and enable our collaborators to play an even more important role: an empowered participant in the development of our contributing to their work.

In a successful tutorial, we end our session by asking our students where they plan to go next and how we can be a part of that future work. These are the same questions that we must ask in our ongoing work with our campus collaborators. When we do this, we move from exporting our rigid expertise to experiencing a more fluid evolution. This invitation to institutional relationships encourages our potential collaborators to engage with us, and in doing so our writing centers can become something new by learning to think together.

There is, of course, always risk in the unknown and the fear associated with change. Many writing center directors will ask whether there is a true need for institutional collaboration and whether there is time in the work day to engage in such relationships. These are valid questions, but fear and resistance to change leads back to "the isolation within which writing centers too frequently find themselves" and a self-imposed marginalization (Macauley & Mauriello, 2007, p. xvi).

So, it is in the spirit of learning to think together that we assembled this edited collection. Many of our authors are learning as they go, finding both the high and low points of institutional collaboration. Our hope is that you will consider their journeys and possibly be encouraged to take the first steps of your own journey.

The chapters of this book are not organized into specific themes, although some lend themselves to pairings because of topical or argumentative similarities. Our decision to avoid deep thematic ties and precisely drawn categories is both practical and ideological. The differences among these chapters allow them to resist such thematic unity; however, they are all united in their efforts to expand writing centers beyond their long-recognized borders. More plainly put, they all seek to build and sustain local relationships, reaching into every corner of the university and even into the local community in order to find them.

In "Horizontal Structures for Learning," Jane Nelson and Margaret Garner (Chapter 1) argue that relationship building and interconnectedness across disciplines is critical to writing center health. The social capital created through one-on-one faculty–tutor relationships and teaching and writing workshops at the University of Wyoming helps resituate the center as a major player in the undergraduate curriculum, rather than as a role player or a peripheral office in relation to the overall effort. Most important, they warn readers that the mission of the institution and the voices of other participants are complex and essential. Hence, even as the writing center advocates interdisciplinary and cross-disciplinary collaboration, it is essential to be mindful of others' voices. Sue Doe (Chapter 2) also attends to the voices of her peers in "Toward a Visible Alliance Between Writing Centers and Contingent Faculty: A Social Materialist Approach." Although both share marginalized status, she recognizes that the contingent faculty member's place on campus is perhaps more tenuous because he or she lacks the stability of location that writing centers enjoy. However, as collaborative partners, writing centers and contingent faculty can draw attention to the labor and teaching needs of contingent members of the university community. Meanwhile, Lisa Whalen (Chapter 3) discusses her transition "From Reactive to Proactive: Lessons of a First-Year Writing Center Director." This chapter shares two narratives of faculty–director relationships: one productive, one not so productive. These experiences led Whalen to a set of suggestions that are useful not only for any new or inexperienced writing center director but also as reminders for those of us established in the field.

Ann N. Amicucci (Chapter 4) continues the exploration of relationships with her chapter, "Writing Across the Web: Connecting the Writing Center to Nursing Distance Learners." Working to address a specific departmental need can lead a writing center beyond the tutorial, into internet tutorials, workshops, lesson designs, and online resources. However, academic departments are not the only places for writing center relationship building, as "Creating Alliances Across Campus: Exploring Identities and Institutional Relationships" demonstrates. The authors, Maggie Herb and Virginia Perdue (Chapter 5), recognize the significance of other university offices in the professional development of tutors at Indiana University of Pennsylvania. In opening dialogue with both disability services and SafeZone, they encourage dialogue, some of which is surprising and unanticipated, concerning the identities and concerns not only of writing center clients but of the tutors themselves. Yet although these authors discuss bringing specialists from other departments into the center, Sue Mendelsohn takes the center into the university. "If You Build It, They Might Come: Constructing Writing Center Satellites" provides a valuable portrait of the complexities created by that activity, noting that department values, beliefs, location, and other factors are critical to the success of a writing center satellite. Through stories of success, failure, and transformation, Sue Mendelsohn (Chapter 6) provides readers with valuable insight into the complexities of relationship building among faculty, students, and writing center staff. In the end, she recognizes a principle that many directors may miss: There are positives in failure and negatives in success.

Although residence halls exist on a majority of campuses, the mutual benefits of linking writing centers with living-learning communities remains relatively unexplored. In "Writing Centers and Living-Learning Communities," Nicole Kraemer Munday (Chapter 7) provides one such exploration, arguing that the common tenets of these residence hall communities and writing center theory and pedagogy make them natural allies. Among the benefits, she argues, are the possibilities of situating a tutor where the action of writing is happening and allowing compositionists ground for further insight into writing processes. One part of the university student body, the English as a Second Language (ESL) population, is much more diverse than many faculty members realize. "Working to Identify and

Meet the Instructional Needs of a Diverse ESL Student Population" by Judy Dyer and Christine Modey (Chapter 8) chronicles the efforts of the University of Michigan to meet not only the demands of traditional ESL students, but of ESL 1.5 students, who are both American citizens and bilingual or non-native speakers. For these authors, the conversation should go well beyond the tutorial, both across the faculty and into the administration, in order to provide the best possible support for these populations. Following their work, a pair of contributors examines the idea of Centers for Writing Excellence. First, Emily Isaacs (Chapter 9), in "The Emergence of Centers for Writing Excellence," makes a strong argument for the transformation of the university writing center into a Center for Writing Excellence as a means of resisting marginalization and shaping a positive message about writing in the university community. Isaacs addresses a range of issues that any writing center administrator would need to consider, including naming, funding, staffing, and programming, and provides a comparative look at some of these centers. "Centers for Writing Excellence and the Construction of Civic Relationships," in contrast, allows Robert T. Koch, Jr. (Chapter 10) to explore one specific aspect of his center—community relationships with both the public library and the local high school. Free creative writing workshops and support for the high school writing center create linkages that engender good will between the institutions and strengthen the quality of student entering the university from the local community.

For Laura Bowles and Joanna Castner-Post (Chapter 11), concurrent enrollment, which provides college credit for high school courses, is fertile ground for building writing center relationships. In "Writing Centers as Nexus of Transformation: Strengthening Education and Institutional Relationships through Concurrent Enrollment Partnerships," these authors argue that, by providing professional development for high school faculty participating in the program, the writing center has a golden opportunity to affect the way high schools approach writing and writing instruction. In addition to strengthening both the high school and university populations, this work includes high school teachers in the discourse of the composition and university communities, improving the overall educational climate. As prior contributors reach into the high schools, Pamela B. Childers (Chapter 12), in "Getting Beyond Mediocrity: The Secondary School Writing Center as Change Agent," examines how the work already taking place can affect multiple constituents, including students, teachers, and parents. "Making Friends With Web 2.0: Writing Centers and Social Networking Sites" by Jackie Grutsch McKinney (Chapter 13) explores the relationships that our tutors are already building through social networking sites such as Facebook. Rather than eliminate or limit such potential resources, she argues that writing centers may wish to learn more about them—that there may be important room for them in the development of a tutor's and a writing center's identity. The development of identity not only happens among tutors, students, and writing centers but at the university level as well.

In "Applying Accreditation Standards to Help Define a Writing Center's Programming and Its On-Campus Relationships," Alan Reinhardt and Crystal Bickford (Chapter 14) discuss the myriad relationships that one writing center director has nurtured and navigated in order to play a role in the college's reaccreditation. Their argument is an important one, in that when writing centers begin to take active roles in reaccreditation and agree to participate in the transformation often created through that process, they can move out of the margin and into a more centralized role in life and livelihood of the university community. Then Kelly L. Latchaw (Chapter 15) looks at writing centers from the perspective of a faculty member whose relationships with writing centers has been varied, sometimes tenuous, and other times strong. In "Insider, Outsider: Reflections on Writing Centers From a Faculty Advocate," she recognizes that no faculty–writing center relationship is perfect, and although they all have their benefits, they also have their dangers. To conclude this exploration of writing center relationships, Michael A. Pemberton takes us "Revisiting 'Tales Too Terrible to Tell': A Survey of Graduate Coursework in Writing Program and Writing Center Administration." Pemberton surveys the field of Composition to examine the type of WPA and WCA training in place today to see whether much has changed. Although his findings suggest that there is room for improvement, he notes that increasing recognition of institutional relationships as significant factors in the success of a WPA or WCA is one positive trend that will help the field overall.

REFERENCES

Bruffee, K. A. (1984). Collaborative learning and the "conversation of mankind." *College English*, *46*, 635–652.

Eodice, M. (2003). Breathing lessons, or collaboration is. In M. A. Pemberton & J. A. Kinkead (Eds.), *The center will hold: Critical perspectives on writing center scholarship* (pp. 114–129). Logan: Utah State University Press.

Harris, M. (2007). Writing ourselves into writing instruction: Beyond sound bytes, tours, reports, orientations and brochures. In W. J. Macauley & N. Mauriello (Eds.), *Marginal words, marginal work? Tutoring the academy in the work of writing centers* (pp. 75–84). Cresskill, NJ: Hampton Press.

Macauley, W. J., & Mauriello, N. (2007). *Marginal words, marginal work? Tutoring the academy in the work of writing centers. Research and teaching in rhetoric and composition.* Cresskill, NJ: Hampton Press.

Readings, B. (1996). *The university in ruins.* Cambridge, MA: Harvard University Press.

chapter 1

HORIZONTAL STRUCTURES FOR LEARNING

Jane Nelson

Margaret Garner

In his 2006 assessment of higher education titled *Our Underachieving Colleges: A Candid Look at How Much Students Learn and Why They Should Be Learning More*, former Harvard President Derek Bok identifies one of the trends causing the overall lackluster performance of college faculties in their primary mission of preparing undergraduate students. An explosion of knowledge and discovery in the last few decades has resulted in increasing specializations that make their way into the undergraduate curriculum through more majors, more departments, and increasing numbers of specialized courses required to complete a concentration. At the same time colleges and universities are requiring increasing specializations, they are also wanting students to acquire competency in a set of educational goals the lexicon for which grows larger by the year: writing, oral communication, teamwork and collaboration, quantitative reasoning, information literacy, critical thinking, problem solving, appreciation for American and global diversity, internationalization, moral reasoning, civic virtues, and more. In his review of studies on student learning, Bok notes the disturbing evidence that the creation of concentrations that take longer to complete provides little cognitive gain for students and may even cause students to decline in writing ability, critical thinking, public speaking, civic engagement, and other important aims of undergraduate education (p. 141).

The solution to this problem is not likely to be a renewed commitment to general education. As Bok points out, students give their highest ratings to courses in their majors. Two book-length studies of undergraduate education from the students' perspective verify the importance of the major for learning skills as well as knowledge. Richard Light (2001), Bok's colleague at Harvard, reveals in *Making the Most of College: Students Speak Their Minds* that Harvard students believe they learned most about writing during their junior and senior years when they took writing- and research-intensive courses in substantive disciplines (p. 59). In their recent study of undergraduates at the University of Washington entitled *Inside the Undergraduate Experience*, Beyer, Gillmore, and Fisher (2007) discovered the same value of disciplinary focus not only for writing but also for several of the skills they examined, especially critical thinking and problem solving, quantitative reasoning, and understanding and appreciating diversity. The strong message that students give about the value of learning in the majors mimics what the faculty themselves believe: the disciplines contain entry into discovery, knowledge making, and educational value.

The authors of all three of these studies conclude that current structures in higher education impede the institution's ability to fulfill its promises about undergraduate education, and they suggest that a way to stimulate change, short of major reform, is the creation of some alternative structures. Reaching the same conclusion in his analysis of higher education, William G. Tierney (1999) drafts some language and ideas for creating alternative structures. In *Building the Responsive Campus: Creating High Performance Colleges and Universities*, Tierney says, "I am advocating an intense form of working relationships that can develop organizational excitement and camaraderie and ultimately produce demonstrable goals" (p. 73). He wants to reward risk taking: "An intellectual organization, a learning community, must comprise a collection of risk-takers who study, teach, and work in ways that are experimental, innovative, and unique" (p. 81). In contrast to the vertical silos or walled villages that characterize disciplinary and departmental structures, Tierney advocates for "soft projects" (pp. 36–47), temporary structures that gather people—faculty, administrators, and sometimes staff—in the short term to accomplish goals with lasting value, goals that enhance student learning and fulfill university-level goals. In his later work, *Trust and the Public Good: Examining the Culture Conditions of Academic Work*, Tierney (2006) adapts the concept of social capital in his analysis of informal and formal faculty networks. To meet the changing obligations that higher education institutions face, Tierney argues that they need to be both better organized and differently organized. They need to create ways for broad and deep faculty engagement in order "to generate capital and overcome the concerns, fears, or objections of those who are reluctant to participate" (p. 87).

The creation of horizontal structures within universities is a way to provide this cross-campus and deep faculty engagement. By a horizontal structure, we are referring to a network that allows broader faculty engagement than is possible through the narrow confines of departments and programs within departments. This structure goes across departments and colleges, incorporating faculty and administrators in fluid, collaborative groups whose members desire to develop the broader student learning outcomes that transcend department boundaries.

In a set of articles on "Faculty Leadership and Institutional Change" in the fall 2007 issue of *Liberal Education*, the authors converge on recommending this concept of horizontal structures to build social capital and promote the kind of broad faculty engagement that Tierney finds essential to fulfill the public good of higher education. Among his recommendations, for example, Jerry Gaff (2007) suggests that institutions promote "academic leadership for important programs that transcend departments" (p. 9), such as critical thinking, quantitative reasoning, and writing. Keeling, Underhile, and Wall (2007) promote the concept even more strongly. They recommend that institutions intentionally create abundant horizontal structures to complement the vertical structures of colleges, schools, divisions, disciplines, and departments.

> The ability to do good work within one's discipline or program area must include both competence in a specific area of knowledge or function and commitment to horizontally defined and broadly held student outcomes. . . . The process of developing commonly held student learning outcomes requires a strong centripetal force along horizontal lines. (p. 30)

Like Tierney, these authors suggest that restructuring along horizontal lines is an ethical responsibility.

Writing centers have always lived comfortably in the world of alternate, horizontal structures. In fact, they offer a model to those who are looking for examples to emulate. In the past 30 years, writing centers have grown exponentially and demonstrated beyond a doubt their value to student learning. Most writing centers no longer have to argue for their worth and existence. Those currently threatened are facing the tight financial situation in higher education rather than skepticism about their worth. Instead of justifying their position or their discipline, writing center professionals engage now in two broad discussions about their institutional roles: strategies for building social capital and debates about their administrative and geographic homes. Although many writing centers now enjoy institutional stability and longevity, they often report about challenging physical spaces, and labor problems remain endemic, including minimal compensation and low academic status. These issues of social capital remain annoyingly serious features for writing center administrators. In terms of intellectual debate, lively discussions revolve around questions of administrative location. With some exceptions, four possibilities exist for writing center homes: English departments, academic success or learning centers, teaching and learning centers, and stand-alone units that report directly to academic affairs. We are proponents of the latter two possibilities because they incorporate horizontal rather than vertical structures. The arguments of the authors we have cited above, all of whom have considerable expertise in dissecting the nature of higher education, substantiate the value of horizontal structures. Our experiences with directing a writing center under the auspices of a horizontal organization corroborate their claims. This structure has allowed the University of Wyoming Writing Center to establish meaningful and productive relationships with people across campus.

THE UNIVERSITY OF WYOMING WRITING CENTER'S MOVE TO A HORIZONTAL STRUCTURE

From its conception, the University of Wyoming Writing Center has had a cooperative mode of operation: those consulting in the Writing Center see writing clients as designers of ideas and text, and the consultants regard themselves as contributors to this process. This mindset was present when the center began in the 1970s in the office of Tilly Warnock, a writing teacher in the Department of English who wanted to create a place for students to come for assistance in writing. She then elicited graduate students to help with the endeavor. Not long after, a center was truly established in a seminar room in the English department building, and faculty became the consultants, working in the Writing Center as a way to complete their required teaching loads. A mixture of consultants from tenured professors to part-time lecturers provided the services.

In the mid-1980s, when John Warnock was directing the center, the Wyoming legislature funded a five-year basic writing project for the university. Funding supported a placement system that consisted of scoring timed writing samples written during summer orientation sessions. Funding also allowed the Department of English to hire through national searches several basic-writing specialists who received three- to five-year temporary appointments. Because the Writing Center was conceptualized as a central support service for the basic writing program, these experts received teaching appointments in the Writing Center as well as in the classroom. The effect on the Writing Center was profound. During staff meetings and project sessions, it became a center for theorizing and debate about rhetoric and composition, while it continued to serve its primary mission of assisting student writers during open hours. After the five-year funding cycle, the basic writing program was discontinued, but the Department of English continued its commitment to staff the Writing Center with teachers of writing. The Writing Center has enjoyed the stability of this commitment ever since.

When the Warnocks directed the University of Wyoming Writing Center during the 1970s and 1980s, it reflected their view that writing centers should keep a critical distance from the institutions that house them. In their seminal work on writing center theory, "Liberatory Writing Centers: Restoring Authority to Writers" (1984), they advocate for revised power relationships between writing teachers and students, and they argue that their revisionary view borders on the revolutionary. They entitle the concluding section to their piece "The Writing Center as 'Outsider.' " They explain, "We are suggesting that the liberatory center remain on the fringes of the academic community, in universities or public schools, in order to maintain critical consciousness" (p. 22). Their argument identifies the problems with vertical structures that position power at the top, but their defense of existing at or migrating to the fringes dodges the responsibility of transforming the institution. A writing center on the borders does not help to position student learning at the center of an institution's mission. Although the Warnocks try to establish the writing center director as an authority figure, Stephen Ferruci (2001) shows that positioning the director in opposition to the establishment causes directors to have unequal power relationships with their administrative and faculty peers. At the University of Wyoming (UW), university-level developments showed a way to define a more predominant place for the Writing Center without creating yet another vertical structure.

In the late 1980s and early 1990s, three major institutional developments precipitated UW's Writing Center both out of the English department as its administrative home and into the university's core. Interestingly, before she and John Warnock left UW for the University of Arizona, Tilly Warnock was involved in one of these developments, and thus she helped to create the groundwork for some powerful horizontal structures at the center of the university designed to support learning. The Writing Center may continue to have revisionary features, but after nearly 20 years of existing at the institutional core, it cannot now be identified as an outside operation. It has strong institutional standing, and it represents a notable alternative to other support services that remain in the vertical structures of the university.

The development of a general education program formally launched in 1991 as the University Studies Program (USP) has constituted a significant curricular change for UW and is one of the developments that moved the Writing Center into the university's core. UW is a land-grant institution with a strong commitment to professional education as well as to the liberal arts. Six of the seven colleges at UW educate professionals in the fields of agriculture, business, education, engineering, health sciences, and law. Prior to 1991, only the College of Arts and Sciences (the seventh and largest college) required a common set of requirements in such areas as history, science, social science, languages, humanities, and fine arts. The decision to require a common core for all undergraduate students at the university has required the professional colleges to institute major curricular changes in their undergraduate programs and to accept unfamiliar teaching roles. In the menu-style system that provides the process for certifying general education courses, faculty agree that as long as a course meets the criteria, it can be taught in any department in any college. A science course or even a humanities course, for instance, can be taught in the College of Agriculture; a fine arts course can be taught in the College of Engineering.

The same holds true for the three writing courses required in the new program. Prior to the USP, students were required to take a two-semester sequence of first-year writing. With the USP, students take three writing courses distributed across their undergraduate career from the first-year composition class to a senior-level class focused on professional writing in the disciplines. Tilly Warnock, a member of the general education planning committee, lobbied successfully for this writing-across-the-curriculum (WAC) structure, and she also successfully lobbied for conceptualizing the Writing Center as the central support system for the expanded university writing requirements. The university committed to a half-time administrative appointment for the Writing Center director, which was defined as both WAC coordination as well as Writing Center administration. The other half of the appointment depends on who holds the director's position. The current director, for instance, holds teaching and professional development responsibilities in the Department of English. The Writing Center director became an ad hoc member of the University Studies Committee charged with reviewing all course proposals, and duties included helping faculty from across the disciplines to create writing-intensive courses, incorporate writing pedagogies, and develop evaluation systems. The Writing Center thus became two kinds of a horizontally structured center: students (and a few staff and faculty) across the disciplines came for assistance with their writing at all levels, and faculty across the disciplines consulted with the director and staff on the teaching of writing.

As the USP was being launched, the university also received some state trust fund monies to create the first computer-writing classroom. The English department chair, who was charged with this task, asked the newly appointed Writing Center director to take it on. After a year-long soft-money project involving collaboration with the Information Technology division, the university space manager, instructional technologies specialists, and a computer science graduate student, a computer-writing classroom was successfully created. The project required that the Writing Center move out of its English department space to new space in the Business Building in order for the center to manage the classroom. Relocating away from the English department constituted the visible signal to the university that writing instruction and support had indeed become a horizontal function.

The same trust fund grant that helped to create the computer-writing classroom also included monies for creating a center for teaching excellence, an initiative that had been identified by the faculty as a high-priority project during one of the periodic university review cycles. Because the WAC component of the Writing Center's new mission included significant faculty development, academic affairs decided to locate the 50% administrative component of the director's position in this center. When physical space opened up in the university library, the Writing Center relocated once again into remodeled quarters co-located with the teaching center. Thus, at nearly the same time, two significantly new horizontal structures were created by the university, and the administrative merging of the two turned out to be an inspired decision. As a division in what is now called the Ellbogen Center for Teaching and Learning (ECTL), the Writing Center has built over the last 19 years considerable social capital around the teaching and practice of writing. The fusion of a writing center with a teaching and learning center has resulted in a powerful horizontal force for learning at the university.

STRENGTHS OF A HORIZONTAL STRUCTURE FOR STAKEHOLDERS

Four groups of writing center stakeholders benefit from the kind of social capital they gain by working in and with our horizontally structured writing center: faculty, Writing Center staff members, students, and the ECTL. In identifying and cataloging the benefits, we have been impressed by their depth and variety, and we find these benefits to be a major reason to advocate for more horizontal structures within programs, departments, and colleges at the university.

Faculty

Although an important goal of the Writing Center is helping students with writing, its outside-of-tutoring activities are equally important and perhaps more important in regards to the faculty's vision of the Writing Center's place on campus. Three kinds of programs are available to faculty and graduate students to assist them in teaching writing. Those who use these programs regard the Writing Center and the ECTL as partners in the hard work of helping students to progress as writers. The programs engender collaborative relationships that are possible because of the horizontal structure of the Writing Center.

One program involves a direct partnership between a faculty member and a staff member in the Writing Center. Upon request and with advance notice, the Writing Center will develop specific workshops conducted in faculty members' classes. Usually, the classroom teacher collaborates with the Writing Center consultant in both the planning and execution of these workshops.

A workshop for a marketing class is a recent example. The Writing Center director talked with the professor before the workshop about his assignment and expectations. The professor had given students several topics from which to pick. For example, one was an analysis of whether Wal-Mart was helpful or hurtful to other businesses. The professor asked the students to look at both sides of the topic but did not make clear that he wished them to argue for one side. With the help of the Writing Center director, the professor clarified his instructions. He and the director also talked about how he expected the students to structure the analysis, and he then included this information in the assignment as well. The professor fully appreciated the changes that were negotiated, and part of the reason the negotiations went smoothly was that the professor and the director were on the same level and had the same desire: a clear assignment that would lead to the professor's expectations.

After students wrote their first drafts, the Writing Center director then gave a revision workshop in the classroom with the professor participating. In this workshop, the director led students through revision for content and organization. After this revision session, students talked about their papers in peer groups. Then the director, the professor, and the students discussed questions about the assignment, especially about the construction of an argument. The professor was involved in all parts of the workshop, especially the question time. Without him there and contributing, the workshop would have been less useful. It is an example of collaboration at its best. In the weeks after the workshop, some of the students had Writing Center consultations to help them further with the revisions.

After workshops like these, faculty often remark on the advantage of observing effective techniques for dealing with various aspects of writing and the writing process. The workshops create a mutually beneficial situation, allowing both faculty in other disciplines and Writing Center consultants to learn from each other. In the prior example, the professor learned how to write a more effective assignment that led to his expectations and how to help students with revision. He also learned the roadblocks that students face in such an assignment and the questions they have. The director learned more about the expectations in marketing papers and the learning outcomes that this professor desired. The main result from this and other collaborative workshops is greater learning for the students.

A second program is designed for faculty and graduate students across the disciplines to learn from each other as they develop ways of teaching and evaluating writing. The Writing Center and the ECTL sponsor numerous workshops on the teaching of writing that include one- to two-hour brown bag lunch meetings, two- to five-day workshops, and semester-long seminars. Every year, in its specialized series for graduate students and for new faculty and lecturers, the ECTL devotes at least one session and usually more to issues of writing in the classroom. Topics on teaching writing have proven to be very popular for the "Planning for Teaching" workshops that occur in summers and in January prior to the second semester. Because the ECTL has a budget for sponsoring numerous teaching programs, it is able to provide substantial materials for its workshops, all of which are free to faculty and graduate students. Over the last 17 years, it has distributed thousands of books on a variety of teaching topics. By far, the most popular book has been John Bean's (1996) *Engaging Ideas: The Professor's Guide to Integrating Writing, Critical Thinking, and Active Learning in the Classroom*. We estimate that we have provided this book to well over 500 faculty over the last decade. After faculty work their way through this book in concert with other faculty in disciplines far removed from their own, they often make substantial changes in their syllabi, borrowing the good ideas from their fellow faculty and then checking in from time to time in following semesters for support and verification. When they design writing-intensive courses as a result of these kinds of workshops, they are not always convinced that students become vastly improved writers, but they are convinced that students become much more engaged with the course content and with the instructor. The Writing Center's involvement in the prior programs is possible because it is part of the ECTL, a center that serves the entire university, and not part of a vertical structure. If it were part of a department or program on campus, this level of involvement would not be possible.

The third program involves the scholarship of teaching and learning, which requires major commitment and thus has the fewest numbers of participants. Because we are a research university, this kind of program is intended to serve equally well the research and teaching responsibilities of faculty. Once again, the programs vary from serving a single faculty member to involving groups of interdisciplinary faculty. We give two examples to show the possibility for high-end results when horizontal structures support teaching and learning:

- A pharmacy professor teaching a writing-intensive public health class for the PharmD program experienced writing-teacher fatigue: he became convinced that his 70 students not only failed to improve but even might have lost writing ability under his instruction. In collaboration with the Writing Center director and staff, he designed a research project that included statistical analysis of error, double-blind rubric scoring of two sets of papers, and analysis of responses on a writing apprehension index (Ranelli & Nelson, 1998). Not only did the project convince him that his students improved in writing with his instruction, but he also learned some new teaching strategies and forged research relationships with other Writing Center staff.

- A semester-long seminar featuring a study of Bean's book for some 20 College of Agriculture faculty in several disciplines inspired this group to name themselves the WAGs, an acronym for Writing in Agriculture Guild. Over the course of two years, they successfully wrote a federal grant to support the sponsorship of a national conference on writing and critical thinking for agriculture faculty. Back at home at UW, a group of WAG faculty from two departments instituted curriculum mapping and conducted qualitative research with their students in department-wide assessment projects that earned them the NACTA 2004 E.B. Knight Journal Award for their report on the results (Williams et al., 2003).

Writing Center Staff

In a collaborative relationship that is endorsed by the College of Arts and Sciences, the English department assigns five to seven of its faculty to serve as staff members for the Writing Center every semester. An assignment in the Writing Center is considered to be equivalent to teaching a course and counts toward the semester's teaching load. This staffing system generally has positive outcomes. Many staff members find that the one-on-one consulting in the Writing Center, so different from classroom teaching, is their most fulfilling and most successful teaching experience. They also value the many faculty relationships that they develop across the disciplines and the opportunity to be involved with writing on a university-wide level in addition to the narrower department level. The Department of English benefits from being able to enhance the faculty's teaching load with this opportunity. The Writing Center benefits from having very effective staff members who can conduct workshops and help faculty as well as consult with students. One of the major benefits of this arrangement for student writers and faculty program participants is that the staff consists of people who teach writing at various levels, care about this teaching, and want to help people with writing. This collaboration, made possible by the horizontal administrative structure, thus benefits all involved.

In addition to the Department of English staff members, three or four undergraduate interns consult in the Writing Center each academic year. The English department provides funding for one intern, and the Honors Program funds two or three who may or may not be English majors. These interns bring an important undergraduate perspective to the center's staff. In turn, the interns receive background in the writing and learning expectations of disciplines other than their own. Although the undergraduate interns typically do not work with graduate student or faculty writing projects, they often gain trust and respect from those who seem far more advanced. Writing Center promotional materials include a photograph of an undergraduate intern in psychology working with a PhD student in statistics. The intern helped not only with the dissertation but also with application materials for a faculty position. When the pharmacy professor completed the study mentioned in the previous section, he used a student intern majoring in English and secondary education to create and then pilot an amended rubric for his revised graduate-level course. The placement of the Writing Center in a university-wide structure allows these interdisciplinary and cross-level interactions to occur.

As the faculty learn from the Writing Center staff during workshops and projects, so, too, do the Writing Center staff and director learn from other faculty members. When the Writing Center staff work with faculty across campus, a level playing field is possible because all are on the same teaching-writing turf, all striving to help students become effective writers. Writing Center staff members may have more experience in rhetoric, and they may know more about the teaching of writing. But the learning goals are the same across disciplines, and most faculty members welcome insights about teaching writing. At the same time, the staff and director have learned innovative ideas for writing projects and fresh approaches for incorporating writing in their own classrooms from the faculty members with whom they have worked.

Because many of the level-2 and level-3 writing courses are taught in disciplines other than English, Writing Center staff members acquire knowledge about the various kinds of writing occurring on campus, an especially important benefit. Writing Center staff members who also teach the first-level writing course find it useful to know about the writing their students will be expected to accomplish in the second- and third-level writing courses. The staff members especially discover the range of demands on students. Sometimes consultants see writing assignments that they would have difficulty approaching, although they are able to help the clients tackle them. Sometimes consultants see assignments that include confusing directions or expectations that the writer just cannot meet, and the staff members can apply this discovery to their own assignment writing. In addition, staff members grapple with all the documentation questions that writers—from faculty through freshmen—struggle to solve. They become very familiar with the headaches that writers have when using complex disciplinary style guides such as APA, CBE, and MLA.

The knowledge that staff members develop in their work with students and faculty becomes the basis for change and growth in the Writing Center organization. For organizational longevity, collaboration and cooperation are essential in the horizontal administrative structure because they are the means by which power is executed. As Tierney (1999) points out, individuals need to find ways to work with the concepts of power and control so that individual creativity is enhanced and group ownership is established. Because the power is shared by the director and the staff members within the Writing Center itself, both individual creativity and group ownership are possible. Writing Center staff members share in decision making with the director. Most often these decisions are discussed in biweekly staff meetings. These meetings also afford a time when staff members discuss individual difficulties with clients, and they share success stories. If one staff member has found an effective approach for a client, then other consultants typically adapt that approach. Because writing center work depends on both an overall sense of shared purpose as well as specific practices, periodic staff meetings are important. The cumulative result of these meetings over the course of a semester, a year, and decades is the development of a specialized and local knowledge base about teaching and practicing writing in one place, UW.

Over the course of many years, for example, the Writing Center has been able to address questions such as the following: How do ESL international students fare at UW? What kinds of technical writing skills must engineering students develop for their senior capstone projects? How are thesis requirements changing for the increasing numbers of professional graduate degree programs? As a literacy site for both students and faculty, the Writing Center is a location for the staff to collect, analyze, and distribute information about these kinds of questions. The horizontal administrative structure within the Writing Center itself, in addition to its horizontal administrative placement within the university, allows this developmental growth and collaboration to take place.

Students

The complexity of interdisciplinary work receives considerable attention from Beyer, Gillmore, and Fisher (2007) in *Inside the Undergraduate Experience*. The authors report that students' learning about writing is largely mediated by their majors, but also that this learning is complicated by contrasting expectations and contradictory standards. A professor in one discipline may praise a paper that a professor in another discipline regards as inadequate. The authors conclude that "what counts as good writing varies from discipline to discipline" (p. 202). When they examine other kinds of learning, they come to the same conclusion. Whether learning occurs in general education courses or in a student's major courses, "learning in college is mediated in all areas by the disciplinary context in which it occurs" (p. 374). This conclusion has important implications for university structures. Does a horizontal administrative structure that encourages interdisciplinary or collaborative work actually deter student learning by mixing disciplines that do not naturally mix? Do the advantages of interdisciplinary work outweigh the disadvantages, especially because students report that they value professors who can apply their course content to other disciplines (Light, 2001)? Whatever the case, those working in interdisciplinary areas, such as writing centers, must decide how best to serve students under the circumstances.

Student use of the UW Writing Center demonstrates its WAC orientation. In a typical semester, the percentages of student visits are distributed among these various colleges: 36% student visits from arts and sciences, 14% from business, 14% from engineering, 13% from education, 15% from health sciences and pharmacy, and 8% from agriculture. Significantly, and always amazing to us, these statistics follow fairly well the numbers of majors in these colleges. In terms of academic class, these Writing Center visits have the following distribution: 15% visits by freshmen, 6% by sophomores, 20% by juniors, 31% by seniors, 19% by master's students, and 9% by doctoral students. In addition to demonstrating the WAC orientation of the Writing Center, the distribution by class reflects what both Light (2001) and Beyer, Gillmore, and Fisher (2007) report: students become more interested in writing as they work on more substantial projects related to their majors and disciplines. Consequently, juniors and seniors tend to be more invested in their writing projects and use the Writing Center more than freshmen and sophomores. An increased difficulty in their assignments may also play a part. The percentage of use by sophomores has remained consistently low for several years, and it is a feature of our campus life that our university needs to discuss.

The tutoring practices and policies of the UW Writing Center necessarily reflect the needs and circumstances of the student writers who use it. Chief among the concepts that need to be adopted by consultants is the idea that writing means different things to faculty in different disciplines. To some, writing is primarily the pragmatic statement of facts; to others, writing is primarily persuading others to buy a product; and to yet others, writing is primarily analyzing all sides of an issue. Moreover, teachers in different disciplines value different aspects of writing. For some, mechanics and grammar are most important; for others, correct documentation is most important. Views about good writing vary among disciplines, and students acquire their views of good writing from the professors in their major.

To fulfill the mission of helping all on campus, the Writing Center consultants must acknowledge the changeable circumstances of a student's writing instruction. Inherent in this help is the understanding that student writers need to comprehend shifting expectations in the courses they are taking in various fields, not just in their major field. This situation is a logical component in any WAC program. To be effective, Writing Center consultants must be able to understand writing with a much broader view than the one often held by English department writing instructors. To most benefit students in all fields, they need to find the similarities in writing within the various disciplines rather than the differences. For example, clear sentences, organization logical for the task, concern with audience, and statements supported by evidence are important in all fields. The consultants need to help student writers gain confidence by recognizing the similarities and then realizing that they can deal with the differences, which are often format, subject matter, and approach.

The cooperative mode of operation also allows consultants to have true conversations with student clients in the Writing Center, conversations in which they discuss the clients' writing and alternatives for improving a piece of writing without evaluation. Part of the staff mission is to help student writers understand how to work on writing cooperatively.

The Ellbogen Center for Teaching and Learning

The Ellbogen Center for Teaching and Learning (ECTL) is a small organization of four directors or coordinators supported by one full-time office associate. Its mission is to provide teaching support to faculty. The Writing Center, as part of the ECTL, is located in close proximity to the ECTL offices. Although the Writing Center's main mission is to help student writers, it also gives assistance to faculty in their writing and teaching.

In addition to the ECTL director and the Writing Center director, two technology coordinators in the ECTL assist the UW teaching community in computer-mediated instruction, especially online teaching, and in the creation of instructional media materials. The ECTL hires student lab assistants to support the technology labs. Recently, a new two-person office called LeaRN (Learning Resource Networks) has been closely associated with the ECTL. LeaRN's mission is to assist students in the six undergraduate colleges with the difficult transition issues they face as first-year students and to assist faculty who teach first- and second-year courses to engage their students in success strategies. Thus, a third horizontal organization has joined the ECTL-Writing Center consortium with the ability to combine and redistribute resources of all kinds to support student learning.

Both the ECTL and LeaRN report directly to Academic Affairs and receive substantial programming budgets to conduct their horizontal work. In contrast to departmental budgets, which are rapidly consumed by faculty demands for travel, copying, technology, and research support, these programming budgets are highly flexible. By combining monies from several sources of discretionary funds from the college deans and other horizontal programs, the ECTL and LeaRN can sponsor university-wide seminars with outside experts in addition to smaller programs that run year-round. In addition, both the ECTL and LeaRN create small competitive grant projects of $1,000 to $3,000 for faculty teaching projects. In the vertical departmental and disciplinary structures at a research institution, money for classroom projects is nearly impossible to get in any other way.

The Writing Center director and staff have been beneficiaries of ECTL program funding in many ways. We are impressed with how the simple availability of a copy machine that is not governed by any rigidly monitored copy limits can help to relieve the stress of a staff member who is teaching three writing courses in addition to staffing the Writing Center. The ECTL has been able to provide supplementary travel support for staff members. Many Writing Center staff have benefited from professional development opportunities related to the ECTL or LeaRN grant projects, either as co-Principal Investigators (PIs) or as designated professionals for some of the project activities. As an ECTL associate closely connected with the governing and planning of all ECTL activities, the Writing Center director benefits from the ECTL and LeaRN programming, especially in terms of professional development. An ECTL associate has numerous possibilities for multidisciplinary collaboration and co-authorship.

As a division of ECTL, the Writing Center benefits from a prime location, high visibility, and high accessibility to students. The space itself is comfortable and inviting, furnished with university-purchased furniture. The ECTL supports and maintains numerous websites, including the Writing Center's OWL, which serves a substantial population of UW outreach students. The ECTL also produces and widely distributes numerous marketing materials to acquaint faculty and students with its services. Because the organization is small, the Writing Center director and staff have access to all of the ECTL professionals for technology support, materials development, and advice in the running of its operations.

Since the teaching center's founding, the ECTL has always been infused with a hefty measure of writing center theory and practice that is easily generalized to the ECTL's mission of providing teaching support and leadership. Writing center theory recommends that writing center consultants avoid evaluating a writer's text, preferring instead to discuss rhetorical effects and possibilities. In the UW Writing Center, students are not considered to be deficient but instead developing writers. The consultations are collaborative efforts between consultant and writer. In the early development of the ECTL's operating principles, similar choices were articulated. No faculty member would ever be considered deficient, and the center would discourage department heads from sending instructors to the ECTL for getting fixed. Although the center received pressure to accept assessment as part of its mission, it steadfastly refused to accept this task. The center made no claims for expert knowledge about excellent teaching. Instead, it created opportunities for faculty to collaborate in course design, assignment creation, and discussions of pedagogy.

Writing center and WAC principles have also infused some of the major ECTL projects. A notable example was a three-year, $350,000 Fund for the Improvement of Postsecondary Education (FIPSE) grant, the co-PIs of which were the ECTL director and the Writing Center director. In this project, entitled "Connecting Learning Across Academic Settings," faculty in the sciences, fine arts, and humanities identified the kinds of literacies students needed to have in order to successfully learn in their courses, and then they developed ways to teach these literacies within the courses. The faculty participants in this project testify that it had a profound effect on their understanding of student learning, and several have gone on to lead major initiatives at the university. For example, two of the science faculty in the project conducted a two-year collaborative study of scientific literacies with participation from 25 science faculty and science education faculty. This group forwarded to the Office of Academic Affairs an action item for the university's next planning cycle that calls for the establishment of a center for the teaching and assessment of science literacies. After two years of interdisciplinary collaboration, these faculty members came to understand the value of horizontal structures for teaching and learning.

HORIZONTAL VERSUS VERTICAL STRUCTURES: A BRIEF COMPARISON

The Writing Center is not the only support service at the university. The LeaRN website lists nearly 20 sites for tutoring, ranging from supplemental instruction in specific courses to generalized help in oral communications, math, foreign languages, and many sciences. However, the Writing Center is the only support service that has created a strong horizontal presence. Most of the other support services have narrowly defined missions that remain tethered to vertical structures, and thus they are unable to easily provide support for broader goals.

We provide our university's math lab as an example of a support service tied to a vertical structure. As a service devoted largely to the mission of helping students pass the lower division math courses required in the general education program or in related disciplines, the math lab cannot help with one of the most critical needs in both undergraduate and graduate education: assisting students in broad ways with problem solving and applications of quantitative reasoning.

This inability is due in part to the university's failure to create a horizontal structure for the math lab. Recognizing the importance of quantitative skills across the disciplines, UW undertook a bold initiative in its first iteration of the USP in the early 1990s. In concert with requiring three levels of writing courses, it required three levels of quantitative reasoning courses. The third level was defined as courses in the majors designed to help students apply algebraic principles to disciplinary problems. Faculty in a variety of fields became intrigued with the concept and created some innovative classes, such as a marketing class in the textiles major and a "numeric imaginings" class for literature majors. However, a major support piece was neglected. In contrast to the support for writing that consisted of a WAC coordinator and a WAC-focused writing center, no person was identified to coordinate the development and support for these courses. Nor was there any indication that the math lab should expand its tutoring capabilities to help students with problem solving or quantitative reasoning in these applied courses, especially at the upper division level. Thus, when a 10-year review and revision of the general education program occurred from 2000 to 2003, the level-3 math requirement was dropped. Faculty had not received enough development time to incorporate and teach a rich set of problems in their courses, and no interdisciplinary culture had been built to provide encouragement and support. The university now finds itself unable to fulfill the demands of faculty, students, and employers who would like to see substantial teaching and learning in a variety of quantitative and problem-solving skills.

Interestingly, during the same revision period of the USP, some upper level administrators lobbied strongly to delete the upper-division writing requirement, arguing that a general education program should be limited to lower division courses. Uneasy with what they called a "bloat" in USP offerings, they wanted to prune course offerings and rely on departments to see the good in substantial upper division writing courses. In a show of confidence about WAC, the faculty voted to keep all three writing courses in the second iteration of the USP. We regard this vote as strongly confirming the power of the horizontal structure created to support writing instruction at the university. After 10 years of persistent and wide-ranging support, faculty across the university had built and learned to value the social capital around the teaching of writing, and they did not want to lose the opportunity to participate in this horizontal community.

CONCLUSION

We have been painting a bright picture of the UW Writing Center's horizontal position, but we do not want to leave without acknowledging some of the obstacles. Because the teaching and practice of writing involve the highest levels of cognitive skills, anxiety always accompanies any major writing enterprise, whether it be a student writing an argument paper, a researcher responding to an editor's comments on a manuscript, or a faculty member designing a new writing-intensive course. The anxiety often translates to criticism or frustration.

Writing clients at the Writing Center sometimes pressure the staff to suspend "just this once" its policies of 30-minute appointments or collaborative discussions of writing. In the press of time, students would love for staff to edit their writing. Graduate students and faculty writers would love for the staff to devote one or even two continuous hours to their manuscripts, especially given their length. Our ESL students in particular often express dissatisfaction with policies that limit their time or require them to be active English-speaking discussants of their ideas and prose.

Faculty who use the Writing Center to assist with teaching also can misconstrue its mission. Sometimes they send students to the Writing Center with the admonition to have the Writing Center "fix" the students' papers or proofread the papers, and they express frustration or even anger when their hope is unfulfilled. Some faculty misinterpret the collaborative nature of the classroom workshops the Writing Center offers and assume, instead, that the Writing Center consultant is the substitute teacher of the day. It is perhaps inevitable that faculty will always complain about weak student writing at all levels. In U.S. higher education, these kinds of complaints have prevailed for more than 100 years, and we forecast that they will continue to be voiced until writing is no longer considered to be an essential tool for learning and communicating.

As expected, the relationship with the English department since the physical move out of the building some 19 years ago has been a road with many bumps and detours. English department faculty members largely support the Writing Center, but some members' attitudes have included hostility and suspicion as well as indifference. The director has little or no influence on the staff assigned to the Writing Center from semester to semester, and most of the department's literature or creative writing graduate students have little professional contact with the director and slight desire to understand writing center theory or practice. Perhaps the most negative feature of occasional cool relationships with the English department is the impact on Writing Center staff, who sometimes struggle to validate writing center work in their promotion and review materials. These kinds of workforce issues, which result from the move away from a department's support, are most certainly serious ones.

In terms of faculty development and student learning, however, the Writing Center's horizontal position has proven to be a robust structure that yields positive results. The Writing Center has built considerable social capital, and it always has immediate access to administrative support and additional funding from the ECTL and from the Office of Academic Affairs. It serves a university-wide audience, and it supports the learning and practice of a skill that everyone values. As a result, it can quickly organize substantial programs to address concerns that become high priority. At our university, there are few centers other than the ECTL that can address university-wide issues related to important undergraduate goals identified by Bok (2006) or Beyer, Gillman, and Fisher (2007): goals like critical thinking and problem solving, understanding and living with diversity, quantitative reasoning, preparing for citizenship or for a global society, and acquiring scientific literacies. There are no other centers that act as the nexus for two constituencies, serving both students and faculty in such a way as to act as a conduit for communication and as interpreters for each other.

In a final illustration of the power of the horizontal structure for writing centers, we provide this brief case study of a successful project that involved a significant number of the tight couplings between vertical and horizontal structures that Keeling, Underhile, and Wall (2007) find to be essential for dynamic organizations. UW is experiencing pretty good success with assessment of student learning across the disciplines, but assessment of the general education program remains a challenge. There is one notable exception. The university has achieved a substantial assessment of the third-level writing course, and this project provides a model for collaborative leadership across disciplines. An accounting faculty member wrote a successful internal grant to provide the funding. An animal science faculty member took the lead in organizing the project. When she issued a call for assistance to create a rubric for assessing student samples, she received participation from more than 30 faculty who teach upper division writing courses in a broad array of disciplines: pharmacy, geography, literature, religious studies, history, family and consumer sciences, accounting, kinesiology, and more. Many of the faculty who responded to this call had worked with the Writing Center director and staff on a variety of projects for many years running. They had revised syllabi, learned how to coach and evaluate writing, coaxed their departments into curriculum mapping, found collaborators for team teaching, and participated in substantial research projects. The sessions on creating a rubric for a university-wide assessment of student writing were intellectually rich and stimulating. The Writing Center and the ECTL provided a venue for these discussions and helped the organizers to revise the rubric based on the complex discussions about it. When the time came for gathering and scoring the essays, many more faculty willingly participated. Aside from gathering data about student writing, this assessment project has had some lasting effects. Several faculty continue to use the rubric for their courses. They publish it with their syllabi, they sponsor conversations with their students about its terms, and they report that it is highly useful for teaching and evaluating writing. As Writing Center professionals, we can achieve no greater satisfaction than to see a group of faculty work in such a collaborative way.

Perhaps the most important lesson we have learned in our roles of directing the Writing Center is to maintain a realistic understanding of the complex missions and practices of our institution. Claims of moral imperatives for writing centers seem disingenuous in the setting of a land-grant research university because these claims do not honor the experiences of students and faculty. Although we agree with Stephen North (1994) that we should no longer regard writing centers as "centers of consciousness," we do not find his revision much better when he says that the center is an "institutional conscience, that small nagging voice that ostensibly reminds the institution of its duties regarding writing" (p. 15). In our experience, universities are well aware of their duties but struggle to find resilient ways to fulfill them.

We find Daniel Mahala (2007) to provide a more accurate characterization of a writing center's multifaceted roles. In "Writing Centers in the Managed University," he argues that writing centers should form multiple alliances to provide intersections with a wide range of literacy sites. In other words, he confirms that writing centers should reside in horizontal structures for learning. Our experiences verify Mahala's conclusions. Having teaching experience in academic departments, we understand how stifling vertical structures can be. In contrast, we have seen how the multifaceted relationships that can develop through a horizontal structure benefit each other as well as the university at large. We encourage writing center directors and university administrators to consider placing their centers in a horizontal structure for the benefit of students as well as the writing centers themselves.

REFERENCES

Bean, J. C. (1996). *Engaging ideas: The professor's guide to integrating writing, critical thinking, and active learning in the classroom.* San Francisco: Jossey-Bass.

Beyer, C. H., Gillmore, G. M., & Fisher, A. T. (2007). *Inside the undergraduate experience: The University of Washington's study of undergraduate learning.* Bolton, MA: Anker Publishing Company.

Bok, E. (2006). *Our underachieving colleges: A candid look at how much students learn and why they should be learning more.* Princeton, NJ: Princeton University Press.

Ferruci, S. A. (2001). Composition's professionalism and the writing center director: Rethinking the director as a teacher. *The Writing Instructor.* Retrieved July 7, 2008, from http://www.writinginstructor.com/essays/ferruci.html

Gaff, J. G. (2007). What if the faculty really do assume responsibility for the educational program? *Liberal Education, 93*(4), 6–13.

Keeling, R. P., Underhile, R., & Wall, A. F. (2007). The dynamics of organization in higher education: Horizontal and vertical structures. *Liberal Education, 93*(4), 22–31.

Light, R. J. (2001). *Making the most of college: Students speak their minds.* Cambridge, MA: Harvard University Press.

Mahala, D. (2007). Writing centers in the managed university. *The Writing Center Journal, 27*(2), 3–8.

North, S. M. (1994). Revisiting "the idea of a writing center." *The Writing Center Journal, 151*(1), 7–19.

Ranelli, P. L., & Nelson, J. V. (1998). Assessing writing perceptions and practices of pharmacy students. *American Journal of Pharmaceutical Education, 62,* 426–432.

Tierney, W. G. (1999). *Building the responsive campus: Creating high performance colleges and universities.* Thousand Oaks, CA: Sage.

Tierney, W. G. (2006). *Trust and the public good: Examining the cultural conditions of academic work.* New York: Peter Lang.

Warnock, T., & Warnock, J. (1984). Liberatory writing centers: Restoring authority to writers. In G. A. Olson (Ed.), *Writing centers: Theory and administration* (pp. 16–23). Urbana, IL: National Council of Teachers of English.

Williams, K. C., Nelson, J. V., McLeod, D. M., Meyer, S. S., Cameron, B. A., & Wangberg, J. K. (2003). A collaborative faculty approach for improving teaching of writing and critical thinking across disciplines: A Wyoming case study. *NACTA Journal, 47*(2), 53–59.

TOWARD A VISIBLE ALLIANCE BETWEEN WRITING CENTERS AND CONTINGENT FACULTY: A SOCIAL MATERIALIST APPROACH

Sue Doe

September 10. Location: The University Writing Center. At the weekly staff meeting, our writing center's graduate assistant recites, with exasperation, a litany of recent missteps by non-tenure-track faculty from across the campus. One adjunct, she says, sent students to the writing center for grammar remediation. Another sent a student to the writing center as punishment for arriving unprepared at a class peer review session. Still another mandated that students seek writing center assistance and required documentation of the visit. Some contingents were from English, others were not. "Don't they understand," our graduate assistant asks, "that we're not a fix-it shop or a babysitting service?"

September 15. Location: My office in the English department. A non-tenure-track colleague visits me soon after learning I've become associate director of the writing center, perhaps assuming that our mutual status as contingent faculty makes me the better person to approach than my tenured director. She tells me that my director and I have just hired two undergraduate writing consultants who were among the weakest writers she had in class last year. They might be carrying a grudge, she worries, as they earned low grades in the class. She asks, "Can you assure me that they won't undermine my course and assignment goals as they work with my current students?"

These scenarios are emblematic of the shifting sands of relationship-building between writing centers and faculty within a context of sharply increased reliance on contingent faculty. They serve as reminder that faculty employment trends in higher education directly affect the work of writing centers, that writing centers have a stake in labor discussions, that writing centers influence other instructional workers in addition to being influenced by them, and that many within university settings share the material conditions of marginalization. Drawing upon these present realities, this chapter argues that writing centers and contingent faculty might begin to reframe their separate experience of marginalization, characterizing it more as opportunity for collective effort and less as fighting over scraps. In short, these groups might work together for the good of themselves and the good of students.

I make this argument as one who has worked in both worlds, first as a 20-year non-tenure-track faculty member who recently moved to the tenure-track and second as a recent associate director of a writing center at a large public university. My goal is to develop a rationale for collective action between these two groups. In seeking this, I am well aware that I am not alone in having experienced contingency in both roles. In this synthesis, I am motivated by a desire both political and pedagogical to bring these two groups together since often in my experience it has seemed they were working at cross purposes. Writing centers and contingent faculty, perhaps especially in Composition but not limited to it, have much in common, and they have much to gain from working together, both from the point of view of improving student learning through writing as well as to mutually enhance their political presence. Yet too often they re-enact university politics of a by-gone era, making assumptions about one another's agency and authority even as their ability to liaise with one another may foretell their future success. I believe both writing centers and contingent faculty are aided in this effort by their mutual possession of literatures that embrace an initiatory agenda. At the same time, only writing centers have a site from which to locate this work, and therefore, it may be within the writing center that we can best situate these efforts.

In this chapter, I first establish the parallel forms of marginalization experienced by writing centers and contingent faculty, discuss the activist approaches articulated by seminal theorists in writing center and contingent faculty literature, and then draw upon a materialist lens to bridge these similar initiatory agendas. Focusing on the special case of the Composition contingent, I show why a solidarity narrative must be preceded by an acknowledgment of difference and suggest that Pratt's contact zones provide a theoretical approach for this work. I then offer, by way of example, a re-reading of the writing center notion of deprivatization and propose it as a concrete topic for contact zone discussions of policy and practice as they are differently valued and experienced by writing centers and contingent faculty.

From this example, I then suggest concrete steps writing centers and contingent faculty might take to construct local directions for shared discussions and negotiated agendas. Finally, I argue that this effort be undertaken within the walls of the writing center, adding a new chapter to the extracurriculum of writing instruction, this one functioning in the margins between academic and public settings.

To contextualize this argument, however, it may be important to first foreground it in discussions of management strategy and rhetorics, in discussions of resistances borne of marginality, and in both feminist-materialist and social-materialist theories. In particular, Gary Rhoades (1998) defines today's faculty as managed professionals functioning within a fully stratified academic workforce run by managers with increasing levels of managerial discretion and flexibility of staffing, the implications of which most faculty are only vaguely aware (p. 4). Such stratifications work to undermine the authority and agency of faculty, Rhoades argues, since a compartmentalized workforce deepens distrust and division among workers and increasingly ensures that "management discretion is broad and expanding" while "Professional involvement in decision making is limited" (p. 6). Dana Cloud (1998) has described this phenomenon as increasingly typical of the American workplace, arguing that therapeutic rhetorics have become predominant, placing responsibility for well-being (and, by extension, blame for failure) on the individual, rather than on institutional shortcomings. Therapeutic rhetorics are a function of ideologies of liberal individualism, which have led, Cloud maintains, to "a decline of public political engagement" (p. 17) fueled by belief in a form of "Liberation [that] is equated with the transformation of selves presumed to possess the economic and cultural means of self-articulation and enlightened consumption" (p. 146).

That not all peoples have equal access to such means has been well established, but in the literatures of marginality, some, like bell hooks (1990), have argued that to be in the margins is actually to be in a "site of radical possibility, a space of resistance" (p. 341). Contingent faculty member Cynthia Nichols (1994) argues from just such a space, identifying with postcolonial theory in her conceptualization of what it means to be a "long-time university adjunct" (p. 42). Through her analysis of tenured faculty's response to a contingent faculty call for voting rights in her department, Nichols explains how the power and privilege associated with tenurable positions can work to infantilize, pathologize, and thus disempower contingent faculty. As she describes it, "Our ability to state our own needs and to identify solutions to those needs is unrecognized. . . . Rather than subjects in our own right, we are inscrutable objects who cannot or will not be understood or reasoned with; we are feminized others with emotional problems; we are object screens onto which those with power project their fears" (p. 54). At the same time, Nichols also acknowledges that her characterization of adjuncting may elide distinctions between adjunct studies and the "penetrating and 'expansive force' " of colonialism (p. 55). Care in making this distinction is important. As bell hooks (1990) points out, the scholarly discussion of postcolonialism has tended to involve an appropriation of the languages of resistance by the non-colonized or those who "participate in the construction of a discourse about the 'Other' " (p. 342), yet have no direct experience of it. Nichols acknowledges this problem, saying, "And my white, middle-class American life . . . bears little resemblance to that of third-world colonized and globally displaced peoples. It is perhaps an ugly habit of privilege that I would presume the right to claim kinship with them or to appropriate their scholarship and critical tools" (p. 55). However, Nichols then adds a clarification that is helpful for our purposes here: "But I believe . . . that my position as academic adjunct is part of a continuum, a global-corporate or even corporate-feudal phenomenon which includes, however distantly, postcolonial diaspora and the real colonial subaltern" (p. 56). Like Nichols, most contingent faculty and most writing center professionals would be loathe to suggest any degree of equivalence between their experience and that of the third-world colonized, but they may nonetheless recognize their institutionalized subordination and marginalization within market-driven economies.

Teresa Ebert (1992), Eileen Schell (1998; Schell et al., 2001), Teresa Enos (1996), and Bruce Horner (2000) apply materialist perspectives to discussions of labor and academic labor specifically. Ebert calls for a critique that counters the anti-theoretical, passive nature of ludic ("playful") feminisms that merely describe "what is," and instead she seeks a feminism that disrupts, resists, and transforms, arguing for "what could be." Working for a materialist feminism that involves "political practice aimed at social transformation of dominant institutions that, as a totality, distribute economic resources and cultural power asymmetrically according to gender," Ebert focuses her attention specifically on divisions of labor. Ebert believes that ludic feminisms tend to mask serious labor issues, such as the invisibility of certain forms of labor; in contrast, she wishes to call attention to and dignify all forms of labor. As such, she advances an inclusive definition of labor, one that includes the "human activity . . . involved in the reproduction of human life itself as well as the basic means to sustain that life . . . that is, products for the direct use and survival of the producer and not for commodity exchange, such as food, clothing and care giving—areas of work that are overwhelmingly the province of women in the gendered division of labor" (pp. 40–41). While she does not address *academic* labor stratification specifically, it is reasonable to extrapolate that Ebert would include teaching among the invisible forms of work left out of ludic feminist discussions. She argues for a materialist feminism that critiques, resists, politically transforms, and demands self-reflexivity. In the academic setting, this approach would certainly include support for instructional workers in writing centers and among teaching faculty.

The work of Eileen Schell (1998; Schell et al., 2001) and Teresa Enos (1996) also takes up this feminist task and directly applies critique and resistance to the issue of contingent labor, particularly in writing studies. Enos' (1996) *Gender Roles and Faculty Lives in Rhetoric and Composition* and Schell's (1998) *Gypsy Academics and Mother-Teachers* bring us face to face with both statistical and personal accounts of the gendered nature of contingent labor in university settings, acknowledging in material terms the very factors Ebert refers to in her re-defining of labor. Enos and Schell point specifically to teaching, service, and program administration as particular forms of labor that fall to women and are marginalized in terms of academic rewards. Further, theirs are calls to action. For her activist approach, Enos states her belief in associations such as the Writing Program Administrators (WPA), which she believes represents an organized source for galvanizing change among its constituency and encouraging shifts in academic reward structures at least within rhetoric and composition. She also calls on the individual to resist "other people's limitations on one's work" (p. 128). Schell's social materialist feminism calls for transformation that is at once personal, institutional, and collective. Arguing for unionization and action, Schell et al. (2001) offers direct refutation to the tendency to fix responsibility on the contingent, as individual or as group, via the "rhetorics of lack," which she describes in similar terms to Cloud's representation of therapeutic rhetorics, specifically as a "problematic rhetorical move that shifts responsibilities from institutions to individuals who occupy the problematic positions" (Moving, p. 326). Schell argues that a "rhetoric of responsibility," fixing responsibility on institutions, must replace rhetorics of lack.

Like Ebert, Enos, and Schell, Bruce Horner (2000) believes that the materiality of academic labor has been inadequately addressed. By "materiality," Horner refers to the conditions of academic work, including institutional support for that work in terms of office space and access to teaching resources, as well as the individual's experience of the context as mediated by such factors as personal history, home culture, and health. By "social," Horner refers to the relations shared among entities engaged in the workplace practices of the academy—faculty to faculty, faculty to staff, faculty to administration, faculty to students, and so on. "Work," Horner says, "denoting simultaneously an activity, the product of that activity, and the place of its practice—encourages us to think of what we do as located materially and historically: as material social practice" (p. xvii). Horner adds that work also "is the occasion for both reproducing and revising material social relations" (p. xix), suggesting we are neither independent of the forces that make our social experience of materiality nor subservient to them. Horner's definition of work sheds light on certain divisions that have grown up between what is often considered the "work" of the academic professional class—principally research and publication—and the "labor" of the sub-professional classes—teaching, service, and program administration—forms of labor that are very familiar to both writing center personnel and contingent faculty.

While Gary Rhoades (1998) argues that the professions are "groups seeking to establish and maintain monopolies of expertise" (p. 20) and are not "proletarianized 'workers' " (p. 28), he does not seem to speak to instructional workers who labor off the tenure-track. In contrast, Horner points out that there is an uncontested elevation of some forms of professional faculty work over others. It may be, therefore, that while researcher-scholars are more easily excluded from the academic proletariat, teaching faculty and instructional staff form a kind of subclass of professional, an increasingly pervasive and stable academic proletariat. Further, Cynthia Tuell (1993), like Schell and Enos, has argued that these labor divisions reflect the gendered nature of labor division within the academy, and perhaps particularly within writing programs. As such, women are associated in the university with motherly roles, with failures of the "normal progression" of the academic career, with "lower" (vs. "upper") division courses, and with practitioner knowledge versus scholar/theoretical knowledge (Tuell, 1993, p. 127).

Drawing upon the claims of these varied materialist perspectives, I argue here for a prioritization of discussions between writing centers and contingent faculty around material forces shaping university instruction, particularly as those forces affect writing. In conducting these discussions, writing centers and contingent faculty might simultaneously increase the visibility of their work while also redefining academic work itself, which has increasingly come to mean one thing only—scholarship "deemed to be one's own work, treated as divorced from material social conditions, a product of the autonomous scholar" (Horner, 2000, p. 2). This trend can be understood as part of larger market forces at work in the university, in which "A significant fraction of the tenure-stream faculty readily engage in . . . the commercialization of research, the enclosure of intellectual property, and market behavior such as competition for scraps of 'merit pay' " (Bousquet, 2008, p. 26). Working in opposition to this view, writing centers and contingent faculty might together more fully articulate a perspective on academic work that acknowledges its varying forms and the mutual dependence of all strata of academic workers upon one another. As such, they might work together to provide leadership for what Bousquet (2008) calls the emerging "oppositional culture," of contingent faculty and graduate employees (p. 26), distinguishing the fomenting resistance to market forces among contingent faculty and staff from the relative silence of those in tenure lines.

But let us return to the introductory scenarios, which depict well-prepared writing center consultants doing what they've learned so well to do—listening deeply and carefully to writers, employing non-interventionist approaches in their responses, helping clients talk through their writing plans—and hence developing a degree of skepticism about the adequacy of writing instruction across the curriculum and even within English and Composition programs. In turn, non-tenure-track faculty undertake the teaching of lower-division and developmental courses and wonder about the bounds of tutoring in the university setting, puzzling over the qualifications of consultants, the constraints on their authorization to critique faculty assignment of writing, and the extent of their understanding of academic labor issues. These scenes remind us that even under the best of circumstances, a reciprocal appreciation of the challenges separately confronted by writing centers and teaching faculty is unlikely to occur naturally but instead must be fostered. The challenge of fostering such understanding becomes more complicated when faculty are nomadic, occasional, or demotivated by contingency from creating ties to university entities like the writing center. In turn, writing centers may ask what possible motivation they would have to build relationships with faculty as transient and deauthorized as the adjunct masses.

The answer is simple: to be fully effective with student writers, both parties need each other, particularly as the enterprise of teaching undergraduates depends increasingly upon contingent faculty. This emerging context creates new opportunities and obligations for writing center–faculty relationships, and these relationships necessitate a re-examination of North's (1984) historic characterization of writing center restraint in critiquing faculty integrations of writing, a characterization built on the premise of a privileged faculty and marginalized writing centers. Where once such restraint was a strategy of self-preservation for writing centers, the ever-enlarging population of at-will faculty employees deems such an approach anachronistic. Instead, as Rhoades (1998) points out, the dependence upon a sub-faculty for lower-division and core curriculum instruction is part of a "managerial strategy, which is to maximize flexibility vis-à-vis all faculty" (p. 264). As such, it may be teaching faculty for whom the stakes are now highest since the dangers associated with exposing instructional failure are entirely theirs. At the same time, these new stakes suggest areas for discussion around teaching, learning, and writing undertaken within a context of material uncertainty. Writing centers could seize this opportunity to engage contingent faculty in the work they both value and could envision this moment as a chance to support and influence teaching more fully than ever before. Such ideas lead to a series of questions: practically speaking, how do we more fully engage a non-residential teaching faculty in such discussions, including the role of writing and writing centers in student learning? What would motivate writing centers and contingent faculty to do so? How might the pursuit of these goals bring heightened awareness to the work of both writing centers and teaching faculty in our institutions? In the pages that follow, I hope to provide both rationale and mechanism for answering these questions.

PARALLEL CONTEXTS AND NEW LIAISON SPACES

Marginalized Faculty

It is by now well established that what was once a temporary solution for a short-term hiring gap—the hiring of the contingent instructor—has become a persistent, if not codified, strategy for meeting ongoing institutional needs (see e.g., change over time in Schuster and Finkelstein, 2006, Figs. 6.5a, b, and c). According to the National Center for Educational Statistics (2006), 38% of faculty across the curriculum were tenure-line, whereas 60% were non-tenure-track, full-time, or part-time (Jacobe, 2006, "Table"). Reliance upon contingent faculty extends across disciplines, with surveys conducted by, among others, the Association of Women in Science, the Status of Women and Minority Groups, and the seven-discipline humanities survey (the American Historical Association's Staffing Survey of 1999, published by the Coalition on the Academic Workforce [CAW]). Schuster and Finkelstein (2006) describe this increasing reliance upon non-tenure-track faculty as "the single most dramatic redeployment of academic staff" in national history (p. 233). They further report that *"term-limited full-time positions have become the modal type of full-time appointment for new entrants to academic careers"* (italics original) and describe this trend as "astonishing" (p. 195). Perhaps most important for this discussion, however, is Schuster and Finkelstein's finding that the activities of term faculty, which is to say their "differentiated . . . work roles" (p. 232), are more specialized than the activities of their tenured colleagues, often focusing on research *or* teaching (p. 232). Those contingent hires whose responsibility is exclusively teaching, especially at the lower division, would seem to represent an important and enlarging constituency for writing centers.

Marginalized Writing Centers

Statistics compiled for the 2003–2004 *Writing Center Research Project* (*WCRP*) suggest that writing centers are on nearly as unstable ground as contingent faculty. This recent analysis of writing center data suggests that while writing centers are the main and often the only writing support available to students on campuses—more than 60% of reporting institutions said their campuses offer no other form of student support (see *WCRP* 2003–2004, "Whom Do Writing Centers Serve?")—writing center presence on many campuses remains tentative. Staff are composed largely of a contingent staff consisting of undergraduates, graduate students, professional staff, and non-tenure-track faculty, and directors report that they have little say in regard to the compensation of these varied personnel. Further, while over half of the director staffing is accomplished through faculty positions (65.2% reported in the 2003–2004 report), fully 24% of these director positions are part-time or full-time non-tenure-track. Directors who are tenure-track are generally not full-time directors but rather have writing center work as a relatively small percentage of a full-time position, most commonly between 25% and 35% of the workload. Further, slightly less than half (49%) of directors possess a PhD, although the percentage of faculty with a terminal degree appears to be rising (from 40% in 1995 as reported by Clark & Healy, 1996), a possible indicator of a deepening professionalization of director roles.

The ability of writing centers to command institutional authority and demonstrate autonomy in curriculum, policy, and research decision making is arguably jeopardized by the absence of tenure among many directors. It may be further eroded by a lack of proximity to writing programs if such proximity to disciplinary expertise is an indicator of the ease with which writing centers and their directors may expect to work together and take positions of practical and theoretical importance. Indeed, fewer than a third of writing centers enjoy such affiliations; only 41% of responding writing centers in the 2003–2004 WCRP were affiliated with English departments or rhetoric and composition programs, whereas 27% were "independent," 10% were associated with learning skills centers, and 8% were affiliated with college or university-wide entities.

Space Needs and Undergraduate Clientele —Shared Concerns

Writing center independence refers mostly to funding sources and mechanisms, but independence is also reflected in the space dedicated to writing center operations. As the *WCRP* states, there is a statistically significant relationship between the size of a writing center and its overall impact. Similarly, the ability of faculty to function effectively is impacted by the absence of dedicated office or other meeting space for out-of-classroom work with students. Much has been made of reports by Andrea Jaeger and M. Kevin Eagan (2008) that undergraduate persistence (measured as both retention and transfer) is jeopardized by adjunct faculty. Yet what Jaeger and Eagan clarify is that, "With increased incentives, part-time faculty members may make a more concerted effort to be more available to students" (para 51), and so "administrators and policy makers actually have some control in addressing the issue" (para 52). In their description, Jaeger and Eagan point to a 1% reduction in students' likelihood of earning an associate's degree for every 10% increase in their exposure to part-time faculty (para 51), positing that it is the inaccessibility of adjunct faculty that is to blame for these negative impacts. However, Jaeger and Eagan ultimately declare that statistically their findings fail to demonstrate the detrimental effect they anticipated, saying, "The results from this study suggest that neither the proportion of faculty members employed in part-time appointments at community colleges nor the proportion of instruction offered by part-time faculty members had a significant effect on associate's degree completion rates" (para 56).

A constructive analysis of space and accessibility issues might point out that writing centers and contingent faculty share not only a need for appropriate space in which to conduct their work but also a primary constituency—undergraduates. Indeed, writing center directors describe their clientele as mostly undergraduates—92% of the users at comprehensive universities, 91% at four-year liberal arts colleges, and 82% at research universities (*WCRP* 2003–2004 report), whereas according to the American Historical Association-CAW 1999 Staff Survey, more than 50% of the introductory courses in English are taught by contingent faculty, 51% of introductory Foreign Language courses, 37% of lower-division philosophy, and 34% and 32%, respectively, of lower-level art history and history courses (American Historical Association-Coalition on the Academic Workforce , 1999, Table 2). Clearly both writing centers and contingent faculty play an increasingly important role in the education of undergraduates; it would seem as well that their overlapping, lower-division student constituencies provide a powerful rationale for partnering.

As this section suggests, writing centers and adjunct faculty share a great deal in terms of the marginalized spaces for their work and their important role with undergraduates. Indeed, those in writing centers well understand how precious space is for working closely with students on their writing. They understand that the absence of a stable physical presence for contingent faculty to work with undergraduates makes their work especially difficult while also complicating the building of relationships within the institution. A writing center contingent faculty initiative could help to build relationships between these groups, providing a material location for these efforts and creating new outreach to the undergraduates of contingent faculty who would benefit from working with writing centers.

Parallel Literatures on Care and Activism, Horner's Social Materialist Stance, and the Special Case of Composition

In addition to a shared experience of institutional marginalization, both writing centers and contingent faculty have been represented in their separate literatures along similar lines advancing self-advocacy and collective activism. Writing center theorist Nancy Grimm (1996) and contingent labor theorist Eileen Schell (1998) separately yet similarly identify an ongoing challenge for their constituencies in relation to activism—the need to transform traditions (and ethics) of care into strategies of self-advocacy. Both theorists also suggest that these groups have legitimate claims to make on their institutions in the interest of student learning. As such, both Grimm and Schell advance an initiatory agenda related to labor and pedagogy. In addition, Bruce Horner's (2000) social materialist lens on writing and academic work may provide a bridging mechanism for theorizing the commodification of instructional work that is shared by writing centers and contingent faculty.

Arguing that "anxiety about change" can lead to writing center perspectives that "suppress knowledge that challenge culturally accepted norms" (p. 532), Nancy Grimm (1996) has argued for a self-advocacy approach to address issues of the traditionally disempowered writing center, urging writing centers to "legitimate themselves as academic units rather than as service units . . . to justify their practice theoretically rather than numerically. . . to define their own priorities and beliefs in a context that exceeds yet respects the local context" (p. 535). Grimm has further urged writing center personnel to take a strong intellectual stand to resist hegemonic forces, rejecting a narrative of victimization. The new writing center that has emerged from the influence of Grimm and other theorists reflects both a grounding in specialized theory and the resolve to achieve legitimacy within university structures.

Like Grimm (1996), Eileen Schell (1998) similarly distances herself from the nurturing stereotypes often associated with non-tenure-track faculty as "mother-teachers." Arguing from a socialist-feminist position, she says that "A feminist ethic of care also is concerned with finding ways to revalue caring through the transformation of the working conditions of those engaged in care" (p. 81). Schell adds, "One way a feminist agenda can transform equity into reality is through the reform of the working conditions of part-time and non-tenure-line faculty, the majority of whom are women" (p. 81). But Schell is also pragmatic, arguing for "resistance to the 'adjunct-as-object-of-pathos narrative' " (p. 70) and the creation of "more democratic conditions for women's lives, not . . . a model of revolution endlessly deferred" (p. 11).

Like Grimm, she rejects the victimization narrative commonly used when discussing contingent faculty issues, pointing out that "characterizing contingent faculty as 'victims' strips them of agency, making them into 'passive objects,' not active subjects" (p. 89). She adds, "When full-time faculty assign 'victim status' to part-time teachers, they do not acknowledge these faculty members' contributions, resourcefulness, resilience, and efforts to organize and change problematic working conditions" (p. 89). Placing herself within the framework of historical materialism, Schell argues for a self-advocacy strategy that is similar to Grimm's.

Horner's (2000) social materialist argument provides a bridge between these literatures, particularly through his discussion of "intrinsic value" versus "economic exchange value" (p. 18), as they often function in the field of Rhetoric and Composition. Horner points out that, unlike sanctioned academic disciplines with long histories, which enjoy intrinsic value within the university, Composition is often expected to produce "commodified literacy skills" and to demonstrate exchange value that meets public and university demands. Such a position, Horner argues, leaves Composition perpetually vulnerable to redesign and to calls for "outcomes" that are in direct contradiction to the theoretical foundations of the field, outcomes that would not be presumed to be known, much less inflicted, upon any other discipline in the academy. Indeed, Composition must constantly resist facile notions about writing and literacy while trying also to be responsive to local contexts.

Similarly and perhaps reflecting writing centers' relationship to Composition studies, the history of writing centers can be characterized as a case study in mostly successful resistance to commodification. While writing centers often still struggle to gain legitimacy in university settings, they nonetheless have built a culture of professionalism around radical self-determinism, leading to student outcomes that are highly valued by universities. In contrast, while contingent faculty have made progress in their organizing efforts, they lag behind writing centers in terms of the development of a professional ethos, which might include, for instance, a unified stand on pedagogical innovation as a legitimate form of scholarship or design of an oppositional and unified set of positions resisting market forces in higher education.

The Special Case of the Composition Contingent

As discussed in the previous section, Composition is a discipline that is particularly prone to commodification. By extension, within this environment, the contingent may be particularly vulnerable to such pressures, as public and campus audiences tacitly convey their expectation for lower-division teaching faculty to produce undergraduate writers whose writing is "cleaned up" and ready for the consumption of those teaching upper-division courses. This problem has direct relevance to writing centers and contingent faculty, in part, because both groups have experienced these pressures but also because the hard-wrought, highly theorized positions of writing centers sometimes bump up against the still-commodified practices of contingent faculty, even or perhaps especially those teaching Composition. Indeed, given their double vulnerability due to both contingency and the status of the field of Composition, contingent writing faculty may find it especially difficult to resist influences that directly conflict with best practices in the teaching of writing. At the same time, contingent faculty retention is directly influenced by measures of student satisfaction. The contingent Composition faculty member's work may thus be especially susceptible to compromising pressures that come from varied directions.

In specific terms that spell out the potential conflict between writing centers and contingent faculty, it may be useful to consider the non-tenure-track Composition faculty member who, endangered by contingency, comes to believe it is her job to "smooth out," if not to utterly homogenize, the multiple literacies of the basic writers she meets, to erase markings of difference so that faculty teaching upper-division courses from across the campus will be untroubled by time-consuming, error-laden papers. Ironically, while she may believe she is doing the work that is expected of her, she might also prefer that such low-level work be done at the writing center, which she may perceive to have an even more pronounced service obligation than her own—an assumption suggested by the second of the opening scenarios.

In contrast to this contingent faculty member is another who believes just the opposite and imagines the writing center to be a location of opportunity, theorization, and thus competitive advantage. For this Composition contingent, her sense of marginalization is heightened by the confrontation between highly theorized writing center practice and the grim, daily grind that is the substance of her professional life. She may thus come to believe that writing centers function on a different plane that is associated with differences in professional opportunity. To this contingent, writing centers, with their codified time for individual conversations about writing, their non-hierarchical and non-expert relationships with writers, and their interest in the writer's development rather than the writing—no pencil in hand, please!—may seem to exist in a rarified world in which issues of writing problem and solution are matters of mere intellectual curiosity rather than concrete teaching imperative. It may seem to this Composition contingent that the professional writing center's respect for literacy differences is a bitter pill that lies in direct opposition to the work she believes she is expected to do.

Indeed, the belief of these two instructors may reflect, as Horner (2000) explains, why contingent faculty capitulate to dominant expectations. He says, "To give this argument a more concretely materialist inflection, we can say that the working conditions of part-time and adjunct faculty increase the likelihood that their teaching will conform to dominant expectations of the academic institution and the public, whether because such conformity is written into their contracts in the form of required texts and syllabi, or because they have neither the incentive nor time to teach differently" (p. 96). For each of these contingent writing instructors, it may seem that when her students go to the writing center, her practices are being inspected and her work is critiqued by persons who know little and care less about her instructional circumstances. While these are familiar concerns, for the contingent faculty member the stakes associated with such inspection are higher than for her tenured colleagues.

It is essential that writing center consultants be apprised of these pressures in order to complicate their beliefs about teaching faculty. A consultant's understanding of the conformity she sees in the adjunct's assignment or the adjunct's written comments will be deepened if she is exposed to the material experience of writing instruction, perhaps particularly in English departments. Looking at writing centers and Composition contingent faculty from a materialist perspective, consultants might imagine and discuss the experience of commodification, learning that writing centers themselves have been down the path of capitulation to mainstream literacy demands and emerged from it. There would be value in developing a strand of work in writing centers focused specifically on such discussions and particularly the effect of commodification on student writing.

We might anticipate two results from such discussions, one political and the other pedagogical. Politically, as writing center personnel and contingent Composition faculty develop new awareness of the similarity of the forces upon them and even the hollow effect of blaming the other—recalling here the opening scenarios—they might together develop new recognition of the material costs they *share* within the managed university. They might challenge Horner's (2000) expectation that, "Being 'political' is . . . a luxury only those comfortably ensconced in the 'professional' class . . . can readily afford" (p. 97). Contingent faculty might begin to challenge their own assumptions that they need to fit in, stay under the radar, and meet mainstream goals for writing instruction, while writing centers might show how "being underpaid, overworked, and disrespected has a politicizing effect" (Horner, 2000, p. 97). As a result, new levels of mutual positive regard and materialist critique might result in pedagogical improvements, innovations, and partnerships between writing centers and contingent faculty. Together, then, contingent Composition faculty and writing centers might begin to develop an oppositional culture, a teaching resistance, that springs from the shared experience of marginality and focuses on maintaining undergraduate learning as the highest priority of colleges and universities. The positive implications for student learning of such collective resistance could be significant.

Discussing Writing Center "Deprivatization" Policy:
A Scenario of Negotiated Alliance

The previous section suggests that we might open up conversations between writing centers and contingent faculty that interrogate classroom practices. In this section, I suggest that we begin that work by querying one or more writing center practices or policies, worrying the social and material implications of such policies by acknowledging how they are understood by those in the marginalized professoriate. A particularly rich opportunity for discussion lies in the topic of deprivatization, which makes concrete many of the challenges associated with writing center interactions with contingent faculty.

But first, it must be admitted that such discussions will necessarily involve confrontation and difficulty, both of which are essential to understanding the stakes of those involved in the conversation. Such a moment may provide opportunity to apply Mary Louise Pratt's arts of the contact zone to a question of importance *within* the academic setting. It must be remembered though that Pratt's approach lies in direct (and essential) contrast to the eidolon of community that too often masks real differences in experience and perceptions of experience. Utilizing the notion of the contact zone may work to challenge, Pratt (1991) says, the "utopian quality" of the "social analyses of language by the academy" (p. 36). The space of this contact zone, while full of peril, Pratt reminds us, is also full of the literate practices of inquiry and dissent, critique and mediation, denunciation and collaboration. These can be understood to be the inevitable and healthy genres of engagement among people with differing perspectives. We might also draw upon the work and literature of those working in community literacy. As Peck, Flower, and Higgins (1995) have argued in their rationalization for community literacy, "intercultural communication on community problems . . . brings together people who normally do not sit down and solve problems together" (p. 210). This work, they say, "asks us to go beyond the celebration of difference . . . to take rhetorical action together, across differences, to change their relationship from that of commentators . . . to collaborators" (p. 214). It is through such processes — processes which we do well to recall are described in the literatures of rhetoric and composition — that shared objectives may be identified and collective gains won.

As we discuss deprivatization, then, we might recall that writing center theorist, Elizabeth Calhoun Bell (2005), describes the record-of-visit as providing a location for gathering crucial information about writing center processes, which can be used to make public the practices of the writing center, to demonstrate writing center accountability to local and tertiary audiences, and to build the case for the important work that goes on inside writing center walls. As Bell points out, the record-of-visit not only deprivatizes the writing that goes on inside an institution, it quite consciously deprivatizes teacher efficacy. Clark and Healy (1996) imagined this moment, though perhaps under the quite different circumstances of a disempowered writing center functioning in the domain of a privileged faculty. Arguing for an emboldened stance, Clark and Healy wrote, "Although we have called for the people who work in writing centers to be less timid in their encounters with writers, teachers, texts, assignments, syllabi, and curricula, they must not let a sense of ethical liberation lead to arrogance or tactlessness" (p. 45). They added, "But what happens when a specific writer brings to the writing center a specific paper based on a specific instructor's poorly designed assignment and already subject to the specific instructor's obviously unconstructive commentary?" (p. 45).

It was a good question then, and it's a good, though different, question now; indeed, it is doubtful that Clark and Healy could have imagined the sweeping changes represented by higher education's increasing reliance on non-tenure-track faculty and the implications of this trend for writing center work. It seems safe to assume that they could not have envisioned working with a faculty as marginalized as writing centers nor writing teachers as contingent as the writing center consultant. When we think of deprivatization today, as a specific context for building collective effort, we must consider the policy from the perspective of today's teaching faculty as well as from the perspective of writing center theorists. Doing so takes us instantly into a new contact zone. Here we see, from the contingent teacher's point of view, the record-of-visit less as "potentially rich data source" than as "potentially damning documentation." While such concerns may seem anachronistic, they are concerns that nonetheless need to be answered anew within the context of an at-will faculty. These contingent faculty may wonder: What precautions are in place to protect faculty who are identified in records-of-visit? What policies help consultants understand the material working conditions of untenurable faculty?

Such questions compel us to consider how consultants and their directors might newly consider faculty, their assignments, and responses to writing within a context of both deprivatization *and* contingency. Indeed, such concerns might guide a good portion of consultant training. For these consultants, it is important that their training reflect the fact that disappointing faculty performances in assigning and assessing writing are catholic, implicating the most senior of faculty as well as the uninitiated, the best paid as well as the worst. North (1994) himself pointed to a retired, senior colleague of his own, who used four different colors of ink to mark "every feature he deemed worth commentary" ("Revisiting" p. 13). Yet today, when teaching increasingly belongs to just one category of faculty, writing center professional development sessions must directly address the material conditions of university labor. Indeed, without an administrator's leadership in this regard, consultants might understand too little about the conditions under which writing instruction is currently provided. Given opportunity to learn about non-tenure-track faculty, consultants would come to understand that labels such as "part-time" and "adjunct" are both inaccurate and systematically deployed; that universities cannot conduct their teaching missions without contingent faculty; that institutional pressures keep contingent faculty at the lower division with a disproportionate number of basic writers when compared to tenure-line faculty; that such faculty are often overloaded with courses; that they are often paid, even as full-timers, less than half that paid to tenure-track faculty; that they often lack office space; and hence that they represent an entirely new form of "inaccessible faculty" that is quite different from the traditional image of the distant, tenured professor who does not *make* time to talk to undergraduates. In general, then, consultants might learn something about institutional complicity in the circumstances that keep adjuncts shamefully compensated, dizzyingly busy, hard to find, and demotivated by contingency to invest in professional development or even to join an "instructional resistance" such as the one being argued for in this chapter.

In addition to consultant training, however, a consideration of North's (1984) recommendation for restraint in critiquing faculty writing assignments might offer a rich area for contingent faculty-writing center conversation and inquiry. Together they might ask, What motivated North to take this position? How have things changed since 1984? Does it matter if faculty circumstances have changed? Together these groups might address the implications when instructional failure belongs exclusively to one category of faculty, the contingent, who alone appears to weakly design, write, and assess writing. Writing center personnel and contingent faculty might study Cloud's (1998) work in therapeutic discourses of blame and consolation that constitute "a powerful rhetorical strategy" (p. 1) deployed by employers. It might be productive as well for writing center personnel and contingent faculty to examine why critiques of institutional shortcomings have been slow to arrive to the academic setting. As Helen O'Grady (2001) has pointed out, "the discourse on critical pedagogy and literacy tends to construct writing teachers as a privileged group" (p. 133). This inadequate discourse, she contends, "relies on the notion that teaching is primarily performed by privileged tenure-track or tenured full-time faculty" (p. 134).

Going consciously into the contact zone, contingent faculty and writing centers might mutually examine and challenge this incomplete understanding. Writing center personnel will need to acknowledge their negative views on the adequacy of university teaching generally and writing instruction more specifically. They may need to acknowledge as well the history of writing center marginalization and the long-standing tradition of writing center consultants proceeding with near pathologic care to avoid confronting a faculty member. Contingent faculty, in turn, will need to admit their concerns about the qualifications of consultants while also calling attention to the relative safe distance from which a consultant draws upon theory to judge an assignment or question an instructor's feedback on a student's paper. As Pratt suggests, we do not become more successful as teachers when we eliminate "oppositional discourse" in the classroom, nor can we take solace in policies and practices around which there is silence rather than discussion and debate. But we might go beyond debate, too, and appropriate the practice of "rivaling" offered by community literacy theorists Peck, Flower, and Higgins (1995). Through this strategic approach to mediating conflict, writing center personnel and contingent faculty might "speak for the responses of others who belong at the table" to inquire "into other images of reality" (p. 217). Each party might begin to imagine the perspective of the other and then extend this imaginative act to include students, administrators, parents, and the public, among others. What would each party have to say about our practices and policies?

But this is only part of the story, of course, because to accomplish this scenario, our well-informed writing center's director must work behind the scenes as an activist rhetorician, laying the groundwork for collective action by getting these two groups talking about the implications of their own marginalized labor on student writing. She promotes new kinds of literacy among these educated and articulate participants who may nonetheless be subordinated rhetors when it comes to issues of labor. She provides space for them to consider public audiences who need to hear about managerial discretion and flexibility of hiring in university settings. She provides them with the tools to discover the genres that will get university administrators to take them seriously. And finally, whether she consciously seeks it or not, she becomes part of a new extracurriculum (Gere, 1994), one that draws upon a long line of non-school literacy efforts, for this work is occurring within an educational environment but is not aimed at producing academic genres; it is rhetorical activism aimed at improving the material circumstances of those involved in instruction. as such, it only indirectly relates to student outcomes. In providing the means and location for this work, our writing center director becomes part of a sweeping revision to historical accounts of writing instruction, one that includes self-help efforts undertaken, to use Gere's words, on kitchen tables and in rented rooms (p. 75) — and yes, in writing centers as well.

A NEW INITIATORY AGENDA—
PRACTICALLY SPEAKING, HOW DO WE DO IT?

1. *As discussed, get conversations started by applying contact zone and rivaling strategies to specific writing center topics such as deprivatization.* Doing so assumes a mutual interest in topics and issues that lie beyond the practices of the writing center, but it will help to begin by opening up the writing center to inspection, by in fact "deprivatizing" writing center policy and practice.

2. *Extend professional development to include contingent faculty.* We might actively extend the professional development and training sessions of writing centers to include contingent faculty—offering incentives, if possible, in the form of small stipends. Consultants and instructors might take turns or pair up on staff development presentations. Building on these, they might together develop conference proposals that provide opportunities for building vitae while also benefiting writing center practice. Where contingent faculty are not yet part of the daily fabric of the writing center, we might open up specialty consultant-tutor positions, with instructors working in slots requiring experience and pedagogical savvy, for instance, as dedicated tutors for the disciplines or in long-term tutorials with basic writers. In these ways and others, writing centers might begin to address contingent faculty directly, as professional to professional, a notion consistent with Eileen Schell's (1998) admonishment that we should neither patronize nor infantilize adjunct faculty. Further, during early professional development sessions, writing center tutors might be called upon to consider questions such as these: What pressures are adjuncts under? What expectations do they have of their students and how do these differ (*if* they differ) from the expectations of writing consultants in the writing center and of those publishing in writing theory?

3. *Develop a research agenda that includes non-tenure-track faculty and focuses on pedagogy.* Writing centers might take the lead on IRB approval processes for projects of interest to both writing centers and teaching faculty. Contingent faculty and writing center personnel, for instance, might together explore the composing processes of non-native speakers, as suggested by Nancy Grimm (1996) in her discussion of directions for writing center research. Or they might query the relationship between specific kinds of commenting strategies and student likelihood of adopting instructor recommendations. Such efforts might launch an entire strand of pedagogical research, calling attention to the importance of classroom research to student learning and enhancing writing center and teaching faculty visibility among local and national audiences.

4. *Work with faculty both in English departments and across the disciplines to challenge policies that threaten student writing and the informed practice of writing instruction. Become visible in the process.* Efforts that provide visible proof of improving student communication abilities, focusing especially on long-term, higher-order strategies, can increase the visibility and relevance of both writing center and contingent faculty work to university missions. In turn, this social capital can be put to work for other purposes that affect the daily life of both instructors and writing centers. As Grimm (1996), Bell (2005), and Brown, Fallon, Lott, Matthew, and Mintie (2007) point out, writing centers have successfully influenced university policies on issues like plagiarism. They might also take a stand on the marginalization of writing instruction itself. Such activism should include contingent faculty, embracing their essential role by providing a site for the development of argumentative discourses around writing instruction, the labor associated with it, and the policies that result.

5. *Provide space and audience for contingent faculty writing and feedback.* As contingent faculty produce their own writing, whether this involves personal, professional, or public writing, writing centers might organize contingent faculty into peer feedback groups. These groups might utilize the space of the writing center to critique and rewrite policy documents that relate to their labor and material circumstances, constructing arguments for varied audiences, and drawing upon writing center expertise in genre options and peer feedback processes.

6. *Advocate for each other.* It is time to deepen writing center understanding of the complexity of faculty roles and the new layers of labor specialization being created in university settings. In turn, contingent faculty might re-examine their relationships with writing centers and recognize the important institutional role that writing centers play in educating students. They might also become more familiar with the history and philosophy of contemporary writing centers, thinking about how writing center pedagogy provides powerful argument for the importance of skilled teaching.

WHY US? IS THIS A JOB FOR WRITING CENTERS?

The deleterious effect of the lack of dedicated physical space for contingent faculty is a matter of crucial importance in part because the material circumstances of teaching clearly influence learning outcomes. Lacking both geographic and political mooring in the quantifiable space of the university, the marginalization of so-called "freeway fliers" is both physical and metaphysical. Frances Ruhlen McConnel (1993) quotes one "frequent flier" who says,

"I am an outsider in relationship to the administration and faculty" and another adjunct who says, "The only time my 'free-lance' status affects the classroom is when students complain about not being able to 'get ahold of me.' When they call the campus . . . , they have a difficult time leaving a message" (p. 53). In both its physical and electronic locations, then, the writing center could provide a kind of safe haven for the wandering faculty, one that would result in new opportunities to liaise, and resulting, almost certainly, in improvements to the work of both groups. In particular, exposure to writing center work might prove transformative to faculty, yielding better assignments and hence clearer contexts for writing center consultants as they work with clients. Additionally, locating this partnership within the writing center could open the doors of writing centers to the many students of contingent faculty.

Beyond these justifications, writing center tradition and ethos provide the strongest rationale for their leadership role in this endeavor. It takes a strong stomach to stand up to power and influence within any workplace setting, and universities are no exception. Writing centers have demonstrated over the years that they possess the theory and strategy that's needed to critique the university from a location within. The fact that writing centers argue for policies such as deprivatization is an indication of their willingness to take on difficult but well-theorized positions to support undergraduate writing and learning. Indeed, writing centers have learned to embrace the Noise that spills from their doorways (Boquet, 2002). They have increasingly extended this vocalization to policy issues of importance, offering theoretically and pedagogically sound rebuttals to ill-conceived approaches such as plagiarism detection as a cure-all for plagiarism. Can the issues of contingent faculty who are involved with student writing be far behind?

Further, while writing centers continue to function, much like adjunct faculty, largely on the margins of universities both physically and fiscally, it may be precisely from this marginal space that the capacity derives for a critical perspective. Writing centers have experienced "the politicizing effect" that Horner (2000) describes as a positive response to being "members of such a proletariat [who] consequently have less to lose by challenging the dominant ideology in their teaching" (p. 98). Writing centers, it might be argued, demonstrate that it is possible to critique the university from a position within.

Further, just as writing centers have emerged philosophically from the service ethos that once positioned them in a deferential role to faculty and to university assumptions about their legitimacy, the same is beginning to be said of contingent faculty. While it is widely accepted that contingent faculty will benefit in the years to come from additional organizing efforts, it might also be argued that contingent faculty need to more fully theorize their positions within the academy. As such, contingent faculty might model themselves after the writing center example, interrogating the politics of their positions to ask, "How are decisions that directly affect teaching and learning, such as the enlargement of enrollment caps and teaching loads, supported by the contingent context of employment, in which the absence of governance makes it possible for such decisions to pass without resistance?" Such questions might also be generative of questions for writing centers, such as, "What assumptions do we make about the autonomy of faculty and how are these assumptions challenged by current employment trends?" Horner (2000) says that "Understanding the politics of pedagogy in terms of social contingencies involves not only exploring its relations to specific students and the demands to be made of them by specific economies, but also exploring its relation to specific teachers and the conditions of their employment as teachers" (p. 101). Contingent faculty and writing centers have much to learn about each other and about the workplace they share. As mutual members of a teaching proletariat, writing centers and contingent faculty might strive together for an initiatory agenda that honors the materiality and significance of their work.

Ultimately, a visible alliance between writing centers and contingent faculty is an argument not just for partnering on initiatives but organizing for a collective response to free market forces operating within our universities. Perhaps others, including tenure-line faculty, will wish to join this oppositional movement, adding their voices to that of writing center staff and contingent faculty, as well as administrative professionals, research associates, post-docs, visiting scholars, and the many other academic workers whose employment within universities is far more contingent than anyone cares to admit. As Studs Terkel (2007), America's foremost oral historian of working people's lives, explained in his final memoir: newspaper people came to realize with the formation of the Newspaper Guild in 1937 that professional people can and sometimes must organize (p. 95). Of course, a widespread collective movement by academic workers will come as something of a surprise to those on the outside who often believe that academics somehow escape free market managerial strategies like the division and outsourcing of labor. We can expect, therefore, that public reviews will be mixed as people consider whether university instruction qualifies as work, much less labor. Perhaps we should try to imagine that moment when non-academic workers look upon us with furrowed brows. It may be as socialist-activist and poet Carl Sandburg described it in his 1912 poem, "Muckers," which depicts 20 common people watching a group of ditch diggers:

> "Of the twenty looking on
> Ten murmur, 'O, it's a hell of a job,'
> Ten others, 'Jesus, I wish I had the job.'"

REFERENCES

American Historical Association. (1999). *Who is teaching in U.S. college classrooms? A collaborative study of undergraduate faculty.* Table 2. Retrieved January 13, 2009, from http://www.historians.org/projects/caw/

Bell, D. C. (November 2005). Deprivatizing writing center work. *Writing Lab Newsletter* (pp. 11-14). West Lafayette, IN: Purdue University and the International Writing Centers Association with the Rich Company Publishers.

Boquet, E. H. (2002). *Noise from the writing center.* Logan: Utah State University Press.

Bousquet, M. (2008, November–December). Battling for hearts and minds. *Academe,* pp. 26–28.

Brown, R., Fallon B., Lott, J., Matthew, E., & Mintie, E. (2007). Taking on Turnitin: Tutors advocating change. *The Writing Center Journal, 27*(1), 7–28.

Coalition on the Academic Workforce. (1999). *Fall 1999 Survey.* Retrieved June 1, 2008, from http://www.historians.org/caw/cawreport.htm

Clark, I. L., & Healy, D. (1996, Fall/Winter). Are writing centers ethical? *WPA: Writing Program Administration, 20*(1–2), 32–48.

Cloud, D. (1998). *Control and consolation in American culture and politics: Rhetorics of therapy.* Thousand Oaks, CA: Sage.

Ebert, T. L. (1992). Ludic feminism, the body, performance, and labor: Bringing "materialism" back into feminist cultural studies. *Cultural Critique, 23,* 5–50.

Enos, T. (1996). *Gender roles and faculty lives in rhetoric and composition.* Carbondale: Southern Illinois University Press.

Gere, A. R. (1994). Kitchen tables and rented rooms: The extracurriculum of composition. *College Composition and Communication, 45*(1), 75–92.

Grimm, N. M. (1996, December). Rearticulating the work of the writing center. *College Composition and Communication, 47*(4), 523–548.

hooks, b. (1990). Marginality as site of resistance. In R. Ferguson, M. Gever, T. T. Minh-ha, & C. West (Eds.), *Out there: Marginalization and contemporary cultures* (pp. 341–343). New York: New Museum of Contemporary Art; Cambridge, MA: MIT Press.

Horner, B. (2000). *Terms of work for composition: A materialist critique.* Albany: State University of New York Press.

Jacobe, M. (2006, November–December). Table: Tenure status of instructional faculty, by principal field of teaching. *Academe Online, 46.* Retrieved July 14, 2008, from http://www.aaup.org/AAUP/pubsres/academe/2006/ND/Feat/jaco.htm

Jaeger, A. J., & Eagan, M. K., Jr. (2008). Unintended consequences: Examining the effect of part-time faculty members on associate's degree completion. *The Free Library.* Retrieved January 13, 2009, from http://www.thefreelibrary.com/ Unintended consequences: examining the effect of part-time faculty...-a0191264566

McConnel, F. R. (1993). Freeway fliers: The migrant workers of the academy. In S. I. Fontaine & S. Hunter (Eds.), *Writing ourselves into the story: Unheard voices from composition studies* (pp. 40–58). Carbondale: Southern Illinois University Press.

National Center for Educational Statistics. (2006). *2004 national study of postsecondary faculty (NSOPF:04) methodology report: Technical report.* Washington, DC: U.S. Department of Education, National Center for Educational Statistics.

Nichols, C. (1994). Uppity subalterns and brazen compositionists: Confronting labour abuses with theory, rhetoric, and the potent personal. In R. Teeuwen & S. Hantke (Eds.), *Gypsy scholars, migrant teachers and the global academic proletariat: Adjunct labour in higher education* (pp. 41–57). Amsterdam & New York: Rodopi.

North, S. (1984). The idea of a writing center. *College English, 46*(5), 433–446.

North, S. (1994, Fall). Revisiting the idea of a writing center. *The Writing Center Journal, 5*(1), 7–19.

O'Grady, H. (2001). Trafficking in freeway flyers: (Re)viewing literacy, working conditions, and quality instruction. In E. E. Schell & P. Lambert Stock (Eds.), *Moving a mountain: Transforming the role of contingent faculty in composition studies* (pp. 132–155). Urbana, IL: National Council of Teachers of English.

Peck, W., Flower, L., & Higgins, L. (1995). Community literacy. *College Composition and Communication, 46*(2), 199–222.

Pratt, M. L. (1991). Arts of the contact zone. *Profession*, 33–40.

Rhoades, G. (1998). *Managed professionals: Unionized faculty and restructuring academic labor.* Albany: State University of New York Press.

Sandburg, C. (1912). *Muckers.* Retrieved January 12, 2009, from http://www.americanpoems.com/poets/carlsandburg/12664

Schell, E. E. (1998). *Gypsy academics and mother-teachers: Gender, contingent labor, and writing instruction.* CrossCurrents: New Perspectives in Rhetoric and Composition. Portsmouth, NH: Boynton/Cook-Heinemann.

Schell, E., Stock, P., & National Council of Teachers of English. (2001, January 1). *Moving a mountain: Transforming the role of contingent faculty in composition studies and higher education* (ERIC Document Reproduction Service No. ED447500). Retrieved May 14, 2009, from ERIC database.

Schuster, J. H., & Finkelstein, M. J. (2006). *The American faculty: The restructuring of academic work and careers.* Baltimore, MD: Johns Hopkins University Press.

Terkel, S. (2007). *Studs Terkel touch and go: A memoir.* New York: The New Press.

Tuell, C. (1993). Composition teaching as "women's work": *Daughters, handmaids, whores, and mothers.* In S. I. Fontaine & S. Hunber (Eds.), *Writing ourselves into the story: Unheard voices from composition studies* (pp. 123– 139). Carbondale: Southern Illinois University Press.

Writing Center Research Project. (2003). Retrieved April 1, 2008, from http://coldfusion.louisville.edu/webs/a-s/wcrp/ (Can also be obtained by contacting the University of Louisville, 312 Ekstrom Library, Louisville, KY 40290, or wcrp@louisville.edu)

FROM REACTIVE TO PROACTIVE: LESSONS OF A FIRST-YEAR WRITING CENTER DIRECTOR

Lisa Whalen

On a crisp fall morning four years ago, I walked across our urban campus of approximately 2,300 students, anticipating the day ahead. For the two months I'd been director, my primary goal had been to increase awareness of our underused, underfunded writing center (WC)—a room the size of a faculty office (in fact, that's what it had been previously). My efforts hadn't been working, so I was surprised to encounter 26 students sprawled on the floor outside the WC. Inside, a frazzled tutor was helping two students at once. What was going on? I doubted my promotional efforts had become successful overnight, and this wasn't exactly the success I envisioned.

Before I could ask, a student shoved a paper under my nose and said, "Can you sign this? I don't need help." The paper was a form that tutors were to sign for each tutorial with Professor John Wilson's[1] students, who were required to visit the WC before turning in their papers that evening.

Required WC visits weren't new to me. As an assistant director at another institution, I'd seen the director successfully implement a policy that eliminated required tutorials without banning them outright. Her rela-

---

[1]Pseudonyms are used to protect the instructors' identities.

tionships with faculty were excellent in spite of the policy — or, I now realize, because of it. She introduced policies by inviting faculty to tour the WC
and meet tutors, at which time she handed out policy sheets. She explained
the reasoning behind each policy within a narrative about what happens
during tutorials. Instead of being told what they could and could not do in
using the WC, faculty saw for themselves what contributed to and detract-
ed from effective tutoring. The director couched her request to refrain from
requiring tutorials within offers to collaborate in finding creative ways to
encourage WC visits. This resulted in effective promotional strategies tied to
individual courses as well as original collaborative research on student writing. Her approach helped combat the "obstacles with public relations" that
Byron L. Stay (2006) says are typical at small institutions (p. 147). From the
start, she was proactive in establishing the tenor of her relationships with
faculty as equal partnerships based on a common goal: helping students
become better writers.

   I drafted a similar policy but neglected to seek faculty buy-in. I know
now that my single-minded focus on student outreach stemmed partly from
lack of confidence in myself as an educator and professional. I bought into
the common perception that WC directors are contingent faculty (Lerner,
2006). I considered myself a former graduate student who had fooled the
"real" faculty into thinking she could walk among them. Unfortunately,
John Wilson also saw me as contingent, something less than "a full faculty
member who teaches and engages in scholarly research" (Olson & Ashton-
Jones, 1984, p. 50). Ultimately, our perceptions were more than just unfortunate; they ruined our relationship. However, I had an opportunity later to
apply what I learned, and I achieved better results.

   As I stared at the form in the student's hand, I envisioned what I
thought were my options: talk to John about his failure to inform (much less
consult) me about requiring WC visits or figure out how best to manage
such appointments. Today I'd have no problem talking to John, but at the
time the choice seemed complicated. What I didn't know was that the complicating factors were not unique to my situation. Stay (2006) explains that
WC directors at small institutions struggle with how faculty perceive their
status because the directors "wear a number of hats. They are most likely the
scheduler, administrator, tutor trainer, and tutor" (p. 148). Michael
Pemberton (2006) also lists rank among the factors that complicate directors' relationships with faculty: "Directors may be untenured, and therefore
their continued employment may hinge on maintaining the good will of faculty. . . . [R]eporting lines may be muddled or conflicted" (p. 408). Both of
these descriptions applied to my situation.

   John was a 60-something, tenured, full professor with 20+ years at the
institution. He was an "insider," a member of the church that owned and
operated the university. He taught in the institution's fastest-growing and

most profitable program, and he answered to the dean of that program. He prepped for classes in a corner office with two windows. He wasn't shy about confronting anyone about anything, and he wasn't diplomatic.

At a time when the university was battling enrollment and budget short-falls, and when "credit-generating" (i.e., income-producing) was the most oft-used adjective on campus, I was a first-time teacher in a department with eight student majors and a handful of surviving upper-level classes. I answered to the dean of a small- to moderate-sized program who had already told me he knew English faculty viewed directing WCs as a stepping stone to teaching literature—a common misperception not true in my case (Lerner, 2006). I was also an adjunct in a windowless offshoot of the WC.

I was a female and an "outsider," not a member of the church that owned the university and that did not allow women to serve in some religious offices. I was the youngest faculty member and looked younger than I was. Though dressed professionally, I was frequently mistaken for a student and seemed to elicit paternal attitudes in some of my male colleagues.

I was also a first-time director of a WC that didn't generate credits but cost money to operate. I worried that administrators would assess the WC's success by its number of tutorials (or cost-effectiveness). I couldn't afford to alienate this group of students on a small campus where news traveled quickly—another example of the PR problems to which Stay (2006) refers.

I told the student who approached me that I couldn't sign his form unless we went through his paper together. He pressed. I refused. He seemed to sense a turf war and knew he was on the winning team.

I told the students in the hallway that the WC could not accommodate all of them before their deadline. Some students acknowledged that their procrastination had caused this situation; others were angry they would not receive a service funded by their tuition; a handful was resentful they were forced to seek tutoring in the first place. By telling them they would not receive a passing grade on their papers without signed forms, John had created "the perception that writing center use is an unpleasant bureaucratic task" (Fritzsche & Young, 2002, p. 54). That perception didn't exactly fit with my promotional scheme, and it made what might be students' first or only contact with the WC a negative experience.

John also told students to have tutors check their final, rather than rough, drafts, sending the message that proofreading was the priority. Irene Clark (1993) explains that this message pits students and tutors at odds in their goals for tutorials, increasing the likelihood that tutorials will be unproductive. She describes her own experience with excessive demand for such tutorials, concluding that it caused "exhaustion and irritation among writing center consultants, not to mention its effect on the receptionist and director" (pp. 518–519). She adds that it resulted in tutors providing "illegitimate assistance" (p. 521). Had I known about her article, existing WC communities and Wcenter, or done a quick Internet search, I'd have discovered other WCs whose policies banned required visits for the same reasons I wanted to do so:

1. The WC did not have the resources to provide quality tutoring for entire classes.
2. Required tutorials fostered student resentment of the WC, the tutors, and the writing process.
3. Resentful students were less engaged in learning and less likely to retain new skills.

Knowing other, more experienced WC directors shared my reasoning would have boosted my confidence, perhaps enough to be proactive in building relationships with faculty and salvaging my relationship with John. However, being new to academia, I figured I was on my own.

Deciding that the bad PR for turning away John's students would be too damaging, I resorted to triage. The tutor and I helped as many of the students as we could and ended up providing the proofreading and "illegitimate assistance" Clark (1993) describes (p. 521). Most students were polite, if unengaged, but some took out their frustration on us. We were demoralized, which Stay (2006) cautions can happen quickly at small institutions. These writing centers "can easily be overwhelmed by programs needing their services" (p. 149). Stay suggests directors "make careful judgments about time" and how to make the most of it (p.148). I decided required tutorials were not a good use of time, but I didn't know how to convince John.

Before I had a chance, John stopped me in the hallway to complain about the tutoring his students received. He pointed to unacceptable theses and abundant grammar errors. Caught off guard, I got as far as "About the required tutorials..." before he interrupted, talking over me to explain what he wanted tutors to do differently next time. *Next time?!* I was paralyzed: Did I have the authority to tell him there wouldn't be a next time? If I did, would it be career suicide? WC homicide? I began to understand the kinds of encounters I imagine led Stephen North (1984) to write "The Idea of a Writing Center."

In his article, North (1984) claims "misunderstanding is something one expects—and almost gets used to—in the writing center business" (p. 71). He cites faculty comments that belie the extent to which their misunderstanding contributes to WC misperceptions. Nancy Grimm (1996) echoes North's claims, adding that such comments stem from the fact that "few faculty are knowledgeable about what goes on in their writing center" (p. 538). Like the faculty North describes, John thought tutoring was for error correction, an outlook that perpetuates a "fix-it shop" mentality (North, 1984, p.66). Because the WC had been on campus for years, I assumed faculty knew what it did. John's perception of tutorials was wrong, but what I perceived as my tenuous standing at the institution prevented me from correcting him.

The prevalence of the fix-it shop metaphor is evident in Malcolm Hayward's (1983) study: Faculty ranked grammar, organization, and punctuation as their top reasons for sending students to the WC, while tutors ranked awareness of language, cognitive development, and organization as top priorities. Hayward's results make it easy to see why faculty charge tutors with performing error correction; some consider it a means to hastening their grading process. It also leads to the fallacy that Grimm (1996) calls the Laundromat metaphor: Papers must "go through" WCs to get cleaned up before they appear before the instructor (p. 523). While I felt comfortable correcting such fallacies among students, I didn't have the confidence to challenge them among faculty.

Another common fallacy that contributed to our poor relationship was that the English department was solely responsible for teaching writing (North, 1984; Zamel, 1995). John's refusal to discuss the assignment with students and his insistence that they visit the WC to "fix" their problems made it clear that he didn't consider teaching writing part of his job. My failure to address these fallacies early led to a situation in which John felt I was just trying to make his life difficult.

I thought publicizing a new policy in the faculty bulletin the next semester meant I was following Fitzgerald and Stephenson's (2006) advice to "explain to faculty the less than optimal results of sending all of their students to our centers without contacting us first" (p. 124). The policy prohibited required tutorials, explained why, and offered help in encouraging students to visit the WC.

However, the following semester, John's students arrived with their forms. My confidence was high enough that I decided to defend the policy but not high enough to confront John face-to-face, so I emailed him.

John,

Thank you for supporting the Writing Center. I appreciate it when faculty encourage students to use our services. However, I need to let you know that I implemented a policy last semester (posted in the faculty bulletin) that the Writing Center cannot comply with requirements for an entire class to visit.

The intent behind this policy is not to create obstacles for students to use the Writing Center—in fact, that's the opposite of what I want to do—but I've found from experience with many courses that requiring an entire class to come doesn't work. Students wait until right before the deadline and all come at once.

We don't have enough tutors to help every student within a short span of time. The students we are able to tutor receive rushed, superficial editing as opposed to tutoring that makes them better writers. In a few cases, students become so desperate for signatures that they pressure tutors to sign forms without reading their papers.

I want to help your students, and I'm confident you and I can find an alternative to required tutorials. I'm happy to visit your class. I can tailor the visit(s) to your assignment. If you don't have enough class time available, I can set up online chats so students can ask specific questions about writing, citation, etc. With every assignment, there are usually a handful of things all of the students struggle with, so everyone would benefit from seeing questions asked and answered in a public forum. (I can also provide you with chat transcripts so students can refer to them later.) If you have other ideas we can certainly discuss them.

Again, thank you for your continued support of the Writing Center.

John seemed to view my email as insubordination. He replied cordially, but his students later asked me if it was true tutors didn't want to help them. The students had become pawns in a power struggle I had no desire to engage in, but I also didn't want them thinking we didn't want to help them.

Later, John copied my department chair and me on a complaint he emailed to his dean. My department chair confirmed my suspicion that his perception of power differentials between us influenced his behavior when she read his email and said, "In all the years I've known him, I've never seen him act like this."

Before I could do damage control, the dean replied that John's required tutorials were an inappropriate use of the WC. I appreciated the dean's support, but the forum in which he'd displayed it was a nightmare—one I'd created. By establishing email as my mode of communication with John, I'd not only increased the chances he could misunderstand my intentions, I'd also inadvertently caused him to receive a semi-public dressing down on my behalf. I suspect this is why he later ignored meeting requests from my department chair and me. John's power on campus was sufficient that even the dean wouldn't push him to meet with us.

The following semester I followed Michele Eodice's (2003) suggestion to "carry on deliberate, productive conversations about writing" (p. 129) by drawing on a WC strength: collaboration. I requested 10–15 minutes at departments' regular meetings to inquire how the WC could help prepare their majors for academic and professional success. In a credit-generating environment, help strengthening departments' majors was welcomed warmly.

I showed examples of a few discipline-specific materials the tutors and I had already created and asked faculty if they would like to work with us in creating similar materials for their students. When they asked about required tutorials, I had a perfect opportunity to explain how encouraging but not requiring WC visits fostered proactive behavior that would help their majors succeed. They agreed to suggest WC visits during their one-on-one advising appointments with majors, a situation much more likely to result in voluntary tutorials than my five-minute, dog-and-pony shows in classes. For the first time, I felt equal with other faculty.

Unfortunately, I hadn't met with every department when Professor Mike Thompson's students began trickling in for required tutorials. Mike was a tenured, full professor, but he was younger than John and an outsider like me. My successful partnerships with other departments, along with Mike's age and outsider status, made him less intimidating. I had also detected an unspoken bond among outsiders; we found security in knowing we could speak freely among ourselves without repercussions. Implicitly, I drew on Mike's pride in being a "rebel" to explain how required appointments forced students to submit to a requirement rather than think independently about the costs, benefits, and consequences of deciding whether or not to seek tutoring. I hinted that required appointments, in their almost inevitable focus on proofreading, emphasized conformity to grammar rules rather than expression of original ideas. To my surprise, the approach worked. Mike became one of my staunchest supporters in battling required appointments.

Much of what I learned comes from reflecting on my relationships with John and Mike. I've culled the following suggestions from those experiences:

- Ask questions, a lot of them. Don't assume colleagues' rank trumps your right to set policy. You may be surprised by the conversation and collaboration your questions foster.
- Reconnoiter. Look outside of your institution for support from Wcenter, regional associations, and other resources. They can provide data to support your ideas or policies.
- If you are a new director, consult your predecessor. He/she can be a valuable source of information, but keep an open mind. Don't make decisions based solely on secondhand information, and don't assume others' perceptions portray exactly the way things are. The previous director's input was helpful when I started my job; however, my assumption of what he meant in saying John was "supportive" of the WC led to a host of prob-

lems. I assumed he meant supportive of WC pedagogy. What he actually meant, I think, was supportive in boosting the number of tutorials with required WC visits. Your impressions of people may differ from others'. Trust your gut.

- Define your role early. To the extent you are able, clarify your job description, authority, and role within the institution as soon as possible. This can prevent you from making embarrassing assumptions and from feeling paralyzed when your policies are challenged, as I did when John told me how tutors should help his students. Perhaps most important, being clear about your role helps prevent WCs from performing "institutional martyr-dom" (North, 1994, p.18) or being viewed "as eager-to-please wives, ready to serve the needs of students and faculty whatever they may be" (Zamel, 1995, p. 532). In other words, knowledge is power.

- Consider the context. What works for a large state university may not work for a small private college, and vice versa. Take into account what you know about your institution, its students, its faculty, and its resources before drafting policies. Ask, what will work best for *this* WC?

- Consider your audience. When I framed WC policy in terms of Mike's rebellious tendencies, I was more effective in gaining his support than when I tried to force policies on John without enough explanation.

- Consult your supervisor. Ask for feedback on policies you want to draft. Supervisors often have big-picture views of their insti-tution; they can provide helpful information and alert you to potential problems. Including them helps build some of the most important relationships you'll need; it pays to have their support if your policies are challenged. Had I consulted my department chair earlier in my conflict with John, she would have suggested how best to communicate with him to avoid neg-ative outcomes.

- Be intentional. For any policy, be clear about the reasons behind it. Put policies in writing and publicize them. It also helps to emphasize that you are willing to collaborate in creating alterna-tives to controversial practices, such as required appointments. Present the WC as a partner rather than a completely autonomous entity.

- Establish open lines of communication. Consider asking to visit department meetings. This can prevent the awkwardness of hav-ing to contact faculty after they have inadvertently violated your policies.

- Meet with instructors about their assignments. This way you can ensure tutors will understand the instructor's expectations and the instructor understands WC procedures. Consider asking instructors about their objectives for tutorials: Do they hope to encourage students to start early and write multiple drafts? To use a complex organizational structure? To focus on paragraph development? Asking these questions gets faculty thinking about their roles in teaching writing.
- Offer to visit class before students come to the WC. Class visits can provide insights into students' perceptions of writing, WCs, and tutorials. You can distribute copies of WC hours and policies, ensure students know what to expect from tutorials, and encourage them to plan ahead. I found that leading a class in pre-writing exercises helps to reduce students' frustration and procrastination. It also uncovers parts of the assignment students find especially difficult, and tutorials can then focus on those parts first.
- Gather supporting materials. Obtain copies of assignments, rubrics, and other relevant materials in advance so tutors don't have to guess or track down answers to questions. It also helps prevent tutorials like some of mine with John's students: based on a student's misunderstanding of the assignment, we spent an hour polishing a paper that didn't fulfill basic assignment requirements.
- Prepare tutors for an onslaught. Alert tutors to deadlines. Make sure they understand policies for establishing priority (e.g., first-come, first-serve; priority for pre-scheduled appointments; etc.). To preserve morale, protect tutors from getting caught between the instructor and the student, or the student and WC policies, as happened in my relationship with John. Assure tutors they can send angry students to you, and then be available whenever you can. If you can't be there, help tutors withstand peer pressure to subvert policies by brainstorming and rehearsing replies for such scenarios.
- If you think it will work, consider offering group tutorials that cover common stumbling blocks, such as MLA or APA style. Then, tutors can focus on higher-order concerns during one-on-one tutorials.
- Once the papers have been graded, ask the students and the instructor for feedback about the tutorials' effectiveness. This shows your commitment to supporting the instructor and his/her students. However, make sure you frame your request as a mutually beneficial exchange of information rather than a will-

ingness to conduct tutorials according to the instructors' specifications.

As a result of collaborations with faculty and other WC professionals, I am in a better position to approach John about reestablishing a relationship. Most helpful was the confidence built through proactive visits to department meetings, which prompted all involved to see me as their equal.

Our relationship led Mike and I to share ideas and teaching spaces, which was mutually beneficial. My visits to his classes helped break down the border between teaching writing and teaching course content. Students, having met me during class, were less intimidated by the idea of seeking tutoring. Mike's acknowledgment of my expertise made students more willing to revise their writing based on tutors' feedback.

I used Mike's assignments in tutor training, which made tutorials more effective. Tutors not only learned about discipline-specific writing but gained deeper insights into helping students with those assignments.

Mike's enthusiasm about the rubric he and I created sparked other instructors' interest. Faculty in each college provided input for creating writing rubric templates they could modify to fit their needs. The rubrics placed the WC in the center of teaching writing campus-wide. Department chairs gave the template to new adjuncts, saving time for all involved and leading to more consistent grading. The templates also introduced new faculty to the WC immediately, laying the groundwork for future relationships.

While it's true our WC may not have as many tutorials per semester as if I'd allowed required appointments like the previous director had, students' and tutors' satisfaction with tutorials has increased. I can't say this will protect the WC from a credit-generating environment forever; however, I can say that faculty and student endorsements go a long way toward ensuring the WC's continued growth.

REFERENCES

Clark, I. (1993). Portfolio evaluation, collaboration, and writing centers. *College Composition and Communication, 44*(4), 515–524.

Eodice, M. (2003). Breathing lessons, or collaboration is. In M. A. Pemberton & J. Kinkead (Eds.), *The center will hold: Critical perspectives on writing center scholarship* (pp. 114–129). Logan: Utah State University Press.

Fitzgerald, L., & Stephenson, D. (2006). Directors at the center: Relationships across campus. In C. Murphy & B. L. Stay (Eds.), *The writing center director's resource book* (pp. 115–125). Mahwah, NJ: Lawrence Erlbaum Associates.

Fritzsche, B. A., & Young, B. R. (2002). Writing center users procrastinate less: The relationship between individual differences in procrastination, peer feedback, and student writing success. *Writing Center Journal, 23*(1), 46–58.

Grimm, N. M. (1996). Rearticulating the work of the writing center. *College Composition and Communication, 47*(4), 523–538.

Hayward, M. (1983). Assessing attitudes toward the writing center. *The Writing Center Journal, 3*(2), 1–12.

Lerner, N. (2006). Time warp: Historical representations of writing center directors. In C. Murphy & B. L. Stay (Eds.), *The writing center director's resource book* (pp. 3–12). Mahwah, NJ: Lawrence Erlbaum Associates.

North, S. (1984). The idea of a writing center. *College English, 46,* 433–446.

North, S. (1994). Revisiting the idea of a writing center. *Writing Center Journal, 15*(1), 7–19.

Olson, G., & Ashton-Jones, E. (1984). Writing center directors: The search for professional status. In C. Murphy & J. Law (Eds.), *Landmark essays on writing centers* (pp. 47–56). Davis, CA: Hermagoras.

Pemberton, M. (2006). Working with faculty consultants in the writing center: Three guidelines and a case history. In C. Murphy & B. L. Stay (Eds.), *The writing center director's resource book* (pp. 403–415). Mahwah, NJ: Lawrence Erlbaum Associates.

Stay, B. L. (2006). Writing centers in the small college. In C. Murphy & B. L. Stay (Eds.), *The writing center director's resource book* (pp. 147–152). Mahwah, NJ: Lawrence Erlbaum Associates.

Zamel, V. (1995). Strangers in academia: The experiences of faculty and ESL students across the curriculum. *College Composition and Communication, 46*(4), 506–521.

chapter 4

WRITING ACROSS THE WEB: CONNECTING THE WRITING CENTER TO NURSING DISTANCE LEARNERS

Ann N. Amicucci

As a new writing center director, I walked toward Fisher Hall anticipating a hostile reception by the faculty I was about to meet in the Duquesne University School of Nursing. I had heard plenty of stories about interactions between writing center administrators and faculty, and I had certainly heard many instructor complaints about the writing center in my time teaching college writing. Yet my expectations were quickly dismantled. Not only were the faculty members welcoming, they were willing to talk as equals about writing, knowing that while the writing center provides writing resources, both the center and faculty hold writing expertise.

On that day, I forged ties with Nursing that became a mutually beneficial collaborative relationship. Together, Nursing and the writing center developed an online tutoring program and a set of online writing tutorial modules for graduate nursing distance learners. The success of this relationship relied on an understanding of students' needs, and students' own responses to these services dictated how the relationship developed. The relationship also resulted in the diversification and visibility of the writing center's services on campus. Through this collaboration, Nursing recognized the value of the writing center as a campus partner, making our services an integral part of the Nursing educational model.

My conversation with Nursing began in response to students' needs. Joannie Lockhart, the Nursing Associate Dean for Academic Affairs, explained to me that the distance learners who compose the Master of Science in Nursing (MSN) degree programs were unable to utilize the writing center's on-campus resources and were in need of online tutoring. Through conversation with Joannie, I learned the Nursing students' stories. The school's six MSN programs, each focused on a specialized nursing field such as administration or forensics, have a high concentration of non-traditional students who are returning to school while continuing to work, raising families, and attending class online from many different time zones. To make our collaboration successful, I explored the writing needs these students had, both in relation to the nursing discipline and in consideration of their busy life situations and status as online learners.

Finding common ground with the Nursing students required understanding these needs. I spoke with Joannie about the Nursing students' experiences in the program, and she explained that the students truly needed writing support. "They haven't been writing papers in their day-to-day jobs," she said. "They haven't been writing sentences. They've been writing chart notes." Nurses commonly experience this conflict between workplace writing and academic writing (Johnson, Symes, Berhard, Landson, & Carroll, 2007) when, as students, they "encounter a dichotomy between writing as a professional and writing as a student." Johnson et al. explain, "When writing as a professional during the clinical phase of an academic program, nursing students chart observations and write in terse phrases, in decided contrast to their academic assignments, where faculty anticipate fully developed sentences, paragraphs, and thoughts" (p. 168). Recognizing this division between writing in a clinical setting and in an academic setting enabled the writing center to connect with the Nursing students. In our contact with graduate student nurses, we acknowledged this particular challenge in order to show them that the center understood this obstacle that they face as they learn to write at the graduate level. Establishing this common ground caused the students to come on board with the center's newly offered services, which in turn resulted in the Nursing faculty's increased support.

In addition to finding common ground with the Nursing students, I researched online tutoring to prepare an effective program. While developing the program, I referred frequently to *Wiring the Writing Center* (Hobson, 1998) and *Taking Flight with OWLs: Examining Electronic Writing Center Work* (Inman & Sewell, 2000). Both books cover the basic concerns an administrator faces when developing an online tutoring program, such as how to translate a theoretical approach used in face-to-face appointments to an online setting and how to train tutors to work in an environment in which nonverbal cues are absent. In the years since these books' publication, articles in *Writing Lab Newsletter* and *Writing Center Journal* and countless voices on Wcenter have escorted the online tutoring conversation into more current technology concerns, including the use of more advanced synchronous tutoring software and the need for increased awareness of academic integrity when a tutor's suggestions are written instead of spoken. When applying online tutoring to a nursing context, I had further considerations. I needed to gauge the students' comfort level with online tutoring without presuming familiarity based on the fact that these students were taking courses online. Also, because students were writing in a discipline-specific context, I had to experiment with ways to tutor students in specific writing skills online. Teaching a student how to navigate the American Psychological Association (APA) style manual in person, for example, is much different than explaining to the student how to do so online.

After researching online tutoring, I implemented a pilot tutoring program and made the pilot available to roughly 60 students in three master's level courses. The research and preparation for the pilot program lasted one semester, including training in software for center administrators and in software and online tutoring for tutors. The center offered 15 potential appointments per week, and the online tutor held 18 appointments over the course of the program's first semester. Given the new status of the service, I hadn't had any set expectations and was happy with this number of appointments. The students who used the service shared positive feedback, and many students scheduled multiple appointments, indicating through their satisfaction that the service was valued. In turn, the students' satisfaction encouraged Nursing to promote the growth of our collaboration.

After one semester, we expanded online tutoring into a full program and began serving all of Nursing's doctoral, master's, and undergraduate distance learning students, enlarging the target population to roughly 600 students. We continued to offer 15 potential appointments per week, and the tutor held 21 sessions during the semester. This number was far lower than I had hoped to see. Although it had a significantly greater target audience, the online tutoring service attracted only a few more appointments than the previous semester. In addition, the low usage numbers indicated to Nursing that students weren't taking advantage of the online tutoring service. I attributed the low number of appointments to the lack of information students were receiving about online tutoring. Much of the writing center's correspondence with students happened through faculty members who were asked to post information about online tutoring on their Blackboard pages and to encourage students to use the service. However, students may not have been receiving enough information about the service or understanding the information about online tutoring sent their way. Unlike in on-campus classroom visits, distance learning students hadn't been given the opportunity to talk with writing center personnel and hear first-hand about the services we offer. The writing center needed to attract more students, or we would risk weakening our relationship with Nursing.

Because usage was low, despite a higher number of students to whom the service was available, we expanded communication with students in hopes of increasing student interest. The online tutor and I spoke to master's students during their campus visits, giving students the chance to connect faces to the people they spoke with online and to ask questions and express concerns. We also began e-mailing the Nursing students periodically to remind them of what the service offered and to encourage them to e-mail us with questions about online tutoring. In the following semester, student attention finally rose, and the online tutor held 59 appointments, a number that was encouraging to both Nursing and the writing center. This increase in the usage of online tutoring strengthened the writing center's relationship with Nursing. When usage rose, faculty moved from seeing online tutoring as a trial run of our collaboration to seeing this service as indispensible, making the writing center a permanent and necessary part of the education that Nursing offered its students.

With online tutoring attracting a larger number of students, the Nursing faculty now saw the writing center as a stakeholder in the graduate education of its nurses. Because a strong relationship existed between Nursing and the writing center, the writing center's work had become highly visible in Nursing. As the online tutoring program became more successful, Nursing faculty members began seeing further potential for using the writing center to assist students with their writing needs. MSN Forensic Nursing program coordinator Kathy Sekula and Forensic Nursing faculty member Alison Colbert explored further collaboration with the writing center by expressing interest in developing online writing tutorials for master's students. From this conversation came the second phase of the writing center's collaboration with Nursing, the creation of the online writing tutorial modules, which provided discipline-specific writing instruction to the Nursing students while diversifying the writing center's services.

The Nursing faculty welcomed this diversification of writing center services that specifically targeted the Nursing students' needs. As distance learners, the Nursing students were unable to attend center workshops. In addition, the center's non-staffed resources—those resources that students could access on their own time—were limited to static handouts available in the center or online, through which students had to teach themselves writing skills. In the writing modules, though, writing lessons are taught to students through online tutorials, and students can still make use of the resources on their own time. Each writing module is interactive, requiring a student to walk through a series of steps to learn about a particular writing topic. These steps include watching videos in which a writing instructor explains a writing concept, visiting online resources, and completing short practice writing assignments.

I developed the writing modules collaboratively with Nursing, which further strengthened our relationship. Kathy, Alison, and I worked together to identify the writing skills most necessary for graduate nursing students. Because the strongest expertise on writing in any discipline rests with the professionals in that discipline (Barnett & Rosen, 1999), the success of the writing modules depended heavily on these faculty members' input. I also relied on the expertise of Lyn Benak, a forensic nurse professional who brought to our conversations the perspective of a publishing nurse outside of academia. Were the writing center to have developed these modules independently, I would not have been able to use nursing experience to consider the needs of researching and publishing nurses. Due to the relationship with Nursing, the center was able to combine writing and nursing expertise to bring the most educational product possible to the Nursing students.

We developed 10 modules on writing topics necessary for graduate nursing work. In choosing topics for the writing modules, we recognized that writing as both a clinical and researching nurse (Inman & Inman, 2002) necessitates competence in multiple forms of writing, varying from the chart notes with which clinical nurses are so familiar to academic and professional manuscripts. With attention to the nurses' backgrounds, the modules' first goal is to introduce student nurses to graduate-level academic writing. A module on academic integrity explains intellectual property and the university's policies on plagiarism and teaches students how to borrow material correctly from other authors. A module on research strategies reviews the basics of researching a topic, such as broadening and narrowing search parameters, and demonstrates how to use the university library's Web site to conduct research in databases.

A writing module on APA style became the most popular module among students. Some nurses came into the program having used APA style for citations as undergraduates, while others had been out of school long enough that they were no longer familiar with how to use any citation and documentation style. In addition, most incoming student nurses were unfamiliar with the breadth of a publication style, thinking that a teacher's instructions to use APA style meant simply to put citations in APA format. Nursing students often resist learning APA style (Johnson et al., 2007) if they have not yet been exposed to its use, and their reluctance to share in this common language with professional colleagues "demonstrates that students do not appreciate that citing sources goes beyond avoiding plagiarism by adding credibility to their writing, allowing them to position their research in the context of existing research, and revealing the depth, breadth, and currency of their research" (p. 170). The module on APA style addresses this problem of students' lack of awareness of the purpose of using a publication style in nursing. The module shows nurses why a publication style is used, explains several basic APA conventions, and instructs students in how to use the APA manual effectively while writing.

A writing module on RefWorks introduces students to this resource management program whose use is required by Nursing. In this module, students learn how to use RefWorks and learn the importance of using such software to manage resources, rather than expecting the software to write a student's citations for him or her. Students welcomed the RefWorks module along with the module on APA style because both modules demystify concepts that new student nurses hear about frequently but don't necessarily understand. In addition to students giving these two modules a positive reception, the Nursing faculty lauded the APA and RefWorks modules as excellent resources for helping students transition into graduate writing.

Nursing requires its students to write and submit a manuscript for possible publication by the time of their degree completion, so many of the writing modules focus on helping students understand how the publication process works and how to prepare publishable manuscripts. One module addresses critical reading of researched sources, and several modules address how to write specific parts of a manuscript, including abstracts and literature reviews. In other modules, students learn about writing query letters for publication and about the peer review process. The key to the modules is that they do not simply instruct students in how to write and publish a general manuscript, or even a scientific manuscript. Each module is specifically geared toward students in nursing and, in particular, the Nursing students at Duquesne. Every example is nursing-related. Every lesson is relevant to what publications in the nursing field expect. It is this focus on the specific needs of nurses that has caused the Nursing faculty to eagerly welcome this type of collaboration with the writing center.

In the writing modules' inception, Nursing required MSN students in the Forensic Nursing program to complete the modules. After both students and faculty responded positively to the modules, Nursing decided to take our relationship a step further. Nursing now requires all of its graduate students, at both the master's and doctoral levels, to complete the writing modules. I serve as the go-to person for students working through the modules, and students contact me via email with questions about any of the material contained within the modules or about using the modules themselves. Each semester, I reassess the modules with Nursing faculty members and make updates to their content based on faculty recommendations. As a result of continued collaboration with the writing center, Nursing has a set of resources specifically geared toward its students' needs.

Both online tutoring and the writing modules have received positive student responses, and student responses have become the gauge by which the strength of the writing center's relationship with Nursing is measured.

Many students cited online tutoring as helpful during coursework, and numerous students found the writing modules to be a necessary introduction to graduate-level writing. Students do have complaints, such as the lack of tutoring availability on the weekends. Students have suggested that online tutoring should be conducted over email and that the writing modules should be made into a credit-bearing course. All of the students' feedback, both positive and negative, gives us the opportunity to strengthen our relationship with Nursing through more conversation, continued assessment of these projects, and further collaboration.

Acquiring a common language with Nursing has also strengthened our relationship. Through collaboration, each side has become better versed in how the other side works: Nursing now understands the theory behind a writing center, and the center staff members have a better grasp of writing in the nursing discipline. Because we share the goal of educating nurses in discipline-specific writing, understanding each other's perspectives has been beneficial. The products of our relationship, the online tutoring program and the writing modules, aim to help students write in and understand writing in the nursing discipline because an understanding of a discipline's writing is necessary in order to gain "acceptance into the academic community" (Blumner, 1999, p. 35). Online tutoring and the writing modules fill a void for distance learning nurses, making writing knowledge and support available outside of the classroom in a forum designed specifically for nurses' needs. Addressing the discipline-specific needs of nurses caused the writing center to gain the Nursing faculty's acceptance as a partner in educating these nurses. This acceptance by Nursing, along with new resources coming out of the center, also helped to increase the writing center's visibility on Duquesne's campus.

Online tutoring and the writing modules benefited the writing center by broadening the scope of the center's technology-enhanced work. Of all the accomplishments made in my first year as center director, the services our center provided to Nursing were the most useful in promoting the center's value. When a colleague or an administrator asked what I'd been up to at the writing center, I would list several initiatives, but the items that caught everyone's attention were those involving technology: online tutoring, attention to the needs of distance learners, and online tutorial modules. Technology? That's where education is going, the eyes of a colleague would say. And the writing center is already there? Even better. Harris (2000) writes that, in order to become "recognized campus leaders," "we have to look beyond our campuses to see where the rest of the world is headed." She argues, "[I]t seems that the most obvious forward motion is toward wherever technology is taking us" (p. 13). Technology is not only the direction in which our students are headed but the direction for writing center work that our campuses are most likely to support. The online tutoring program and the writing modules became the banners I waved to show how strong our center's work is. By addressing specific student needs while utilizing the technological resources available at the university, I positioned the writing center as a campus resource able to adapt and grow with the campus community, making it valuable in the eyes of university administrators as well.

The center's increased visibility enhanced the professionalism of its services and its perception by students, faculty, and administration, and this visibility came as a direct result of developing a strong relationship with Nursing. As Eodice (2003) points out, "[W]hat we could be doing to insure visibility is what we do best, and what we do in a powerful collection of moments all the hours we are open: collaborate" (p. 116). Eodice's comment identifies the heart of staying visible: making connections, reaching out to colleagues, and using combined expertise to strengthen the already valuable resources in a writing center. Due to the success of the products of our collaboration, Nursing faculty members now associate the center with more than one-on-one writing assistance and see it as a place for aid specific to graduate Nursing distance learners. In addition, the modules showcase the fact that the writing center is a place to develop discipline-specific and graduate-level writing skills outside of one-on-one consultations. This reception by and success with Nursing translates into increased clout with other schools on campus: Suddenly the writing center is more than a room in College Hall because it exists beyond walls and across time zones, and our success with Nursing is evidence of the strong work happening in the center.

The collaboration with Nursing has ramifications for relationships with other campus schools as well. Before the online tutoring program for Nursing began, the writing center did not serve any distance learners on campus. Within the first year of the Nursing online tutoring program, I began talking with Duquesne's School of Leadership and Professional Advancement (SLPA), which represents another distance learning population, about establishing online tutoring for SLPA students based on the Nursing model. The collaboration with Nursing lends credence to the writing center's ability to offer services online, and its success makes seeking funding for future projects easier. Increased attention to the writing center's potential could pose a threat to our relationship with Nursing, however. The online tutoring program and the writing modules are successful because of the time spent in collaboration with Nursing faculty to develop and maintain resources that address nurses' specific writing needs. Yet if every school on campus approached the writing center with the desire to build similar relationships, the writing center would not be able to provide the same specific attention to each or maintain the same level of relationship with Nursing while operating on its current staff and funding resources. A desire for successful collaboration adds to the struggle for funding that most writing centers face (Schreiber, 2006), but the success of our writing center's Nursing relationship will certainly drive us to continue in that struggle.

Amid its successes, the writing center's relationship with Nursing has room for development. In cross-campus collaborations, we run the risk of talking over students' heads: administrators to administrators or faculty to faculty. While we always have students' needs in mind, having conversations in which students' opinions are consistently absent can cause us to lose sight of students' perspectives. Finding common ground with students was important in developing online tutoring and the writing modules, and it is even more important as this collaboration continues. We need to clearly communicate the goals of these programs to students in ways other than e-mail and information on Blackboard sites. Also, while the writing modules go beyond written handouts in conveying lessons to students, they can still become static resources if students are left alone with them. DeVoss (2002) cautions writing centers against shifting focus to new technologies, advising us instead to maintain our focus on writers. To maintain this focus on the Nursing writers, we need to keep communication lines open. Visiting virtual classrooms, for example, or creating an online discussion board about the writing center's services would keep these services visible to the Nursing students and give students the opportunity to inquire about the services in order to fully understand them. In addition, bringing other writing center staff or Nursing faculty members into collaborative conversations will strengthen our relationship while making all the people with whom students are in contact well versed in the resources we bring to these students.

The challenges that face this relationship, coupled with students' positive responses, show how many more possibilities exist for connecting Nursing and the writing center. The most encouraging aspect of the writing center's relationship with Nursing is that the Nursing faculty members are constantly asking for more: more tutoring, more resources, and more collaboration. As online tutoring and the writing modules continue to draw feedback from students and faculty, we continue to discover ways to help the Nursing students develop as writers.

Collaborations such as the one between the Duquesne University Writing Center and the university's School of Nursing keep writing centers viable as campus partners in the education of professional writers. To truly be at the center of campus writing, we must rely on and complement the expertise of faculty across campus. The first step is saying "yes" when we hear of a need. Beyond that, we can simply keep having conversations: collaborating with the educators around us while keeping one ear on the voices of the students we serve.

REFERENCES

Barnett, R. W., & Rosen, L. M. (1999). The WAC/writing center partnership: Creating a campus-wide writing environment. In R. W. Barnett & J. S. Blumner (Eds.), *Writing centers and writing across the curriculum programs: Building interdisciplinary partnerships* (pp. 1–12). Westport, CT: Greenwood Press.

Blumner, J. S. (1999). Authority and initiation: Preparing students for discipline-specific language conventions. In R. W. Barnett & J. S. Blumner (Eds.), *Writing centers and writing across the curriculum programs: Building interdisciplinary partnerships* (pp. 33–44). Westport, CT: Greenwood Press.

DeVoss, D. (2002). Computer literacies and the roles of the writing center. In P. Gillespie, A. Gillam, L. F. Brown, & B. Stay (Eds.), *Writing center research: Extending the conversation* (pp. 167–185). Mahwah, NJ: Lawrence Erlbaum Associates.

Eodice, M. (2003). Breathing lessons, or collaboration is.... In M. A. Pemberton & J. Kinkead (Eds.), *The center will hold: Critical perspectives on writing center scholarship* (pp. 114–129). Logan: Utah State University Press.

Harris, M. (2000). Preparing to sit at the head table: Maintaining writing center viability in the twenty-first century. *Writing Center Journal, 20*(2), 13–21.

Hobson, E. (Ed.). (1998). *Wiring the writing center.* Logan: Utah State University Press.

Inman, J. A., & Inman, S. L. (2002). Student writers and images of nursing in popular culture: Informed pedagogy, curricular interventions. *Kairos, 7*(2). Retrieved December 20, 2008, from http://www.technorhetoric.net/7.2/binder.html?sectionone/inman

Inman, J. A., & Sewell, D. N. (Eds.). (2000). *Taking flight with OWLs: Examining electronic writing center work.* Mahwah, NJ: Lawrence Erlbaum Associates.

Johnson, M. K., Symes, L., Berhard, L., Landson, M. J., & Carroll, T. L. (2007). Mentoring disadvantaged nursing students through technical writing workshops. *Nurse Educator, 32,* 168–172.

Schreiber, E. (2006). Funding the center through a university line. In C. Murphy & B. L. Stay (Eds.), *The writing center director's resource book* (pp. 417–423). Mahwah, NJ: Lawrence Erlbaum Associates.

CREATING ALLIANCES ACROSS CAMPUS: EXPLORING IDENTITIES AND INSTITUTIONAL RELATIONSHIPS

Maggie Herb
Virginia Perdue

From Gary Olson (1984) to William Macauley and Nicholas Mauriello (2007), the literature of writing center administration contains frequent advice to forge alliances across campus. New and experienced directors alike are urged to collaborate with classroom instructors, to increase writing center visibility within academic programs, and, of course, to communicate frequently with those all-important upper-level administrators from whom funding comes. All of this is good advice, particularly for an academic enterprise whose heart and soul are collaboration and communication.

Rarely, however, do writing center administrators hear about outreach to non-academic offices, to counseling services, disability support services, or other student affairs units that care for the non-academic dimensions of our students' lives. Yet, if we stop to think about it, the professionals in these offices certainly have contributions to make—maybe not to our financial stability, but certainly to our tutor training—as their insights can help tutors to better understand the complex lives of the students with whom they work. After all, we are all in the business of helping students negotiate personal and academic challenges, a common mission to capitalize on. As we discovered, these professionals had far more to contribute than merely expanding our tutors' conferencing skills; their visits sparked our examination of the principles and practices that inform various dimensions of tutor identity.

THE BEGINNING

In spring of 2008, we invited faculty from across campus to speak to our tutors as part of a series of in-depth tutor training meetings at our university's writing center. This decision to reach out to student services faculty happened organically—a result of a fortuitous mix of circumstances. Although the previous fall we had experienced substantial turnover with over half of our tutors newly hired, this spring semester offered us a relatively rare set of circumstances: no turnover and an experienced staff. We realized, as we planned our spring tutor training, that this stability meant that we were able to expand into new areas—in particular, to cover some more in-depth topics. These circumstances coincided neatly with a request a year earlier from "Safe Zone," an outreach program sponsored by our university's Commission on Gay/Lesbian/Bisexual/Transgender (GLBT) Issues; the leadership wished to pilot with writing tutors an undergraduate training module that focused on sensitivity to and awareness of the challenges that GLBT students face. While we were initially excited by the idea, we simply weren't able to fit the program into our training meetings at that time. Our staff of experienced tutors in this new semester allowed us finally to move forward with Safe Zone's pilot program.

Intrigued by the possibilities of this institutional collaboration, we thought our tutors might benefit from the expertise of other guest speakers from across campus. So we contacted several student service faculty members whose areas of specialty overlapped with potential topics in tutor training, and our plan for a semester of staff meetings featuring student services faculty was underway.

We invited faculty members to speak to our tutors about the issues faced by multilingual students, students with physical and learning disabilities, students who identify as GLBT, and students who write about traumatic events, but we focus in this chapter on the meetings that addressed the last two groups. In narrowing our focus this way, we recognize that we run the risk of suggesting a false connection between students dealing with emotional trauma and GLBT students. With homosexuality still classified as a mental illness by the American Psychiatric Association as recently as 1973 ("Homosexuality"), we recognize that a side-by-side look at these two groups of students could be read as problematic. For this reason, we want to make clear that our particular focus should not be interpreted as a suggestion that we view a connection between students who identify as GLBT and students who are experiencing emotional trauma.

Our reasoning for focusing on these particular meetings is twofold. First, while writing center literature has often explored the challenges of multilingual students and students with disabilities, comparatively less has been written about how writing tutors might interact most productively with students who write about traumatic events or who identify as GLBT. Second, despite this lack of literature, these were the meetings that generated the strongest—and the most unexpected—reactions among the tutors. This convergence suggested that a critical examination of these two meetings was in order.

THE COUNSELING CENTER

The common practice in first-year writing courses to assign personal narratives dovetails nicely with those students who are eager to write about their own traumatic experiences. Indeed, several books have been written by composition scholars about the evocation of student trauma in writing assignments and how writing instructors can respond productively to such papers (C. Anderson & M. MacCurdy, 2000; J. Berman, 2001; S. Borrowman, 2005; M. Payne, 2000).

In contrast, writing center literature about trauma writing and tutors' responses to it is far more limited. Most theoretical collections contain essays that discuss ethical, political, social, cultural, technological, and textual issues in tutoring (P. Gillespie, A. Gillam, L. F. Brown, & B. L. Stay, 2002; N. Grimm, 1999; C. Murphy & S. Sherwood, 2008; C. Murphy & B. L. Stay, 2006; M. Pemberton & J. Kinkead, 2003). Emotional issues are addressed only in passing as part of potentially troubling interchanges when tutors' and writers' purposes cross. For example, at the end of an article in which Stacey Freed (2008) questions the standard professional advice to tutors to remain impartial in the face of intellectually disagreeable ideas, she briefly acknowledges the emotional dimension of such encounters. She refers to Muriel Harris' advice to tutors to use standard counseling techniques in order to help students explore deeper issues that may interfere with their writing, but then she asks if such probing might inadvertently trigger emotional problems. Rather than exploring this avenue of thought further,[1] Freed endorses the solution that Emily Meyer and Louise Z. Smith offer: "to make a referral [to the counseling center] as gently as possible" (as cited in Freed, 2008, p.140). Then she ends this discussion by quickly returning to her primary focus on confronting the political and social challenges of students' ideas.

---

[1] To be fair, exploring the potential for emotional trauma in tutoring sessions was not Freed's purpose; however, her handling of this issue is precisely the point: discussions of how tutors might respond to traumatic writing are usually bundled with broader issues.

In contrast, tutor training texts offer practical advice about how to respond in emotionally charged situations: reminding tutors to paraphrase what they hear, to listen carefully, to ask the writer what he or she wants to do, to bring the session back to the writing, and to suggest counseling (P. Gillespie & N. Lerner, 2000; D. McAndrew, T. Reigstad, & J. Strickland, 2001; B. Rafoth, 2005; L. Ryan & L. Zimmerelli, 2006). Nevertheless, this advice rarely acknowledges the tutors' own emotions in such situations, assuming that tutors can and will maintain an emotional distance. One useful exception is a brief but concrete discussion by Corinne Agostinelli, Helena Poch, and Elizabeth Santoro (2005). They offer several strategies for tutors to use when their own emotions are too fully involved, ranging from acknowledging that engagement, playing "devil's advocate," and offering to back out or to bring in another tutor (pp. 38–39). Ultimately, however, Noreen Lape (2008) notes that even this kind of advice does not adequately prepare tutors in advance of emotionally charged tutoring sessions. She offers a sequenced "pedagogy of empathy" that borrows techniques from service-learning theory to help tutors anticipate and actually practice for such situations (pp. 3–4).

Obviously, then, our training goal for this first meeting reflected the practicalities and the limits of our profession's standard tutoring advice. So when we asked Beth, a faculty member in the counseling center, to help us all understand the counseling dimension of our work, we hoped our tutors might feel more prepared to respond effectively to trauma writing. Our institutional goal was equally modest: we were content to lay the groundwork for an ongoing collaborative relationship by learning about each other's services. So, after general introductions, Beth outlined the roles and responsibilities of the counseling center faculty, as well as the limitations of this student service. In turn, we educated Beth about such standard tutoring practices as reading aloud, focusing on content first, and safeguarding students' privacy.

Then we moved into the main purpose of her visit: learning a professional counselor's perspective on how tutors can best respond to students whose papers reveal serious emotional problems. Beth began by describing the range of problems that college students typically experience, among them eating disorders, alcohol and substance abuse, emotional and physical abuse, and depression. Even a brief survey of campus counseling literature reinforces her description, as university counselors report increased demand by students suffering from stress, depression, and abuse issues (A. Levine & J. Cureton, 1998; S. Benton, J. Robertson, W. Tseng & F. Newton, 2003; R. Kadison & T. DiGeronimo, 2004). She emphasized the frequency of this range of issues but also noted that many students who write about traumatic experiences have started to heal, so tutors should probably worry about those students less.

In response, some of the tutors recounted their experiences in responding to papers recounting violent episodes of abuse. Unlike instructors who usually encounter such writing in the relative privacy of their offices, tutors must respond immediately and in the public space of the center, circumstances that challenged these tutors to be simultaneously sensitive to and questioning of painful content. They asked Beth, on the one hand, if it is "ok to focus on editing issues" or to "ask for more detail about abuse." On the other hand, they wondered if it is appropriate to express sympathy or otherwise to react emotionally. Beth's advice to listen carefully and to ask questions mirrored standard tutoring practice, but, more important, she reassured the tutors that the intuitive responses they described were indeed on target.

When discussion turned to how to respond when content crosses that border between troubling and dangerous, the tone of the meeting shifted noticeably. Beth's suggestion that tutors might refer a student to the counseling center was met with surprise and resistance from the undergraduate tutors present. "I'm not comfortable doing that," one commented. "I feel like that's snitching. What if someone overhears? What if the student is embarrassed?" In response, Beth emphasized that tutors are certainly not expected to diagnose or to play counselor, but it is useful for them to be familiar with appropriate resources and willing to pass that information along to students. Despite Beth's assurances, the undergraduate tutors still felt that they were being encouraged to "snitch" on fellow students, even by simply handing them a brochure. So, we resolved this rapidly developing impasse between Beth and the tutors by advising them to talk with one of us if they feel a student is getting in too deep, so that we, not the tutor, would offer the brochure or make the referral call if necessary.

Interestingly, the graduate tutors' response to the invitation to refer students directly or by brochure to the counseling center was one of relief and reassurance. They felt far more comfortable knowing they could call on the resources of the counseling center if a student they were tutoring appeared to need more emotional assistance than they could responsibly offer. As gratified as we were about the graduate tutors' positive response, we were equally intrigued by the undergraduates' resistance, noting it as the subject of future reflection.

Overall, we and our presenter were pleased with the connection that had been established between our writing center and the counseling center. Beth reported that simply knowing more about our environment and practices encouraged her to recommend more students to us for writing help. For our part, we not only learned about what situations would call for a referral to the counseling center, but we also developed an ad hoc policy for making such referrals that respected our undergraduate tutors' sensibilities. So on that level, our first attempt at collaboration and alliance building seemed quite promising.

THE SAFE ZONE

The Safe Zone, the training arm of our campus' GLBT Commission, offers regular day-long workshops for faculty and staff who wish to be part of a network of safe spaces for GLBT students and had long intended to pilot a similar workshop for undergraduate student workers. Due to their daily interactions with a broad slice of the undergraduate population, particularly first-year students encountering identity issues of all sorts, writing center tutors were an obvious choice. The relative brevity of our writing center's training sessions, however, required the Safe Zone presenters to adapt their day-long training session to one hour. As if this time constraint were not difficult enough, our lack of knowledge about how GLBT issues might intersect with writing center work posed an additional challenge.

Certainly, composition studies has addressed the specific needs and challenges faced by GLBT students in first-year writing classes and the adequacy of composition pedagogy in meeting these needs. Harriet Malinowitz (1995) writes about the problematic nature of composition pedagogies that encourage students to share their personal experiences in their writing; although well-intentioned, these pedagogies often do not acknowledge how such an approach could be fraught with tension and significance for GLBT students. Malinowitz's admonitions to writing instructors are certainly applicable to writing center workers. Although the writing center is not a composition classroom, writers and tutors do engage with the products of the classroom in the writing center, so if students bring in confessional writing in which they discuss sexual orientation or gender issues, tutors should be prepared to treat the subject matter sensitively.

Still, in terms of specific discussion or advice about addressing the particular concerns of GLBT students in the writing center, Harry Denny (2005) is one of the only voices to have emerged. While Denny touches on identity issues faced by student writers, his argument for applying queer theory to writing center practice is more theoretical than practical. So, when the Safe Zone leaders asked us about the best focus for the meeting, we emphasized that we were interested in learning specifics about what we, as tutors and administrators, could do to make the writing center a safe space for GLBT students and how we could avoid any inadvertent marginalization.

Following this discussion, we sent several emails to the tutors to explain the focus of the meeting. Immediately prior to the meeting, however, some of the tutors still expressed confusion about its purpose. One tutor even asked, somewhat embarrassed, "What does GLBT stand for again?" We knew then that our explanations had been insufficient; considering the diversity of our group, from age to religion to cultural background, their levels of knowledge about GLBT issues were bound to vary based on their experiences. This was an issue that we should have considered more thoroughly prior to the meeting, as it had the potential to interfere with the collaborative relationship we were trying to establish.

Our Safe Zone presenters were Jules, an administrator in residence life, and Rita, a faculty member in the counseling center. They began the meeting by familiarizing us with the purpose and goals of the Safe Zone program and defining some basic terminology before turning the floor over to us and asking how GLBT issues emerge in the writing center. Several tutors mentioned an incident from the semester before, when a student brought in a paper, full of fire and brimstone, that condemned gay marriage, using the most offensive language possible. The tutor who worked with this student was offended and uncomfortable but was unsure of the best way to respond. While that paper was fairly extreme, tutors encountering a paper that contains inappropriate or troubling language is not an uncommon occurrence. This part of the discussion became quite lively, then, as the tutors shared their experiences, and Jules and Rita offered suggestions on how to tactfully address offensive language in a paper.

Throughout this part of the presentation, the tutors were interested and enthusiastic; we were engaged in a discussion about situations they had directly experienced, and the speakers offered specific, practical advice. However, we detected a subtle shift in attitude as Jules and Rita turned the conversation away from student writing and toward our own roles, asking us how we as tutors and administrators can work to make the writing center a safe space for GLBT students. This question was initially met with a resounding silence. Eventually a few graduate tutors offered some suggestions about active listening and responding to students' cues, but the majority of the undergraduate tutors did not engage in this discussion.

After listening to our suggestions, Jules and Rita advised us further about how to make GLBT students feel safe and comfortable in the writing center. They cautioned us not to assume heterosexuality as the "default" when conversing with students. If a male student mentions going on a date, don't assume that his date is a woman. If a student talks about her parents, don't assume that her parents are necessarily a mom and a dad. Additionally, they cautioned, we also cannot assume that we know a student's gender identity. We should always listen to students' cues before making any assumptions about their gender, their sexuality or that of their significant others and family. As the meeting closed, Jules and Rita reminded us that we can refer interested students to Safe Zone members if they have questions or concerns about their experiences as GLBT students on campus.

Because the silences during the second part of the meeting had concerned us, we were eager to get the tutors' feedback. The next day, Maggie chatted with several graduate tutors who seemed enthusiastic about the discussion. One of them even asked for extra copies of handouts that Jules had provided. However, she received a markedly different reaction during a conversation with three undergraduate tutors later that same day.

The conversation began when one of the tutors motioned her over and asked in a whisper: "Maggie, is someone who works here a . . . *homosexual*?" With a sinking feeling, she sat down with them and tried to unpack the question. As they talked, Maggie realized how much trouble these three tutors were still having understanding the purpose of the meeting, uncertainty that apparently resulted in speculation about the "real reason" for the meeting. She reiterated to these tutors what Jules and Rita had emphasized about the importance of being sensitive to heterosexist attitudes and being aware of other GLBT issues that might present themselves in a tutoring session. Still, she was met with resistance. "My job is to read papers and help students with their writing," one of the tutors told her. "Someone's sexuality is none of my business. It has nothing to do my tutoring," she asserted firmly, regarding any such acknowledgments as an intrusion into students' privacy.

Malinowitz has addressed the problematic nature of such statements that draw a dichotomy between public and private; they place GLBT individuals as outsiders who are erased from the social realm and the discourse used to describe it (p. 38). Similarly, Denny argues that when we discuss students who visit the writing center, we must consider their identities and how these identities affect their writing. When tutors and writers work together, these issues necessarily influence their interaction. Most writing center administrators understand—and celebrate—the reality that tutoring involves far more than simply reading and responding to papers and that the role of a tutor is complex; however, the conversations with our undergraduate tutors as a result of this meeting revealed that their perceptions of their roles were much more restricted than ours or the graduate tutors' were.

As we thought about this second attempt at collaboration, the results surprised us; after Beth's visit, we agreed that we had started to establish a continuing cross-campus relationship. With Jules and Rita's visit, however, the result seemed more like an information trade-off. Our group learned about how to avoid heterosexism in our conversations with students, and we received useful suggestions on how to address offensive language in student writing. For their part, Jules and Rita gained useful initial feedback about developing their pilot program for undergraduate student workers. Thus, although we may not have developed a lasting alliance with the Safe Zone leaders, we both felt that our collaboration was still useful; no one ruled out mutual initiatives in the future.

REFLECTIONS

As we reviewed the results of our cross-campus collaboration a few months later, we drew a number of conclusions about our experience. First, in answer to the question of whether it was worth it, our response was a qualified yes. "Qualified" because we made mistakes that interfered with tutors' benefiting fully from the sessions. Our assumption that all tutors would respond to each presentation with the same interest as we did prevented us from realizing that these sessions covered complicated ground that our diverse group of tutors would respond to very differently. In our eagerness to collaborate with our colleagues, we did not adequately prepare the tutors for the meetings, especially with respect to our goals.

Despite these mistakes, we concluded that our experience was worth it because we began to establish our writing center's connections with other student services, tenuous though they may be. It was worth it because we discovered that the writing center community has not adequately considered how tutors and administrators alike might attend more carefully to making our writing centers safe places for GLBT students as well as for those who write or talk about traumatic experiences. Finally, it was worth it because we gained valuable insights into the variety of ways in which tutors viewed their own roles and responsibilities.

Although we and our presenters were uniformly excited by the possibilities opened up in this collaboration, our tutors had a wider range of responses. If the information was tied to specific advice, reactions were positive across the board. However, when presenters moved into sensitive areas related to gender identity or emotional problems, reactions separated cleanly along graduate and undergraduate lines, giving us much to think about.

On the surface, it is easy to say that undergraduates naturally will be less identified with the institution than graduates; after all, this group of undergraduate tutors was younger and less experienced than the graduate tutors, with ages ranging from 19 to 22 years in contrast to the graduate tutors, whose ages ranged from 28 to 40+. The undergraduates' use of the word "snitching" is telling; "snitching" indicates a greater identification with the students they serve and a greater felt distance from—even a repudiation of—any institutional authority they may wield. In contrast, the graduate tutors' appreciation of these issues indicated a stronger identification with the institution.

It is equally easy to note that these two issues—distinct though they are—each trigger anxiety about invasions of students' privacy. Many people, especially undergraduates, still see a recommendation that someone seek counseling as questioning a person's sanity. Similarly, a suggestion that gender identity might play a role in the apparently neutral space of a tutorial is often regarded as an intrusion into matters best left private. As a result, acknowledging either of these issues in a tutoring session would easily be perceived as, at minimum, a deflection from the proper focus on the paper.

This anxiety is more than an emotional response; its roots burrow deep into ideological factors that shape undergraduate tutors' perceptions of their jobs. In *Good Intentions*, Nancy Grimm (1999) has written at length about how writing centers' immersion in modernist ideology encourages tutors to narrowly define their job as reading papers and helping students with their writing. This instrumental view, says Grimm, grows from interlinked beliefs in individual autonomy and progress that, we admit, probably undergird our own tutor training. This training, in turn, discourages tutors from perceiving that they are indeed institutional agents, whose "help" actually funnels students into producing texts that shut down exploration and questioning (pp. 71–72). Thus, our presenters' invitations to refer students for counseling and to examine our own heterosexual assumptions contributed strongly to the unease the undergraduate tutors felt about these "outside" considerations.

Conversely, the graduate tutors were more comfortable with the terms and ideas presented during these meetings perhaps because the ideological issues of identity, privilege, and institutional roles frequently addressed during their coursework and scholarly activity inoculates them to some degree from the ideological influences Grimm delineates. As graduate students, they also may have been able to connect the ideas from the tutor training with various theories of teaching and learning encountered in their studies, thereby encouraging them to see their tutoring as an integral part of their ongoing professionalization. As a result, they welcomed as appropriate to their role as tutors the very suggestions that so challenged the undergraduates.

OUTCOMES

In the intervening months since these visits, neither we nor the faculty in these student services offices have pursued further official contact. However, changing circumstances, not a lack of goodwill, have discouraged further collaboration—at least for now. The counseling center has experienced both a physical move and a shift in its institutional mission that have consumed the energies of its faculty. And because many counseling center faculty are involved in the Safe Zone program, these changes have affected those initiatives as well. Within our own walls, the spring of 2009 has started with a major turnover of staff, requiring us to attend, once again, to the basics of tutoring. These internal and external changes serve well to remind us that collaborative efforts across campus will ebb and flow as conditions warrant.

When conditions do allow for renewed contact, however, we will need to consider practical concerns like time, as well as more strategic ones such as how to best frame the meetings for the tutors and communicate our needs to our guest speakers. Obviously, we need to be more realistic about what is possible to accomplish within the timeframe available. Due to our tutors' full schedules and our writing center's extended operating hours, we can only afford one hour every two weeks for a staff meeting. Moreover, as the semester progresses and the writing center becomes busier, we need to reassess how much learning can take place during this hour.

The subject matter we are addressing complicates the issue as well. Even under ideal circumstances, an hour-long meeting would never sufficiently address the challenges raised by the topics. Such limits suggest that a credit-bearing course would overcome these constraints, at least in part. But we do not wish to restrict tutor discussion of complicated or challenging subjects to formal tutor training courses. Rather, our experience suggests that more careful planning might allow staff meetings to accomplish much of what we set out to do.

First, we can take steps to ensure that the meetings are as focused as possible. We therefore need to communicate clearly and specifically with our guest speakers beforehand about our needs and goals. Now that we have established relationships with these faculty, it will certainly be easier to develop more focused meetings for future visits; with introductions and other preliminaries already out of the way and our speakers more aware of our needs, they can address tutor concerns more quickly and, we hope, explore them in more depth.

We also need to clarify with tutors prior to the meetings how the subject matter relates to their tutoring. Although we attempted to do so, it is obvious in the wake of the Safe Zone meeting that sending email before each presentation was not sufficient. A general staff meeting prior to the series of guest speakers might be a better way to acquaint tutors with the subjects to be discussed so that together we clarify our goals and expectations for the presenters. An important facet of this planning process is to recognize that the diversity of our tutors (in terms of language, ethnicity, culture, religion, age, and graduate status) allows for various levels of knowledge about and comfort with any given subject matter. We should be prepared to work with these tutors' questions and concerns.

These practical tactics aside, probably the most important lesson our experience reveals is a need to think more critically about our overall approach to working with writing tutors—a process that will take us into territory far beyond the scope of this chapter. We recognize that factors such as gender, ethnicity, national background, language, and social class complicate tutors' divergent perceptions of identity. However, the distinct reactions of our graduate and undergraduate tutors illustrate that the deceptively simple factor of education level is an important influence in the development of tutoring identity. This experience has ultimately led us to speculate

about theoretical and ideological issues of tutors' identity formation, particularly the implications for tutor training.

Writing center literature has begun to explore how these issues affect
graduate students who work in the writing center. Drawing from Connie
Snyder Mick's description of graduate tutors as more than students but less
than faculty, Melissa Nicolas (2008) expands upon the complications that the
writing center community's traditional emphasis on "peer" tutoring poses
for the "in-between" status of graduate tutors (p. 2). As useful as her examination is in illuminating issues of authority for graduate students in the
writing center, our experience indicates that it is just a start: in pointing to
the existence of concerns unique to graduate tutors, it is clear that we can no
longer assume all tutoring is undergraduate "peer" tutoring. The writing
center community needs to acknowledge instead that tutoring involves multiple roles and practices. Specifically, what does it mean to uphold the ethic
of peer collaboration with a staff and a clientele of both graduates and
undergraduates? What does it mean if staff and clientele are exclusively
graduate or undergraduate? How far can we ask undergraduate tutors to
expand their perceptions of their tutoring roles before their identification
with their fellow students is lost?

As the writing center community considers these broad questions, pragmatic issues arise for the daily operation of writing centers and for tutor
training. If graduate tutors are not peers in the traditional sense of the word
for our field, how do they construct their roles and their practices as tutors,
particularly as they diverge from and overlap with undergraduate tutors?
This question, in turn, drives a whole series of questions about differences
in approach to the diverse students who come through our doors. Given the
gaps in writing center literature about approaches to students who write
about trauma or GLBT issues, we need to ask this question in particular
about these groups.

Ultimately, how can we effectively guide a group of tutors, who may
have vastly different perceptions of their tutoring identities, to grow both
more skillful and more reflective in ways that honor their own and their students' diversity yet uphold excellence in writing center practice? This is the
question we started with, albeit expressed rather more modestly and without the recognition of the tutors' own diversity. What began with our pragmatic intention to help our tutors develop their skills eventually led us to
some profound questions about tutor training, identity formation, and
tutoring ideology; more significantly, these questions emerged from the
planning, the listening, and the thinking that resulted from our "simple"
invitations to student services faculty to talk with our tutors. Although we
could not predict these developments, it is clear that when we look outward,
reaching across campus to our colleagues, we may just find that, in unanticipated ways, we are challenging ourselves.

REFERENCES

Agostinelli, C., Poch, H., & Santoro, E. (2005). Tutoring in emotionally charged sessions. In B. Rafoth (Ed.), *A tutor's guide: Helping writers one-to-one* (2nd ed., pp. 34–40). Portsmouth, NH: Boynton/Cook.

Anderson, C., & MacCurdy, M. (2000). *Writing and healing: Toward an informed practice.* Urbana, IL: National Council of Teachers of English.

Benton, S. A., Robertson, J. M., Tseng, W. C., Newton, F. B., & Benton, S. L. (2003). Changes in counseling center client problems across 13 years. *Professional Psychology: Research and Practice, 34*(1), 66–72.

Berman, J. (2001). *Risky writing: Self-disclosure and self-transformation in the classroom.* Amherst: University of Massachusetts Press.

Borrowman, S. (2005). *Trauma and the teaching of writing.* Albany: SUNY Press.

Denny, H. (2005). Queering the writing center. *The Writing Center Journal, 25*(2), 39–62.

Freed, S. (2008). Subjectivity in the tutorial session: How far can we go? In C. Murphy & S. Sherwood (Eds.), *The St. Martin's sourcebook for writing tutors* (3rd ed., pp. 137–140). Boston: Bedford/St. Martin's.

Gillespie, P., Gillam, A., Brown, L. F., & Stay, B. L. (Eds.). (2002). *Writing center research: Extending the conversation.* Mahwah, NJ: Erlbaum.

Gillespie, P., & Lerner, N. (2000). *The Allyn & Bacon guide to peer tutoring.* Boston: Allyn & Bacon.

Grimm, N. M. (1999). *Good intentions: Writing center work for postmodern times.* Portsmouth, NH: Boynton/Cook.

Homosexuality and sexual orientation disturbance: Proposed change in DSM-II. (1973). *American Psychological Association Document Reference No. 730008.* Retrieved August 12, 2009, from www.psychiatryonline.com/DSMPDF/DSM-II_Homosexuality_Revision.pdf

Kadison, R., & DiGeronimo, T. F. (2004). *College of the overwhelmed: The campus mental health crisis and what to do about it.* San Francisco: Jossey-Bass.

Lape, N. (2008). Training tutors in emotional intelligence: Toward a pedagogy of empathy. *Writing Lab Newsletter, 33*(2), 1–6.

Levine, A., & Cureton, J. S. (1998). *When hope and fear collide: A portrait of today's college student.* San Francisco: Jossey-Bass.

Macauley, W., & Mauriello, N. (Eds.). (2007). *Marginal words, marginal works? Tutoring the academy in the work of writing centers.* Cresskill, NJ: Hampton Press.

Malinowitz, H. (1995). *Textual orientations.* Portsmouth, NH: Boynton/Cook.

McAndrew, D., Reigstad, T., & Strickland, J. (2001). *Tutoring writing: A practical guide for conferences.* Portsmouth, NH: Boynton/Cook.

Murphy, C., & Sherwood, S. (Eds.). (2008). *The St. Martin's sourcebook for writing tutors* (3rd ed.). Boston: Bedford/St. Martin's.

Murphy, C., & Stay, B. L. (Eds.). (2006). *The writing center director's resource book.* Mahwah, NJ: Erlbaum.

Nicolas, M. (Ed.). (2008). *(E)Merging identities: Graduate students in the writing center.* Southlake, TX: Fountainhead.

Olson, G. (Ed.). (1984).*Writing centers: Theory and administration.* Urbana, IL: National Council of Teachers of English.

Payne, M. (2000). *Bodily discourses: When students write about abuse and eating disorders.* Portsmouth, NH: Boynton/Cook.

Pemberton, M., & Kinkead, J. (Eds.). (2003). *The center will hold: Critical perspectives on writing center scholarship.* Logan: Utah State University Press.

Rafoth, B. (Ed.). (2005). *A tutor's guide: Helping writers one-to-one* (2nd ed.). Portsmouth, NH: Boynton/Cook.

Ryan, L., & Zimmerelli, L. (2006). *The Bedford guide for writing tutors* (4th ed.). Boston: Bedford/St. Martin's.

IF YOU BUILD IT, THEY MIGHT COME: CONSTRUCTING WRITING CENTER SATELLITES

Sue Mendelsohn

As writing center practitioners, we tend to describe our practice as set apart and in between; our scholarship has long been dominated by topographical metaphors of borderlands, margins, and liminal spaces. The sheer pervasiveness of these spatial metaphors attests to a history of perceived marginalization within academic institutions. Nancy Grimm's 1996 article, for instance, proposes strategies to liberate writing centers from their "subordinate position" to composition programs (p. 527). Carol Peterson Haviland (2007) voices what is likely a common sentiment among critics when she calls the trope of marginalization "an extremely tired horse . . . that of PMU (poor marginalized us)" (p. 79). However, many critics use metaphors of liminality differently—to describe an institutional separateness that enhances, rather than limits, the role that writing centers play as mediators between student writers and the university. "Writing center workers," Grimm writes, "need to think of themselves as fieldworkers, curious about the liminal understandings that occur on the borders of cultural and academic practices, inviting students to articulate their observations about what happens at these crossings" (Grimm, 1996, p. 543).

Scholarly efforts to subvert the "PMU" idea and posit writing centers' liminal status as a privileged position have gone in many directions since

Stephen North's (1984) "Idea of a Writing Center." Centers have been conceptualized as in but not of academic institutions and therefore as sanctuaries from the nomos, the custom-law, of academia—a contact zone for grappling with questions of authority (Carino, 2003; Clark, 1990; Grimm, 1999), race (DiPardo, 1992; Geller, Eodice, Condon, Carroll, & Boquet, 2007), identity construction and sexuality (Denny, 2005), feminism (Lutes, 2002; Woolbright, 1992), peace and conflict (Diab, 2008), and disability (Hawkes, 2006), to mention just a handful. The writing center practitioner's ability to "cross genres and contexts" and "blur the line between the academy and the community" has even been reconceived as a model for speeding up the sometimes glacial pace of change in university administrations: "One might say that writing center work has been light-years ahead of the academy, in a sense, predicting the blurred boundaries now facing our institutions: interdisciplinarity, students from high school concurrently taking college courses, partnerships with community economic groups" (Mullin, Carino, Nelson, & Evertz, 2006, p. 233). Scholars have even envisioned consultants taking on creative roles that play with nomos: tricksters (Geller et al., 2007) and riffing, improvising musicians (Boquet, 2002).

Yet this reconceptualized writing center topography, in which institutional liminality is rewritten as a virtue rather than a limitation, can be an equally restrictive conceptual model. If writing centers' status as separate and between is consistently understood as a strength, how might that limit administrators' ability to recognize the potential benefits of certain institutional partnerships? In other words, what happens when liminal centers become joiners? What happens when centers—to meet the needs of writers, to thrive— form partnerships that demand participation in another academic culture? Louise Smith is one critic who has rejected these either/or characterizations of centers as either playing on the margins or ensconced within institutional systems. She advocates, instead, for "independence and collaboration": decentralized "centers" situated in multiple sites and staffed by people from various disciplines who share ideas about writing pedagogy: "New models for integrating writing centers with writing-across-the-curriculum are beginning to appear. Instead of discarding writing centers, we should find ways of decentralizing them so they can use their knowledge more effectively" (Smith, 2003, pp. 22–23). Ultimately, this approach allows centers to retain their characteristic institutional agility while benefitting from strong cross-curricular partnerships.

During the 2005–2006 school year, the Saint Louis University writing center decided to become a joiner in a big way; it went into the satellite business. At the time, the university's writing center would have been more accurately termed the "Writing Cubicles." The center operated out of two makeshift cubicles placed in a wide hallway in the basement of an academic resources building. Serving a campus of 7,000 undergraduates, the organization needed to grow, and grow quickly, to meet students' and faculty members' demands for writing support. The budget for this initiative? Zippo. The new office space set aside for it? Zilch. So the writing center did what many centers do: administrators identified campus partners who expressed a need for greater or more specialized writing support and provided it in exchange for space and funding. The center opened satellites.

For writing centers that have space, location, and funding limitations—and that describes many centers—satellites can offer solutions. They also allow us to become more of a part of the culture of the partner-college or entity while taking a discipline-specific approach to its writing support needs. In return, colleges and schools receive more writing support and services customized for their needs. But when satellites fail, they can drain time and energy and damage the writing center's credibility. In 2005–2006, the Saint Louis University writing center opened four satellites with partners in the business school, the college of engineering, the college of health sciences, and the library. This narrative recounts the stories of these satellites—one that failed, one that metamorphosed, one that survived, and one that thrived.

At the same time that the writing center needed to expand, the English department was looking for ways to create funding and professional development opportunities for its graduate students. The two organizations' goals dovetailed into satellites. The English department chair negotiated with the deans of the business school and the college of engineering to fund writing consultants for 10 hours per week and provide office space in their respective buildings. Both satellites produced lackluster results the first year. In the second year, the English department chose to fund an additional consultant at each location hoping that the services would take root. The engineering satellite still failed to draw engineering writers in significant numbers and closed. While more encouraging, the business school satellite's usage numbers were not high enough to convince the dean that her school needed to devote scarce office space to a satellite. Thus this location also closed after its second year. However, the writing center's partnership with the business school continued with an arrangement that better suited its needs and the center's strengths. The dean continued to fund one consultant to work out of the library satellite and coordinate a popular business writing workshop series.

Satellites in the library and the health sciences college experienced more immediate success. Funded by the health sciences college, the English department, the provost, and the graduate school, the health sciences satellite proved its worth in its first year and continued to grow busier. The library satellite was an immediate hit. Despite a hard-to-find location in the first year, writers flocked. A subsequent move to a more accessible space within the library, combined with major increases in writing center staffing there, made this the writing center's most popular location.

The experience of getting those four satellites off the ground was akin to drinking from the fire hose: consultants and administrators learned quickly what worked and what did not. Taken together, those satellites tell the story of lessons learned the hard way: when to say "no thanks" to satellites, when to say "yes," and how to make them work. Some of the lessons were no great surprise: satellites take considerable resources, time, and effort to sustain; consultants who work in satellites will feel as though they've been banished to Siberia unless the whole staff works to make them feel less isolated; and the more partnerships formed, the more stakeholders a center has to answer to. The focus here, instead, is on the four lessons that ran counter to assumptions. These are the lessons that, had they been clearer before, would have helped the university build better satellites and have the wisdom to decline taking on at least one of them before it started. The writing center learned about the cultural and administrative transformations required to decentralize the center without destabilizing it.

LESSON 1: WRITING CENTERS
ARE MARVELOUS

Finding partners to provide funding, resources, and/or space for a satellite is not as hard as it might seem. Harvey Kail (2000) explains,

> What distinguishes writing centers in academe is their willingness and ability to engage student writers sentence by sentence, phrase by phrase, word by word, comma by comma, one to one, face to face. No one else in the academy can or wants to do this work, but everyone wants it done—now. (p. 25)

Deans, professors, and students want what writing centers have to offer, so centers can negotiate from a position of strength. But the process of securing partners raises what Elisabeth Piedmont-Marton (2005) calls writing centers' "problems with power." She draws from Stephen Greenblatt's reading of Christopher Columbus' descriptions of the New World as "marvelous," a power-laden term. In a characteristic passage in a letter to Ferdinand and Isabella, Columbus says of a lake, "There are great indications of this being the terrestrial paradise, for its site coincides with the opinion of the holy and wise theologians whom I have mentioned . . . and if the water of which I speak does not proceed from the earthly paradise, it appears to be still more marvelous, for I do not believe that there is any river in the world so large or so deep" (Columbus, 1892, pp. 141–142). While he attempts to claim the lake using a Christian framework, ultimately its unknowable foreignness and greatness make its power all the more an object of marvel that is worthy of mastery. For Columbus, the word connotes wonder, a fear of otherness, and the desire to possess and control.

The strange marvelousness of writing centers provokes others to take possession of them and define them in their own terms, giving rise to the popular trope of frustration that writing centers are misunderstood that goes all the way back to North's "Idea of a Writing Center" in 1984. Piedmont-Marton (2005) says of writing center practitioners,

> We of all people know what it means to be marveled at, converted, and possessed. We both do it, and then, in turn resist it being done to us. My point is not that we should not continue to resist the forces of conversion and possession, but rather that we are going about it the wrong way.

When negotiating for satellite support, the challenge for writing center administrators is to establish a partnership that resists being possessed. Administrators can do that by moving away from a hat-in-hand approach to finding support and instead becoming comfortable wielding the power writing centers' marvelousness brings. Piedmont-Marton (2005) constructs a way to stay open to outside forces of change while taking on the role of leader rather than victim or subject. Saint Louis University writing center administrators learned to go into negotiations with satellite partners ready to stand firm on some praxis and policies and, at the same time, to be changed. This attitude serves as a productive complement to Louise Smith's (1986) stance that writing centers' pedagogical certainty is leading to a sclerosis of innovation; we can spark new ideas, Smith (1986) argues, by spreading out, broadening partnerships, diversifying staff, and sharing best practices. It is entirely fair that academic units would expect to get services customized for their students and faculty in return for space and funding. So writing centers need to enter into discussions about satellites willing to shape a vision to meet the partner's needs while also meeting the pedagogical, intellectual, and administrative needs of the center. The Saint Louis University writing center, for instance, needed to explain to several of the satellite partners why the writing center would not provide faculty members with in-house editing and grading services.

As important as it was to preserve pedagogical integrity, the university's writing center did learn to welcome the ways that satellites changed its culture. When negotiating for the health sciences writing center, for instance, the dean wanted graduate student writing consultants—the people who would be staffing the proposed satellite—to work with faculty members on their publications. At first, we resisted that arrangement because consultants would have difficulty negotiating their authority in that relationship and might be pressured to play the role of proofreader. But as the dean continued to talk, we realized that the writing center needed to learn more about the needs of their faculty members and challenge graduate student consultants to negotiate the power dynamics that come into play when they work with faculty members. The dean described to me the culture of her college where a number of newer faculty members had returned to academe after careers in health care. Many were less experienced with academic publishing than the centers' consultants, and some were working on pieces for the popular media. She was right; writing center consultants probably could act as helpful peers, in a sense, for some health sciences professors, so the center changed its policy at that satellite.

LESSON 2: SATELLITES ARE GOOD AT MEETING DEMAND, NOT AT GENERATING IT

Satellites can fill existing needs for writing center services. But the stakeholder who gets to define what that need is determines whether the satellite will ultimately be successful. The year that Saint Louis University opened four satellites, the writing center made a number of decisions based on the needs identified by constituencies who had little control over whether writers would actually use a satellite. The initial need that motivated building satellites was the English department chair's desire to create jobs and professional development experiences for her graduate students. The department chair brokered three of the satellites by identifying schools and colleges that had deep enough pockets to fund consultants, were under-using the center, and were enough of a hike from the center's main office to make a satellite seem like a convenience.

The other players at the table had their own reasons for the satellites. College and school administrators, responding to faculty members' concerns, wanted to improve the quality of student writing. For the dean of the health sciences college, one need was to kick-start faculty members' publishing. In the engineering college, a number of department chairs wanted data from the satellite to use in the accreditation process. Another driver of decision making was the writing center's need: to serve students and faculty from schools and colleges that typically under-used the center. Anticipating future funding struggles, the writing center wanted data to demonstrate that the center does a good job serving all sectors of the university and is not just a haven for humanities departments. Pie charts with nice even pieces can make persuasive arguments to university administrators.

In the end, the needs that each of those constituencies identified didn't necessarily translate into actual demand from writers and instructors. Just because faculty members wanted their students to write better did not mean that students would choose to visit the satellite. So where should a writing center administrator look to understand whether a need for a satellite exists? An obvious answer, but one that I think is only partly correct, would be to survey students. My experience suggests that undergraduate writers are not the best predictors of what they'll use; students tend to overestimate the extent to which they will take advantage of services. Instead, another factor turned out to be a strong indicator of satellites' success: the existing writing culture.

At the Saint Louis University, business and health sciences departments have active, social writing cultures. A good number of their faculty members talk to both the writing center and each other about their own writing and the writing they teach. They share assignments, request workshops, and recommend their students visit the center. While most engineering students complete more writing projects in their major courses than business students, they seek writing support services in fewer numbers. Not surprisingly, the writing culture in their college seems to encourage a less social approach and one in which some instructors view "content" as divorced from writing. Consultant Sarah Fielding explains that "My sense was that writing there was thought of as an individual, isolating, inferior activity that one does alone and outside of his/her actual work. It is Other" (personal communication, July 10, 2008). They do not often connect their courses to the writing center, seldom requesting workshops or recommending the center's services to classes. Consultant Ty Hawkins also traces the problem back to the engineering faculty but feels the writing center played a part in the dynamic too: "The writing center did not seem to have built the infrastructure there . . . to support a dynamic exchange between Parks [College of Engineering] instructors and satellite consultants. Of course, this was to be expected, as the satellite was new. Yet I personally never was able to develop what I would term workable means of bridging the gap between Parks instructors and myself. This was a real frustration" (personal communication, July 10, 2008). As Hawkins' comments suggest, the satellite was not an effective place to build the key alliances the writing center needed with faculty. Those needed to be in place beforehand. The writing center could not make up for years of inattention to the engineering college by suddenly showing up and hanging out a shingle. Without a long-term focus on relationship building between an academic unit and writing center staff *before* the satellite opens, a satellite will have trouble establishing itself.

The data from 2005 through 2008 suggest that, while the numbers of business, health sciences, and, to a lesser degree, engineering students increased each year, satellite offices were not the clear cause. The numbers of students from other colleges also increased in similar proportions over the same time period. And visits from business and engineering students continued to increase even after those satellites closed. Thus, the data suggest that satellites are not good tools for building demand—they do not do a good job of accomplishing the goals that many deans, department chairs, and writing center coordinators created them for. That conclusion runs counter to the aims many of the Saint Louis University writing center satellite partners had when they agreed to support satellites. Simply putting a satellite in a college or school does not necessarily make people write more, write better, or find a desire for feedback on their writing. Instead, a satellite office is entering an existing writing culture. With careful attention over a long period of time, writing centers can influence that culture to some extent, and it will also change our centers, but remaking it within a few years is unrealistic. What a satellite *can* do is provide more specialized, targeted services than a generalist writing center can.

LESSON 3: VISIBILITY AND A BUCK WILL BUY YOU A CUP OF COFFEE

The visibility of a satellite office is important but not nearly as important as one might think. By the end of its first year, the satellite in the engineering college was still drawing anemic numbers of engineering students and faculty. Writers used just 5% of the available consulting slots. The college agreed to make two changes. The first was to open the satellite to writers from all departments, not just engineering departments, so that the increased usage would make the space seem more vibrant. The second was to move the satellite from its current space in a small office in the back of an office suite in a lightly trafficked hallway to a more visible space within the engineering building. To show its commitment to making it work, the college let consultants share some prime real estate, a glass-walled second-floor conference room that overlooked the building's entryway. The hope was that once students saw the magical interaction of a writing consultant and a writer huddled over a piece of writing, deep in conversation, they would begin to use the service themselves. It would be contagious. What was the result? In the old location, consultants spent much of their time twiddling their thumbs. In the new location, the difference was that the whole college could see the consultants spending much of their time twiddling their thumbs. Students from non-engineering departments were glad for the services, but engineering students remained unmoved. In the second year, engineering students used 15% of the available consulting slots, an increase over the previous year, but hardly enough to justify keeping the satellite open.

    The experience at the library satellite drove home how much less important visibility was than anticipated. The library "office" was a fourth floor shared group study room surrounded by stacks. The room was so difficult to find that consultants posted three signs with arrows, "Writing Center this way!" Writers still had trouble finding it, but that didn't stop them from using the location. In its first year, the library satellite filled 56% of the available consulting slots. Beginning in the 2007–2008 school year, a much more accessible, visible permanent satellite space opened on the third floor, and usage remained steady at 54%. During midterms and finals periods, consultants reported long waiting lists of writers hoping to squeeze in.

What made the hidden library satellite more popular than the highly visible engineering satellite? Consultant Sarah Fielding argues that it comes down to the clash between culture and space, "When the [engineering] satellite first opened, it was back in a bunny hole that no one could find. Then we were given a nice office in a fairly prominent location. But by then, word was out that we had traces of that thing moving in there—writing—that thing they (perhaps) feared most. When they walked by, students and faculty alike averted their eyes, and I felt as if I were manning the Student Health Center instead, and diseases were rampant inside" (personal communication, July 10, 2008). For a culture in which writing is a solitary activity and collaborating on writing was, for some, a sign of deficiency, the office's visibility may have actually dissuaded writers from visiting.

LESSON 4: GO BIG OR GO HOME

For good reasons, satellites often start as pilot projects. Campus partners are more likely to agree to something termed a "pilot project" because it connotes a low-stakes endeavor that is easy to start and equally easy to walk away from if it does not produce satisfactory results. However, writing centers should be wary if "pilot project" is another way of saying a small-scale or short-term experiment for its stakeholders. Writing center satellites and their partners should be prepared to keep satellites open at least a moderate number of hours per week for several years, even if the endeavor is packaged as a pilot project. The Saint Louis University satellites needed to be open 20 hours per week for two or three years before they fully took root. The business and engineering locations highlighted this lesson. Each offered only 10 consulting slots per week during their first year. Writers filled just 13% of those slots in the business satellite and just 5% in the engineering satellite. Clearly these academic units were not receiving sufficient services for their investments. In a last-ditch attempt to prove the value of the satellites (and maintain jobs for its graduate students), the English department elected to fund consultants to provide 10 additional slots per week in the second year of the business and engineering satellites' existence. This critical mass of open hours increased the satellites' business exponentially. While doubling consultation slots, the business satellite more than tripled the number of visits by business students. The engineering satellite tripled the number of engineering writers who visited and saw a seven-fold increase in the number of overall visits from undergraduates from all colleges (see Fig. 6.1).

Why did the 10-slot/week satellites do such a poor job of attracting writers? Here, visibility proved to be a weakness. Students and faculty members grew accustomed to seeing a dark, locked office most of the time they walked past. The few writers who sought out consultations at one of these satellites needed to be on the ball enough to learn when the offices were open and a little lucky to sync up their schedules to match an available slot. These writers are the ones who would have likely walked across campus to the main location anyway if the satellites were not there. By starting with 10-slot/week in that first year, the satellites relied on the most tenacious writers as a gauge for *all* writers' interest in the satellites. The 20-slot/week schedules adopted in the second year reached the critical mass of availability, acting as a more reliable indicator of demand.

Longevity is key as well. The health sciences satellite demonstrated the importance of staying invested in a satellite for several years. While the location has offered 30 consulting slots per week for the past three years, the percentage of those slots that writers used grew from 18% in the first year to 24% in the second and 41% in the third. The only satellite that remained immune from the lesson to "go big" was the library office. This location, despite offering only six hours per week in its first year, was bustling from the start. In fact, its first year was its busiest, with 56% of slots filled. Why did the library satellite prove an exception to the rule? First, it was the only

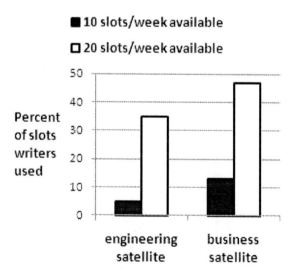

FIGURE 6.1. Percentage of slots used at business and engineering satellites with 10 slots/week available compared with 20 slots/week available.

location that offered evening hours in the place where writers worked, filling a gap in services that the main location and the other satellites could not. The second reason goes back to the issue of culture. Students write, research, and hang out in the library. And a dedicated staff of reference librarians regularly connect students to the center's services.

THE REWARDS OF FAILURE

The lessons that the Saint Louis University writing center learned these past years—that centers can negotiate from a position of strength; that what writers think they need matters more than what deans, instructors, and writing center administrators want; that location matters more that visibility; and that satellites that start as small projects will not have the critical mass to flourish—led to several successes. Chief among them were a four-fold increase in consultations and a sharp increase in workshop requests—both achieved despite lacking additional in-house space or funding. A less visible but perhaps more important change is the writing center's deepening engagement in the university's various writing cultures and the slowly growing ability to shape those cultures and be shaped by them. These benefits, however, still came with a steep cost in administrative time. While satellite funders can easily grasp the need to fund the consultants who directly provide services, the additional time and effort on the part of administrators to make a satellite work is not as obviously essential a cost.

As happened with Saint Louis University's college of engineering, satellite failures can discourage consultants and hurt the center's standing among students and faculty. Yet the satellites' failures can bring some opportunities as well. Before the 2005–2006 school year, the writing center was trapped in a catch-22 which is familiar to many writing center administrators. The center could not make a strong case to the provost for additional staffing and space because, without more staff and space, consultants could not serve more writers and prove that a greater demand for writing support existed. Satellites can help solve that conundrum—even those that eventually fail to thrive can play a role in boosting consultation numbers enough to convince university administrators to support a staffing increase and larger office spaces. The Saint Louis University writing center was able to accomplish these gains by learning with its partners the sometimes counterintuitive lessons of satellite building.

One of the more difficult lessons learned is that marginality carries a certain level of anonymity, and with anonymity comes security. When a center becomes more visible, as it inevitably does with satellites, its failures become more visible as well. Consultants sitting idle in a satellite location may give the university community the impression that an entire writing center is using more resources than it needs or is simply not a relevant service to students and faculty. Elizabeth Boquet (1999) hints at an even more serious outcome of making the center more visible when she writes that, "Foucault shows us, in the first pages of *Discipline and Punish*, that to extend power is to put it at risk. This has certainly been true of the university's relationship to the writing center, a symbiosis highlighting the degree to which institutional power becomes most vulnerable at the very point at which it becomes most visible" (p. 465). The more visible a center becomes, the more marvelous—and therefore the more vulnerable to possession and control—it appears to other university entities. This is certainly the case with the Saint Louis University writing center; in light of the center's current role on campus, the provost is considering restructuring scenarios proposed by three campus entities that would like to house it. If writing center administrators and other partners decide to build satellites together, students might come, but other institutional officials might come too and seek to exert more control over the center's operations. Writing centers that choose to grow through satellites need to be prepared for the positive consequences of not only their successes but their failures and for the negative consequences not only of their failures but their successes.

REFERENCES

Boquet, E. (1999). Our little secret: A history of writing centers, pre- to post-open admissions. *College Composition and Communication, 50*(3), 463–482.

Boquet, E. (2002). *Noise from the writing center*. Logan: Utah State University Press.

Carino, P. (2003). Power and authority in the writing center. In M. A. Pemberton & J. Kinkead (Eds.), *The center will hold: Critical perspectives on writing center scholarship* (pp. 96–113). Logan: Utah State University Press.

Clark, I. L. (1990). Maintaining chaos in the writing center: A critical perspective on writing center dogma. *Writing Center Journal, 11*(1), 81–95.

Columbus, C. (1892). Letter to Ferdinand and Isabella. In A. Stedman (Ed.), *Writings of Christopher Columbus: Descriptive of the discovery* (pp. 105–150). New York: Jenkins & McCowan.

Denny, H. (2005). Queering the writing center. *Writing Center Journal, 25*(2), 39–62.

Diab, R. (2008, October). *Plenary: New voices in writing center scholarship*. Paper presented at the IWCA/NCPTW conference, Las Vegas, NV.

DiPardo, A. (1992). "Whispers of coming and going": Lessons from Fannie. *Writing Center Journal, 12*(2), 125–144.

Geller, A. E., Eodice, M., Condon, F., Carroll, M., & Boquet, E. (2007). *The everyday writing center: A community of practice*. Logan: Utah State University Press.

Grimm, N. M. (1996). Rearticulating the work of the writing center. *College Composition and Communication, 47*(4), 523–548.

Grimm, N. M. (1999). *Good intentions: Writing center work for postmodern times*. Portsmouth, NH: Boynton/Cook Heinemann.

Hawkes, L. (2006). When compassion isn't enough: Providing fair and equivalent access to writing help for students with disabilities. In C. Murphy & B. L. Stay (Eds.), *The writing center director's resource book* (pp. 371–378). Mahwah, NJ: Lawrence Erlbaum Associates.

Kail, H. (2000). Writing center work: An ongoing challenge. *Writing Center Journal, 20*(2), 25–28.

Lutes, A. M. (2002). Why feminists make better tutors: Gender and disciplinary expertise in a curriculum-based tutoring program. In P. Gillespie, A. Gillam, L. Falls Brown, & B. Stay (Eds.), *Writing center research: Extending the conversation* (pp. 235–265). Mahwah, NJ: Lawrence Erlbaum Associates.

Mullin, J., Carino, P., Nelson, J., & Evertz, K. (2006). Administrative (chaos) theory: The politics and practices of writing center location. In C. Murphy & B. L. Stay (Eds.), *The writing center director's resource book* (pp. 225–236). Mahwah, NJ: Lawrence Erlbaum Associates.

North, S. (1984). The idea of a writing center. *College English, 46*(5), 433–446.

Peterson Haviland, C. (2007). Review: The everyday writing center. *Writing Center Journal, 27*(2), 77–80.

Piedmont-Marton, E. (2005, October). *A seat at the big table: Writing centers and institutional leadership.* Paper presented at the NCPTW/IWCA conference, Minneapolis, MN.

Smith, L. Z. (2003). Independence and collaboration: Why we should decentralize writing centers. *Writing Center Journal, 23*(1), 15–23.

Woolbright, M. (1992). The politics of tutoring: Feminism within the patriarchy. *Writing Center Journal, 13*(1), 16–30.

chapter 7

WRITING CENTERS AND LIVING LEARNING COMMUNITIES

Nicole Kraemer Munday

Sitting in a fluorescent-lit conference room, armed with markers and large sheets of paper for brainstorming, my colleagues and I imagined how our university might transform itself over the next few decades—in terms of fostering a culture of intellectualism and attracting a talented, active student body. As individual tables began to report their findings to this assembly of faculty members, student affairs staff, and campus administrators, I heard a chorus of approval for a proposal that would regroup students into Living Learning Communities. And when I heard the room buzzing with what was an almost unprecedented level of consensus, at least on my campus, I began to do a little brainstorming of my own: what did the Writing Center stand to gain or lose if we, too, jumped on the Living Learning Community bandwagon?

I'll admit, whenever I find out about any new programs being instituted at my university, I'm an unabashed opportunist for the Writing Center. My focus on outreach is based on a desire to raise the profile of our relatively new writing center and to build a positive reputation for the Center among its various stakeholders—students, faculty, and administrators. But my agenda is also grounded in a belief that writing center work is fundamental to higher education (Cooper, 1995; DeCiccio, 2006; Kuh, Kinzie, Schuh,

Whitt, & Associates, 2005; Wallace & Simpson, 1991). The habits of mind that we foster at the center, emphasizing collaboration, intellectual curiosity, and self-directed, lifelong learning, should push us to a larger sense of purpose—a goal of making writing center values permeate throughout our respective universities. Like Severino and Knight (2007), I, too, am eager to "export" (p. 20) writing center philosophy and pedagogy throughout the university structure to every corner of every department.

To find "exporting" opportunities, writing center directors cultivate a speculator's sixth sense, staking claims on campus projects that align with our centers' missions and ideologies. When writing centers enter collaborative partnerships, such as the Living Learning Community (LLC) partnership I propose here, they engage in a particularly fruitful form of outreach that allows them to increase their campus visibility, spread accurate information about writing center practice, foster a university-wide writing environment, and gain institutional recognition as a team player while building new alliances with colleagues.

Before entering a discussion about the relative merits and pitfalls of Writing Center–Living Learning Community (WC–LLC) partnerships, it is important to define LLCs and how they typically function. LLCs might seem familiar to writing center directors and consultants who have had long-standing partnerships with learning communities through Writing Fellows programs (Severino & Knight, 2007). However, LLCs differ from traditional learning communities because they are based in residence halls. This means that not only are LLC participants co-enrolled in some of the same courses (a common feature in traditional learning communities), but the community is further strengthened because participants also live within close proximity to one another.

In addition to the residential component, two of the defining features of LLCs are an integrated approach to learning and greater interaction between faculty members and students; therefore, the boundaries between in-class and out-of-class work and the boundaries between faculty members and students are often blurred. For example, faculty members who teach one of the LLC's co-enrolled courses might lead discussion sessions in the residence hall to supplement readings that LLC participants have been assigned for class, or perhaps a faculty member might organize an LLC potluck dinner or camping trip, during which there could be an educational component, like a discussion session, or the event might be more free-form in its structure, allowing faculty and students to learn from one another more organically.

There is often great variation in LLC activities and configurations from one university to another because LLCs are context-dependent: they may be designed to fit the needs of individual campuses (Schuh, 1999, p. 12). This makes it difficult to generalize about all LLCs, just as it is difficult to generalize about all writing centers (Macauley & Mauriello, 2007, pp. xv–xvi). However, the prior description of LLC underlying principles shows a clear connection between LLC goals and the type of work that writing centers have been doing for decades—creating interdisciplinary connections as we work with writers across the curriculum, embracing a non-hierarchical pedagogical model through peer tutoring, focusing on writers rather than individual texts, and viewing students holistically as consultants seek to develop rapport with their fellow writers. Therefore, the common dispositions that writing center and LLC communities share toward student learning, as well as the mutual benefits that both groups would reap in a WC-LLC partnership, suggest it makes a lot of sense for the two entities to band together.

WC–LLC PARTNERSHIPS AS WRITING CENTER OUTREACH

Throughout writing center lore, whenever we depict vibrant writing center settings, whether we are marveling at Harris' (1993) bustling Purdue University Writing Lab (pp. 6–7) or reflecting on the fraught sessions that Boquet (2002) chronicles during her time as an undergraduate consultant (pp. 1–6) and as a director (pp. 48–51), there is always one constant: writers are always present. In order to thrive, writing centers need to draw in writers—regardless of whether our writing centers are stand-alone, bricks-and-mortar units; embedded in libraries or satellite locations; or strictly cyberspace settings. If we are going to make writers aware of our existence and convince them of our worth, we have to make ourselves visible or our centers will likely wither.

As Hughes (1991) notes, "the history of writing centers is largely one of expansion" (p. 39), which implies that directors ought to maintain a speculator's stance when thinking about the existing needs of our home institutions. Both Hughes and Severino and Knight (2007) offer forceful arguments for why the writing center community must move beyond the walls of our writing centers, and they point toward the need for greater visibility as one of the main reasons why outreach is necessary. In "Exporting Writing Center Pedagogy," Severino and Knight note that because writing centers tend to be relatively small departments, "we face a real challenge in making our little country visible on the large map" of our universities (p. 19). To make writing centers visible, many scholars (Adams, 1991; Leahy, 1999; Severino & Knight, 2007) suggest that extended-contact initiatives, such as satellite centers, writing fellows programs, or what Hughes (1991) describes more generally as "instructional outreach" (p. 40), may be the most effective way of "reaching new audiences" (p. 39). With extended-contact instruc-

tional programs, writing center staff members are able to explain writing
center work with greater nuance than a brief class visit might allow. As both
Hughes (1991) and Severino and Knight (2007) point out, extended-contact
instructional outreach affords the opportunity to speak to students and faculty members directly in order to stamp out writing centers' most perni-
cious myths— that they have a remedial bent, that they are places for people and papers with special writing troubles, or that they are only needed by
students who are writing first-year English papers.

Beyond creating an accurate impression about the writing center, another goal of outreach is to demonstrate our value to students so that we provide impetus for writers to visit the center. This latter goal is particularly
important for centers, like mine, that rely on voluntary student visits. With
indirect outreach methods, such as posters, podcasts, and newsletters, writing centers develop and disperse these materials and then can only hope that
potential writing center clients will take notice. But when writing centers
participate in direct, extended-contact instructional outreach where there is
a ready-made student audience—as there is in writing fellows programs or
WC–LLC partnerships—we can address our intended audiences unfiltered.
Because promoting writing centers drains energy from writing center staff
and resources from our writing center budgets, we need to choose the most
effective outreach methods available; WC–LLC partnerships can be a particularly potent form of instructional outreach.

Scholars have argued that instructional outreach also leads to increased
writing center visits, though no statistical data support this claim.
Nevertheless, anecdotal evidence abounds. Hughes (1991) declares, "There
is no doubt that, when they are well done, these [instructional-outreach-]
presentations work; students come for tutorials as a direct result of the
presentations made in their classes" (p. 42). Severino and Knight (2007)
share student feedback from their Writing Fellows program at the
University of Iowa to show how this instructional outreach program
helped draw more visitors to the Main Writing Center. One student who
worked closely with a Fellow commented, "I intend to seek the writing
center more often to help with future assignments and recommend this
[Fellows] group and center highly to friends, peers, and colleagues" (p.
27). In Severino and Knight's model, the Fellows program allows the Main
Writing Center to draft off its efforts, similar to the way runners and bicy-
clists sometimes collaborate with their peers to draft off one another. This
drafting effect suggests that WC–LLC partnerships may draw more writers to the Main Writing Center, and the extended contact that LLC participants have with WC–LLC Liaisons could mean that LLC residents will
be more likely to continue their contact with the Main Writing Center
throughout their college careers, even after they move out of their LLC
residence hall.

LLCS AS AN OPPORTUNITY
TO COLLABORATE WITH RESIDENCE LIFE

So, what added outreach benefits do LLCs offer the writing center community beyond those which extended-contact instructional initiatives, such as writing fellows programs, already bring us? The answer is "Location, location, location!"—especially the location of LLCs within universities' institutional structures and the physical location of LLCs within residence halls. Because LLCs incorporate a residential component, whereas most writing fellows programs do not, LLC initiatives typically fall under the purview of Residence Life instead of Academic Affairs. Although writing centers have long histories of working with faculty members, traditionally, there have been few opportunities for writing centers to collaborate with residence life departments (besides offering workshops as part of a residence hall's programming or asking for space to set up a satellite writing center). Yet Residence Life is a well-funded and deeply entrenched department with considerable institutional clout, making it an important powerbroker on many college campuses, one to which the writing center community perhaps has failed to pay sufficient attention.

Another reason that Residence Life is an important writing center ally is due to its centrality to students' lives, particularly among non-commuting first-year students. As Simpson (1991) notes, first-year residence halls "are the primary source of information about campus services for most freshmen," especially in the first few weeks after they arrive to campus (p. 103). For non-commuting students, the first sustained contact they will have with campus personnel is likely to be through Residence Life. In the days leading up to the start of classes, when many universities host mandatory orientation sessions for new students, first-years are often grouped together according to their residence halls. Residence Life staff leads packs of residents from one event to another, serving as new students' lifelines for navigating campus and learning where to find the library, post office, dining halls, and other essential locations. Because we, as writing center staff members, believe our centers to be essential locations for thinking and learning, we must find ways to reach out to Residence Life staff members, who are the gatekeepers to first-year residence halls. If they, too, recognize the value of writing centers, they can help us promote our services.

Furthermore, we should ask Residence Life departments to grant writing center staff regular access to residence halls so we can provide convenient and accessible writing assistance to their residents. The writing center community has already begun to recognize residence halls as important sites for learning, thinking, and writing; several university writing centers have established residence hall satellites, including those at Bowling Green State

University (*Satellite Hours*, n.d.), Purdue University (*Satellite Location*, 2008), the University of Mississippi (*Stockard-Martin*, n.d.), the University of Nebraska-Lincoln (*Contact Us*, 2008), and the University of Wisconsin-Madison (*About the Writing Center*, 2006). Satellite centers located in residence halls are useful because, as Levine (1994) notes, residential college students spend much more time in their residence halls than they do in their classrooms (p. 94). Residence halls are also promising sites for writing center involvement because we know that some of the time that students spend in their residence hall is devoted to writing and seeking peer feedback on their work (Harris, 1992, p. 370; Munday, 2007).

In my study of peer response practices among writers in a first-year residence hall, follow-up interviews with student participants revealed that writers chose their peer response partners based on proximity, not who might be able to provide them with the best feedback (Munday, 2007). Placing trained writing consultants in the residence hall would be a valuable resource for student writers for a number of reasons. First, someone with expertise in tutoring writing would be available at a writer's moment of need, conveniently located to offer last-minute help on a draft or to answer a quick question. Second, writing consultants could model effective peer response behaviors, delivering assistance to pairs of writers and responders or to large groups. Finally, writing center staff who work within a residence hall may be able respond to writers' needs with more alacrity and flexibility than is typically feasible in the Main Writing Center, particularly if consultants embed themselves in the residence hall community and are able to achieve insider status.

This final advantage for writing centers—increased responsiveness to student need through an increased sense of rapport—is where WC–LLC partnerships begin to diverge from other residence hall-related outreach, such as satellite centers or one-time writing center workshops. Because student engagement and retention are among the main goals of LLCs, and because a student's feeling of connectedness to faculty members and peers is often named as the leading indicator of successful student engagement and retention (Gabelnick, MacGregor, Matthews, & Smith, 1990; Pascarella & Terenzini, 2005; Simpson, 1991), community-building efforts play a prominent role in LLC formation. This emphasis on community building explains why LLCs often include social components and why faculty members teaching linked courses within LLC programs are encouraged to lead and attend out-of-class community events. Writing consultants who participate in WC–LLC partnerships should strive to become fully accepted members of the learning community, and writing centers can help achieve this by providing LLCs with dedicated WC–LLC Liaisons.

THE ROLE OF WC–LLC LIAISONS

Ideally, WC–LLC Liaisons would meet with LLC residents as soon as they arrived on campus, and the same writing center consultant, or consultants, would work within an LLC throughout an academic year. Along with Residence Life staff and LLC faculty members, WC–LLC Liaisons could join any planned LLC trips or other activities, which would increase the sense of camaraderie between writing center staff members and LLC participants, as well as offer WC–LLC Liaisons opportunities at each event to show students and faculty how writing is an integral part of lifelong learning. Writing-to-learn activities might include writing journal entries during an extended camping trip, taking a few minutes before a lecture begins to freewrite about the speaker's topic, or brainstorming a list of questions that LLC participants might like to ask during a question-and-answer session at the end of a lecture event. These activities emphasize the importance of writing as a form of discovery and help reinforce a university-wide culture of writing, something that several writing center scholars have named as an important objective for the writing center and writing-across-the-curriculum communities (Barnett & Rosen, 1999; Severino & Knight, 2007).

WC–LLC Liaisons could also set up an informal satellite writing center, which would require minimal operating resources. Hours for the WC–LLC satellite could be built around the needs of the residents and the amount of funding available to compensate the Liaison. But even if there were not enough funding to pay for regular weekly hours, a few hours strategically planned around writing deadlines for the LLC linked courses could prove effective. As far as space for an LLC writing center satellite, the Liaison could request permission to use the Resident Assistant's office on a temporary basis, or the Liaison and residents might decide they prefer meeting in a more informal setting, such as a study lounge or students' own rooms. Storing some writing materials in the residence hall—such as current MLA and APA handbooks, a comprehensive dictionary, and a laptop computer with internet access—would be helpful, but without these items, the Liaison could easily improvise by relying on the good will of fellow LLC participants because sharing resources is one of the benefits of participating in such a community.

In addition to setting up an LLC satellite and attending LLC activities, WC–LLC Liaisons can perform many of the outreach projects that writing center consultants and administrators customarily carry out: writing center tours, themed workshops, and the distribution of promotional materials. Because liaisons are already embedded in the LLC community, they have the advantage of knowing their audience in advance, making the outreach work they do more likely to have an impact.

In some ways, the collaboration between LLC faculty members and WC–LLC Liaisons might mirror the activities of faculty members and writing center staff working within a writing fellows program. Severino and Knight (2007) discuss the program at the University of Iowa, in which Fellows meet with faculty members to discuss future writing assignments and to offer feedback about how students are responding to their instructors' writing tasks. Leahy (1999) describes a similar process where writing assistants at Boise State University's Writing Fellows program offer feedback to instructors regarding "what worked and what did not" in terms of the assignment (p. 74). These debriefing sessions would help faculty members understand how students experience and interpret writing assignments while WC–LLC Liaisons would gain a greater understanding of faculty expectations and the effort that goes into lesson planning and syllabus construction.

WC–LLC LIAISONS
AS CHANGE AGENTS

From my perspective as the director of a newly created writing center, the most promising aspect of WC–LLC partnerships is its outreach potential for boosting a center's campus visibility and influence; however, more experienced writing center professionals point to a more altruistic purpose for WC–LLC partnerships that should not be overlooked. Rafoth (2007) observes that the writing center community seems to be at a crossroads, where we are taking stock of our discipline and thinking about our future. He writes:

> Today, as writing centers take on expanded roles in programs, curricula, and institutions, the challenge seems rather different than it was, say, twenty years ago. To understand this challenge we need only look as far as our scholarly record during the past two decades, which shows that writing center professionals are now in a position to influence teaching and learning as never before. To realize this potential, we are asked to reach out to colleagues across campus and be prepared to learn from them. (pp. ix–x)

LLCs provide many opportunities for writing center professionals to both teach and learn—to teach by sharing our expertise in peer tutoring, collaborative learning, and writing instruction, and to learn from Residence Life staff members and faculty from across the curriculum.

Murphy (2006) implicitly recognizes the notion of writing-center-director-as-speculator when she suggests that writing centers have an ethical charge to act as responsible agents for institutional change because of "our history of innovation, exploration, and accomplishment" (p. 273). She also argues that writing centers' commitment to peer tutoring means that writing centers are natural leaders in educational movements that focus on "community formation," such as service learning and character education (p. 276). Although Murphy does not mention LLCs specifically, there is a clear link between the interdisciplinary, collaborative learning emphasis in LLCs and the programs she describes. In her aptly titled article, "On Not 'Bowling Alone' in the Writing Center, or Why Peer Tutoring Is an Essential Community for Writers and for Higher Education," Murphy asserts that it is time "to move beyond arguments of marginalization versus adaptation" to enlarge our sense of purpose and "recognize the transformative power" (p. 278) of our tradition of collaborative learning, non-hierarchical power structures, and reflective community formation.

Similarly, Sunstein (1998) makes the case that writing center professionals should celebrate our institutional "liminality" rather than mourn our "marginality" (p. 8). Sunstein acknowledges that living in the liminal spaces, or "borderlands," means being isolated from others, which can make writing center administrators and consultants feel vulnerable. But at the same time, the isolation found in liminality is a type of freedom because those who dwell in liminality are not beholden to a singular power structure. In her article, "Really Useful Knowledge: A Cultural Studies Agenda for Writing Centers," Cooper (1995) identifies undergraduate writing consultants as "organic intellectuals" who hold particular promise for agitating for change in our systems of higher education. She argues that peer consultants straddle two communities—as writing center employees, which makes them part of the institutional hierarchy, and as members of the student body, which affords them a better understanding of student needs than "traditional intellectuals" can acquire. Cooper concludes that undergraduate writing center consultants, dwelling in liminal spaces, are perhaps the best brokers for educational reform. According to Cooper, organic intellectuals "are the intellectuals of an emergent social group, one which is not yet dominant but whose vision is more directly responsive to the current historical conditions of the society than that of the dominant group, whose vision developed out of past historical conditions" (p. 142). Cooper's comparison of traditional and organic intellectuals has significant implications for our understanding of WC–LLC partnerships because it suggests that undergraduate WC–LLC Liaisons are essential elements in the community formation, assessment, and success of individual LLCs, as well as the sustainability and potential scope of the entire LLC movement.

Some Student Affairs scholars identify the lack of buy-in among faculty members as one of the greatest threats to the success and sustainability of LLC initiatives (Schoem, 2004; Shapiro & Levine, 1999; Whitt & Nuss, 1994). Schoem (2004) and Shapiro and Levine (1999) say that faculty's reluctance to become involved with LLCs may stem from university reward systems that privilege faculty research while treating faculty involvement in student development as something less than an intellectual activity. Some claim another possible explanation is that many faculty members construct scholarly identities through their disciplinary allegiances instead of their campus loyalties, which can impede efforts to build interdisciplinary links in LLC programs and can contribute to a culture of compartmentalization and fragmentation at many colleges and universities (Engstrom, 2004; Schoem, 2004; Shapiro & Levine, 1999). One possibility that has not been addressed in the LLC literature, however, is that the sometimes radical rhetoric of a handful of LLC proponents may be repellent to faculty members who fall into Cooper's category of traditional intellectuals—those who are already more inclined toward maintaining the status quo. For example, as Klein (2002) advocates for LLCs as part of a sweeping reform of general education curricula, he predicts that higher education today is facing "a tectonic shift, from a competitive, teacher-centered, discipline- and classroom-based world to a new form of learning" (p. 9). Apocalyptic rhetoric such as this can be perceived as threatening to those accustomed to more traditional deliveries of education, and it is conceivable that some might summarily dismiss pedagogical innovations like LLCs if they are presented as a panacea that will cure all of the problems of the modern-day university.

The writing center's role as a border-crossing department, along with peer consultants' disposition as organic intellectuals, means that we have the capacity to prompt campus discussions leading to what Klein calls "moments of communion, spontaneity, and insight" (as cited in Sunstein, 1998, p. 14). Whether the rhetoric of LLC proponents is overblown or prophetic, writing centers can become a stabilizing force, a familiar entity, helping to promote a culture of collaborative learning on campus, especially because writing centers have a strong tradition of consultants and directors viewing themselves as co-learners—with one another and with the writers who visit us (Boquet, 2002; Cooper, 1995; Geller, Eodice, Condon, Carroll, & Boquet, 2007).

As Murphy (2006) and Sunstein (1998) remind us, because writing centers occupy a unique position in the academy and have a tradition of collaborative and interdisciplinary learning, we can, and should, assume our role as change agents, to help build connections among students, faculty members, student affairs, and campus administrators. Yes, in the process, it is likely that writing centers would gain visibility, increase their campus profiles, and increase our responsiveness to the needs of writers with whom we work. And, yes, we probably should advocate for campus decompartmentalization because, according to many higher education scholars, that is precisely what the American university system needs now (Love, 2004; Pascarella & Terenzini, 2005, p. 647; Smith, MacGregor, Matthews, & Gabelnick, 2004). But perhaps the most compelling reason that writing centers should engage in the LLC conversation is that collaboration is *what we do*; it is as natural for us as the air we breathe (Eodice, 2003). Therefore, I believe it is natural for writing centers to serve as leading advocates for university programs that embrace collaborative learning, as LLCs do. Eodice (2003) writes, "We can and should *demand* collaboration and continue to work toward boundarylessness, even with the knowledge that these actions will never be fully accomplished, completed" (p. 129, italics original). She reminds us that collaborative relationships rarely have neat end-points; they often represent beginnings to an ongoing enterprise that carries both great promise and great risk. Likewise, WC–LLC partnerships, though worthwhile, present writing centers with challenges that require careful planning and ongoing reflection.

CHALLENGES OF WC–LLC PARTNERSHIPS

One of the common criticisms of LLCs is that they exclude segments of the student population—namely, those who live off-campus. Furthermore, as Whitt and Nuss (1994) report, students who are able to participate in LLCs share similar demographics: they "tend to be traditional-age and single," which means that LLCs tend to leave out "older learners or students who for a variety of reasons must commute from home to campus" (p. 152). Because research shows that residential students already have an advantage over their commuting peers regarding academic persistence toward degree, intellectual orientation, and cognitive development (Schuh, 1999), funneling more resources to residential students through an LLC could intensify the performance gap. Writing center directors will need to ask themselves what portion of their resources (time and money) would be taken up by a potential LLC partnership, and how might the needs of commuting students be balanced against the needs of residential students so that both groups have fair and equal access to writing center services?

Another important question that writing center professionals will need to confront is how LLC duties should be divided among writing center staff, faculty, and student affairs. As they discuss the integration of writing instruction in learning communities, Howard and Rice (2004) express concern that writing instructors might be pushed into subordinate positions when teaching linked or co-curricular courses with faculty members from other disciplines. Certainly, Howard and Rice are not being alarmist, considering composition's history of subjugation within the academy, as well as the frequency with which first-year composition courses are taught by part-time adjuncts and teaching assistants who tend to have less academic status than the full-time tenured professors who may be assigned to teach the learning community's "content courses" (pp. 45–46). Howard and Rice depict a scenario where the process of writing may be viewed as central to LLCs, while writing as a discipline and writing instructors as individuals may be viewed as marginal. To avoid this predicament, Howard and Rice offer the following useful guidelines that, while geared toward learning communities, remain applicable for WC–LLC partnerships:

1. Write the contract before beginning the job.
2. Articulate the goals for writing in the learning community.
3. Plan the number of extra meetings or workshops that will be part of the learning community.
4. Determine how the success of the learning community and of the linked writing course will be measured.
5. Consider the labor issues.
6. Assure strong, continuing administrative support (pp. 46–47).

Howard and Rice's guidelines stress the necessity of planning ahead before writing center professionals enter into hasty LLC partnerships. Not only do we need to avoid stretching writing center resources too thin, we also need to ensure that writing centers are viewed as equal members and participants in LLCs.

Lastly, writing center administrators must carefully consider how to train and supervise WC–LLC Liaisons who will be operating in even more informal and autonomous settings than are typically found in many writing centers. Writing center administrators have an ethical obligation to ensure that consultants are not placed in unsafe working situations, so WC–LLC Liaisons need training on how to navigate their new role as peer tutors in an LLC setting. For example, should writing center policy prohibit tutoring sessions from taking place in students' bedrooms? Should we limit Liaisons to more public locations like study lounges or resident assistant offices? Because of the social bonds created in the LLC community, additional ethical issues may arise, such as conflicts of interest among faculty, students, and writing center consultants. For example, how should a Liaison respond if a student admits to plagiarizing a paper written for one of the linked LLC courses? How should the Liaison respond if an LLC faculty member shares information about an LLC student's grades in violation of that student's privacy rights? As these scenarios show, WC–LLC Liaisons may find themselves in thorny situations where they need to respond quickly. Therefore, writing centers should work to develop ethical guidelines for Liaisons to follow while making sure that the guidelines allow for "the roomy space of ambiguity" (Geller et al., 2007, p. 65) so that guidelines do not become prescriptive practices.

CONCLUSION

If WC–LLC partnerships were to become as widespread in the writing center community as writing fellows and satellite centers are now, how might this change our practices and our discipline? I believe that the relationships developed through WC–LLC partnerships would give writing centers the chance to simultaneously constrict and enlarge our scope. Constricting our scope is useful if it allows us to gain a deeper understanding of the needs of writers. Working within smaller communities on campus, like that of a LLC, lets writing consultants use a more narrow lens as they reflect on their own tutoring methods. A single WC–LLC Liaison with membership in a small community can seek feedback from writers on a range of issues. What types of workshops would be most useful to student writers? At which points in the semester would themed workshops draw the biggest crowds? Are there different avenues for discussing writing strategies—other than workshops and one-on-one consultations—that might be more valuable to the LLC members? When WC–LLC Liaisons seek answers to questions such as these, they are able to conduct a micro-assessment of students' writing needs, and writing center directors could use the resulting data to inform practices in the writing center.

Meanwhile, WC–LLC partnerships could enlarge writing centers' spheres of influence in two important ways: writing center staff could extend their research efforts beyond the writing center's walls to begin studying students' writing behavior in the residence halls. Harris (1992) notes that "perhaps the least studied of the widespread uses of collaboration in writing groups is that informal network of assistance and support that goes on in residence halls, study rooms, coffee shops, libraries, and faculty offices—where peers help each other by reading each other's drafts when asked" (p. 370). One of the main obstacles to researching extracurricular peer response is that it occurs in non-academic spaces that are difficult for researchers to access. However, if writing center consultants and directors were to get involved in LLCs, they would be in a unique position to study the processes of student writers in an extracurricular setting. We could learn more about students' timelines for drafting, revising, and seeking feedback about their papers; we could also investigate how students are using new technologies to complete collaborative projects and pursue other lines of inquiry.

Furthermore, if writing center professionals used their LLC involvement to conduct residence hall research, we would be making a significant contribution to the field of composition. Fifteen years ago, Gere (1994), a leader in peer response and writing group research, warned her fellow compositionists that, "In concentrating on establishing our position within the academy, we have neglected to recount the history of composition in other contexts; we have neglected composition's extracurriculum" (p. 79). Since that time, scant research about writing has been done in the residence halls (Munday, 2007). If writing center scholars were to break new ground in composition research by using LLCs as a conduit, our findings might gain recognition among our fellow compositionists, and we might finally become "fully integrated in our own discipline (Ede, 1995, p. 101) while also contributing to the body of knowledge about student writing.

In the opening comments to their book *Marginal Words, Marginal Work? Tutoring the Academy in the Work of Writing Centers*, Macauley and Mauriello (2007) urge writing center professionals to engage in "creative problem solving" so that we can frame our work as valuable to our local institutions (p. xvi). WC–LLC partnerships offer the writing center community another creative problem-solving option. Just as writing consultants model writing strategies to increase the tools in a writer's "rhetorical toolbox" (Murray, 1968, p. 73), we need to consider WC–LLC partnerships as an important tool in our writing center outreach toolbox.

REFERENCES

About the Writing Center: Our locations ("Selected campus residence halls"). (2006). Retrieved January 14, 2009, from http://www.wisc.edu/writing/AboutUs/Ser Places.html

Adams, K. H. (1991). Satellite writing centers: A successful model for writing across the curriculum. In R. Wallace & J. Simpson (Eds.), *The writing center: New directions* (pp. 73–81). New York: Garland.

Barnett, R. W., & Rosen, L. M. (1999). The WAC/writing center partnership: Creating a campus-wide writing environment. In R. W. Barnett & J. S. Blumner (Eds.), *Writing centers and writing across the curriculum programs: Building interdisciplinary partnerships* (pp. 1–12). Westport, CT: Greenwood.

Boquet, E. H. (2002). *Noise from the writing center.* Logan: Utah State University Press.

Contact us. (2008). Retrieved January 14, 2009, from http://www.unl.edu/writing/about/contact.shtml

Cooper, M. M. (1995). Really useful knowledge: A cultural studies agenda for writing centers. In C. Murphy & J. Law (Eds.), *Landmark essays on writing centers* (pp. 135–147). Davis, CA: Hermagoras.

DeCiccio, A. C. (2006). There's something happening here: The writing center and core writing. In C. Murphy & B. L. Stay (Eds.), *The writing center director's resource book* (pp. 187–195). Mahwah, NJ: Lawrence Erlbaum Associates.

Ede, L. (1995). Writing as a social process: A theoretical foundation for writing centers? In C. Murphy & J. Law (Eds.), *Landmark essays on writing centers* (pp. 99–107). Davis, CA: Hermagoras.

Engstrom, C. M. (2004). The power of faculty-student affairs for promoting integrative learning experiences in learning communities. In S. N. Hurd & R. F. Stein (Eds.), *Building and sustaining learning communities: The Syracuse University experience* (pp. 59–75). Bolton, MA: Anker.

Eodice, M. (2003). Breathing lessons or collaboration is. . . . In M. A. Pemberton & J. Kinkead (Eds.), *The center will hold: Critical perspectives on writing center scholarship* (pp. 114–129). Logan: Utah State University Press.

Gabelnick, F., MacGregor, J., Matthews, R. S., & Smith, B. L. (1990). *Learning communities: Creating connections among students, faculty, and disciplines.* San Francisco: Jossey Bass.

Geller, A. E., Eodice, M., Condon, F., Carroll, M., & Boquet, E. H. (2007). *The everyday writing center: A community of practice.* Logan: Utah State University Press.

Gere, A. R. (1994). Kitchen tables and rented rooms: The extracurriculum of composition. *College Composition and Communication, 45*(1), 75–92.

Harris, M. (1992). Collaboration is not collaboration is not collaboration: Writing center tutorials vs. peer-response groups. *College Composition and Communication, 43*(3), 369–383.

Harris, M. (1993). A multiservice writing lab in a multiversity: The Purdue University Writing Lab. In J. A. Kinkead & J. G. Harris (Eds.), *Writing centers in context: Twelve case studies* (pp. 1–27). Urbana, IL: National Council of Teachers of English.

Howard, R. M., & Rice, V. (2004). Roles of and structures for writing courses in learning communities. In S. N. Hurd & R. F. Stein (Eds.), *Building and sustaining learning communities: The Syracuse University experience* (pp. 35–50). Bolton, MA: Anker.

Hughes, B. T. (1991). Writing center outreach: Sharing knowledge and influencing attitudes about writing. In R. Wallace & J. Simpson (Eds.), *The writing center: New directions* (pp. 39–55). New York: Garland.

Klein, T. (2002). The search for a college commons. *About Campus,* 9–16.

Kuh, G. D., Kinzie, J., Schuh, J. H., Whitt, E. J., & Associates. (2005). *Student success in college: Creating conditions that matter.* San Francisco: Jossey-Bass.

Leahy, R. (1999). When a writing center undertakes a writing fellows program. In R. W. Barnett & J. S. Blumner (Eds.), *Writing centers and writing across the curriculum programs* (pp. 71–88). Westport, CT: Greenwood.

Levine, A. (1994). Guerilla education in residential life. In C. C. Schroeder, P. M. Mable, & Associates (Eds.), *Realizing the educational potential of residence halls* (pp. 93–106). San Francisco: Jossey-Bass.

Love, A. G. (2004). A campus culture for sustaining learning communities. In J. L. Laufgraben & N. S. Shapiro (Eds.), *Sustaining & improving learning communities* (pp. 14–30). San Francisco: Jossey-Bass.

Macauley, W. J., Jr., & Mauriello, N. (2007). An invitation to the "ongoing conversation." In W. J. Macauley, Jr., & N. Mauriello (Eds.), *Marginal words, marginal work? Tutoring the academy in the work of writing centers* (pp. xiii–xvi). Cresskill, NJ: Hampton Press.

Munday, N. K. (2007). Peer response practices among writers in a first-year residence hall: An ethnographic study (Doctoral dissertation, Indiana University of Pennsylvania, 2007). *Dissertation Abstracts International, 68,* 4696.

Murphy, C. (2006). On not "bowling alone" in the writing center, or why peer tutoring is an essential community for writers and for higher education. In C. Murphy & B. L. Stay (Eds.), *The writing center director's resource book* (pp. 271–279). Mahwah, NJ: Lawrence Erlbaum Associates.

Murray, D. M. (1968). *A writer teaches writing: A practical method of teaching composition.* Boston: Houghton Mifflin.

Pascarella, E. T., & Terenzini, P. T. (2005). *How college affects students: A third decade of research* (Vol. 2). San Francisco: Jossey-Bass.

Rafoth, B. (2007). Foreword. In W. J. Macauley, Jr. & N. Mauriello (Eds.), *Marginal words, marginal work? Tutoring the academy in the work of writing centers* (pp. ix–x). Cresskill, NJ: Hampton Press.

Satellite hours. (n.d.). Retrieved January 14, 2009, from http://www.bgsu.edu/offices/acen/writingctr/page29900.html

Satellite location: Meredith Hall. (2008). Retrieved January 14, 2009, from http://owl.english.purdue.edu/writinglab/satellitemeredith

Schoem, D. (2004). Sustaining living-learning programs. In J. L. Laufgraben & N. S. Shapiro (Eds.), *Sustaining & improving learning communities* (pp. 130–156). San Francisco: Jossey-Bass.

Schuh, J. H. (1999). Student learning in college residence halls: What the research shows. In J. H. Schuh (Ed.), *Educational programming and student learning in college and university residence halls* (pp. 2–20). Columbus, OH: Association of College and University Housing Officers–International.

Severino, C., & Knight, M. (2007). Exporting writing center pedagogy: Writing fellows programs as ambassadors for the writing center. In W. J. Macauley, Jr. & N. Mauriello (Eds.), *Marginal words, marginal work? Tutoring the academy in the work of writing centers* (pp. xiii–xvi). Cresskill, NJ: Hampton Press.

Shapiro, N. S., & Levine, J. H. (1999). *Creating learning communities: A practical guide to winning support, organizing for change, and implementing programs.* San Francisco: Jossey-Bass.

Simpson, J. (1991). The role of writing centers in student retention programs. In R. Wallace & J. Simpson (Eds.), *The writing center: New directions* (pp. 102–109). New York: Garland.

Smith, B. L., MacGregor, J., Matthews, R. S., & Gabelnick, F. (2004). *Learning communities: Reforming undergraduate education.* San Francisco: Jossey-Bass.

Stockard-Martin satellite. (n.d.). Retrieved January 14, 2009, from http://www.ole-miss.edu/depts/writing_center/satellites.html

Sunstein, B. S. (1998). Moveable feasts, liminal spaces: Writing centers and the state of in-betweenness. *The Writing Center Journal, 18,* 7–26.

Wallace, R., & Simpson, J. (1991). Preface. In R. Wallace & J. Simpson (Eds.), *The writing center: New directions* (pp. ix–x). New York: Garland.

Whitt, E. J., & Nuss, E. M. (1994). Connecting residence halls to the curriculum. In C. C. Schroeder, P. M. Mable, & Associates (Eds.), *Realizing the educational potential of residence halls* (pp. 133–164). San Francisco: Jossey-Bass.

WORKING TO IDENTIFY AND MEET THE INSTRUCTIONAL NEEDS OF A DIVERSE ESL STUDENT POPULATION

Judy Dyer
Christine Modey

"My name is Zhenyi Zhang, but I go by Jane." I hear myself say this to everyone who asks my name. The interesting thing is that I overly emphasize the last part. It has become automatic for me to gloss over my Chinese name, but every time I do that, I feel a deep sense of guilt. . . . As I have grown older, I have realized that I was not in fact ashamed of being Chinese, rather I wanted to make sure that if someone called me by my Chinese name, they would say it with the confidence and the power it deserves. Since I have spent about equal time in the USA and China, I have simultaneously developed parallel Chinese and American dreams. Although these two different sets of ideals sometimes conflict, I have been able to find ways to integrate the two into all of my decisions.

—Zhenyi Zhang, University of Michigan
undergraduate

Over the past five years, the English as a Second Language (ESL) student population at the University of Michigan has become more heterogeneous, with increasing numbers of ESL students being permanent residents rather than international visitors. This chapter discusses the collaborative efforts of two units at the University of Michigan—the English Language Institute (ELI) and the Gayle Morris Sweetland Center for Writing (Sweetland)—to better understand the needs of this changing ESL student population and to work together to develop programs and personnel to meet its needs. Zhenyi Zhang's statement, quoted previously, clearly describes the dual identity of such U.S.-resident ESL students who, in addition to their home language and culture, also share language and cultural characteristics with their American-born peers. Although they share some characteristics with international ESL students in their use of English, such U.S.-resident ESL students are bypassing the classes and language services the university has traditionally offered to international ESL students. Instead, many students like Zhenyi enroll in writing-intensive courses where no extra help is provided for ESL writers. To address these students' emerging needs and to make the needs of all ESL writers better known and better met on campus, ELI and Sweetland began collaborating. In this chapter, we profile briefly the two units involved in the collaboration and the ESL populations they serve. We then describe some of the projects and programs on which they have collaborated. Finally, we undertake an examination of the conditions and relationships that encourage the collaboration while also considering factors that constrain its expansion.

The two units have overlapping but distinct missions. Founded in 1941, the ELI's work is diverse, encompassing the teaching of English for Academic Purposes, training teachers of ESL, test writing and assessment, and Applied Linguistic Research, with special expertise in corpus research. Although ELI offers classes to both native and non-native English-speaking students across the university, the teaching of English for Academic Purposes to international students is the main work of the unit, which offers more than thirty courses in all language skill areas. These courses are designed to enable international ESL students at all levels "to enhance their linguistic and communicative skills to become effective, fully participating members of the academic community both during their time on campus and beyond" (http://www.lsa.umich.edu/eli/). The Sweetland Center for Writing (originally the English Composition Board) was founded in 1978 by professors from the English department to foster a campus-wide writing culture by developing a cross-curricular selection of courses to improve students' writing and also to provide extra tutorial support for students who did not pass the university's writing assessment. During its history, Sweetland has sponsored and initiated a broad range of writing-related programs and activities, the largest of which are SCWRTG100: Transition to College Writing, a course for first-year students who lack confidence or experience in writing; and Writing Workshop, a one-to-one, faculty-staffed, tutorial service. Both provide significant support to ESL writers, who comprise approximately 20 percent of the students in the two programs (C. Lapere, personal communication, March 31, 2008; P. Manning, personal communication, January 13, 2009). As a service unit within the College of Literature, Science, and the Arts offering support in academic written English to all graduate and undergraduate students, Sweetland as part of its work, assists ESL writers to become proficient in academic writing and also networks with many other academic units across campus to support the teaching of writing.

The collaboration we describe between these units began in February 2003 when Professor Martha Vicinus, then Director of the Sweetland, requested additional support from the Dean's office to manage the perceived increase in international students visiting Sweetland's Writing Workshop. In 2002–2003, 1,741 writing workshop clients indicated that their native language was not English, compared with 1,012 in 1999–2000; moreover, the number of times that faculty reported addressing ESL issues in a writing workshop session nearly doubled, from 568 in 1999–2000 to 1,066 in 2002–2003 (C. Lapere, personal communication, July 8, 2008). The Dean asked the ELI to provide that support, so one faculty member from ELI held a writing clinic at Sweetland in the fall of 2004 for six hours per week, while another ELI faculty member held a writing clinic for the same number of hours at ELI. The ELI writing clinic schedule filled up very quickly at Sweetland — evidence that the specialized ESL writing clinic had become more visible and accessible and was meeting a need among students.

As ELI faculty members worked with the ESL students at Sweetland, they observed that the increase in ESL students visiting Writing Workshop was not due to increasing numbers of *international* students, but rather to increasing numbers of ESL writers with four or more years of U.S. education. These students may not have been required to submit a Test of English as a Foreign Language (TOEFL) score and therefore had not passed through ELI on admission to the university or otherwise been identified as needing language help. Indeed, because the University of Michigan administration did not distinguish U.S.-resident ESL students from the general student population and collected no statistics for this group, the exact number of U.S.-resident ESL students on campus was unknown.[1] At the same time, instructors of ELI120, Sweetland100, English 125, and Sweetland's Writing Workshop were also beginning to observe that the ESL population they were encountering was more heterogeneous than in earlier years. The international student who had studied English as a foreign language in his or her home country and had come to the United States for university education accounted for only about one third of the writing class and Writing Workshop ESL population.

---

[1]With other colleagues, ELI and Sweetland faculty and staff are working through university databases to identify such students in the University of Michigan student population. In addition, a new question on a survey given to around 75 percent of all incoming students in fall 2009 will capture just these data.

The ESL students whom University of Michigan instructors were encountering seemed to have more varied and complex relationships with English than the international ESL student population. Indeed, rather than learning English as a foreign language or a second official language in their home country or by attending an international school where part of their studies was completed in English (as had been typical for international students), many of these non-traditional ESL students had learned English by attending a U.S. boarding school while their family remained in their home country or by migrating to the United States with their family and attending high school in the United States. The increase in this final category of students is reflected in U.S. census data, which reports that the proportion of the U.S. population ages five or older who speak a language other than English at home grew from 11 percent in 1980 to 18 percent in 2000. These ESL students have been referred to in the literature as U.S. Resident Language Minority (Reid, 1997) or Generation 1.5 writers (Rumbaut & Ima, 1988). The latter term, however, has been variously defined by so many researchers (Harklau, Siegal, & Losey, 1999; Roberge, 2002; Singhal, 2004) that it has little meaning except perhaps at its most general level. (In this chapter, we use "ESL" inclusively to refer to both U.S.-resident and international ESL students.)

Regardless of how such students are designated, U.S.-resident ESL students, because they move between their home language and culture and the language and culture of the university and the broader American society, show markedly different uses of English in their writing than international students and may require teachers to adopt a different approach to writing instruction.[2] Because of their dual identity as both ESL writers and U.S. residents, Generation 1.5 students have been ignored by researchers who study native English writers (as Generation 1.5 writing exhibits ESL features). They have also been overlooked by ESL writing specialists because they rarely enroll in ESL writing classes (Thonus, 2003). This group therefore

---

[2]While not all Generation 1.5 students have ESL writing issues, their academic writing may display informal spoken language and idioms and errors in non-salient inflections (verb endings, singulars and plurals, auxiliary verbs). Generation 1.5 students rarely possess a meta-language to talk about their English because they have acquired English aurally in an immersion context. They often have the intuitive and unconscious grasp of English grammar of a native speaker but with a narrower range because they have not been exposed to as many written and spoken genres in English. These characteristics differ from those of international students, who often use more formal syntax and vocabulary as a result of learning English from books, have had little exposure to more idiomatic English, have a competence in grammar and the meta-language for discussing it (although they may not be able to perform that competence), and have few intuitions about correct usage of English. See Friederich (2006) for a full description.

stands on a middle ground between the expertise of writing center instructors and ESL specialists. In fact, the type of writing support that they need does not fit easily into any of the institutionalized forms of support already in existence at the University of Michigan, including ELI and Sweetland. For this very reason, collaboration between units such as ELI and Sweetland is imperative, both to raise awareness among those who work with international and U.S.-resident ESL writers—almost every faculty member at the university!—and to create a fund of knowledge and other institutional structures that legitimate students' language identities and experiences as well as the work of the faculty who provide the services and resources they need.

To enhance instructors' abilities to meet the needs of the diverse population of ESL writers and to share knowledge with the larger University of Michigan community, Sweetland and ELI faculty offered workshops and seminars about ESL writers, both describing the heterogeneity of the population and discussing sample ESL essays to help faculty develop instructional strategies to support diverse ESL writers. Judy Dyer and Sweetland faculty member Matthew Kelley gave such presentations at Sweetland's annual faculty orientations and to English department first-year writing instructors in 2005 and 2006. This outreach to writing faculty bore immediate fruit by opening an avenue to dialogue between instructors and the writing specialists at Sweetland and ELI about ESL writers. Sweetland and ELI received emails and phone calls from writing faculty anxious to know how they could best assist their students with writing; faculty made appointments to talk to Sweetland and ELI instructors about their students; and both units received referrals of students from faculty who had attended these workshops. In this way, instructors from Sweetland, ELI, and the Department of English began to learn how best to support their ESL students by improving their own teaching skills and by developing knowledge of additional campus resources for ESL students.

Although the workshops centered on describing the varying instructional needs of ESL writers, building pedagogical strategies, and connecting instructors to available resources, the workshops also made visible the differences in tutoring practices between ELI and Sweetland instructors and opened up a crucial conversation among faculty about best practices in working with ESL students one-to-one. Most Sweetland faculty members—and perhaps compositionists in general—downplay lower-order concerns such as grammar and spelling in favor of higher-order concerns such as argument, organization, and development. The Sweetland faculty manual explicitly states that "Writing Workshop is not a proofreading service" (p. 28), and "If the student's writing shows patterns of error, faculty respond by providing mini-lessons in grammar and mechanics, or by looking beyond the surface features of the paper to find other matters of concern which the student may not have noticed" (p. 29). Moreover, the division in the literature on tutoring writing between more directive and less directive approaches

(Brooks, 1991; Shamoon & Burns, 1995) is reflected among the Sweetland faculty, with some taking an interrogative approach to one-to-one writing instruction, whereas others are more explicit in suggesting revisions. The tutoring ethos of ELI instructors, on the other hand, tends towards a more directive approach, often using explicit correction of errors in the rationale that some of these errors are usage-based exceptions to so-called grammar "rules" and may not be 100 percent remediable, and that time can be spent more wisely correcting more serious errors (Reid, 1997, p. 24) or teaching about those which can help students become better writers. Given such pedagogical divisions, ongoing dialogue seems necessary. Without the opportunity to discuss such issues with colleagues who come to writing instruction from other backgrounds, it is unlikely that any mutual understanding, let alone consensus, about how to work with ESL students one-to-one could emerge. While faculty workshops have not closed the institutional gap into which ESL and Generation 1.5 students fall at the University of Michigan and elsewhere, nor resolved disagreements about approach, instructors have emerged from them better equipped to "see" and to help the students whom they encounter in their own classrooms. Asking a simple initial question such as "Did you spend some of your high school years in the U.S.?" helps instructors to identify the kind of English language and writing support that may benefit a student (Reid, 1997).

In addition to opening up dialogue among faculty about diverse ESL writers, ELI and Sweetland faculty are beginning to create a community of support for undergraduate ESL writers among their peers. Judy Dyer has visited classes for undergraduates training as writing tutors for the Sweetland Peer Tutoring Center and also collaborated with Sweetland faculty teaching the peer tutor training course to pair trainee tutors with ESL students from the undergraduate ESL writing class, ELI 120. For the trainee tutors, the experience of working directly with ESL students from a variety of backgrounds was a valuable "hands-on" addition to the writing center theory they were studying (Gillespie & Lerner, 2004; Harris, 2008). In fall 2008 and 2009, Dyer herself taught one section of the class in peer tutor training. Perhaps even more important than her students' evident interest in ESL issues was the surprising degree to which they began to adopt the role of advocate for their ESL peers, with the perspective of ESL writers themselves appearing in the peer tutors' reports of their practice tutoring sessions. With a foot in each unit and expertise in ESL, Dyer acquainted her cohort of peer tutors with the importance of understanding their peers who speak English as a second language and of developing tutoring strategies that will be most helpful to them. Following her example, the curriculum of the peer tutor training course may evolve to increase emphasis on working with ESL writers, which will have further ripple effects in the larger pool of peer tutors as they share their strategies with each other.

While the prior ad-hoc collaborations, based largely on relationship building, information sharing, and dialogue, have been useful to many writing teachers and tutors on campus, faculty in both units have realized that additional research is needed in particular areas of their work to fully explore the pedagogical issues they encounter. In developing a deeper understanding of ESL writers, several collaborative research projects have been and continue to be helpful to the faculty of both units. Two corpora compiled at ELI, most notably the Michigan Corpus of Academic Spoken English (MICASE) and the Michigan Corpus of Upper-Level Student Papers (MICUSP; http://www.elicorpora.info/), have provided inspiration and models for two additional research projects—one at ELI compiling a corpus of international and Generation 1.5 student essays and the other at Sweetland investigating best practices in the tutoring of writing.

As an offshoot of MICUSP, a specialized corpus project was launched in 2006 to collect essays from first- or second-year student writers whose home language was either Korean or Chinese, with a view to describing in an empirical way the textual practices and discursive characteristics of University of Michigan ESL student writers. The project's main goal is to gain a more nuanced understanding of the differences between international and Generation 1.5 writers on campus. In addition, an investigation into best practices in writing tutoring is underway at the Sweetland with a team of faculty from both units. The project's goal is to describe how writing center faculty and their students work together and the impact of this work on students' revision process. Although the project was not explicitly designed to study ESL students, because the project team includes members from both ELI and Sweetland, analysis of the data for what it can reveal about differences and similarities between ESL and NES (Native English Speakers) writers has become an important aspect of the project.

The faculty who have collaborated on the projects described in this chapter were motivated primarily by their desire to better understand and serve the diverse ESL students at the University of Michigan. However, numerous formal and informal institutional factors have facilitated their work. None of the collaborative activities described above would have been possible without support from university administrators. In an article that appeared in *Change: The Magazine of Higher Learning* in 2005, in which she describes her study of four universities that have created strong collaborative cultures, Adrianna Kezar (2005) identifies administrative support—particularly support from the upper administration—as one of eight factors that promote the transformation of an individualistic college culture to a collaborative one (p. 53). Certainly, the Dean's request that ELI help to support ESL writers at Sweetland sparked the current efforts by bringing ELI faculty into the writing center; receptiveness to including ESL information in faculty development activities and Dyer's teaching of Sweetland's peer tutoring course required support and cooperation from the units' directors. Research, particularly in units where faculty's primary responsibility is for teaching rather than for research or service, always requires administrative support and funding. In the case of Sweetland's research project, grant funding was provided by the Gilbert Whitaker Fund for the Improvement of Teaching at the University of Michigan, and the director of the Sweetland offered course release time, as well as material and administrative support for Christine Modey to work on the project in the winter of 2008.

However, no matter how strong a director's support, a unit is rarely able to facilitate large-scale, campus-wide collaborations, and it certainly cannot, by itself, create a collaborative campus culture. Kezar argues, in particular, that collaborative efforts often founder when they lack support from upper administration. To succeed, they must "be discussed by senior executives, connected to the strategic objectives of the institution, and written into official documents such as strategic plans, accreditation reports, and board correspondence." Collaboration must also be modeled by the administration in the way decisions are made (Kezar, 2005, p. 55). Viewed in this light, the collaboration between Sweetland and ELI regarding the university's ESL students is limited, and its benefits have certainly not extended much beyond the faculties of those two units to the vast majority of faculty who teach ESL students. The units' collaboration with each other is not central to their institutional functions or identities (nor is collaboration central to the University of Michigan's mission), and until it becomes so and receives concomitant support from upper administration, it is unlikely that collaboration between the units will extend beyond the two units themselves to become a formal campus-wide network that supports all faculty who want to be better teachers for ESL students.

Despite lack of support from upper administration, a nascent faculty network between ELI and Sweetland does exist. Indeed, the informal networking among faculty—literally, around the water cooler in the Sweetland kitchen—has been a main force behind the expansion of the connections between ELI and Sweetland described in this chapter. However, a more influential network—one that Sweetland is already well positioned to facilitate—would depend on a core of faculty members in each unit with functional links to many other faculty members in various departments with an interest in supporting the writing of ESL students. Faculty networks, Kezar (2005) argues, are crucial for the success of any collaborative efforts, because they "provide a vehicle for the ideas to flow and to gain momentum and energy . . . the networks overcome resistance to new structures and processes on campus" (p. 53). Developing a network of those interested in ESL issues remains a challenge, particularly for a group of faculty—lecturers—for whom the usual rewards of academic labor—tenure, promotion—are absent, and for whom the usual supports—sabbaticals, grants, release time—are either non-existent or very limited. Such rewards and incentives, Kezar

(2005) argues, are also important in promoting collaboration (p. 54). For lecturers these are difficult to obtain, so the additional work of collaboration, while personally satisfying and professionally fruitful, is generally not rewarded by the institution and must be regarded by the collaborators as a good in itself.

In addition to support from university administrators and faculty networks, institutional structures can also foster collaboration by coordinating and facilitating efforts and by providing places for faculty to work together, as well as necessary infrastructure (Kezar, 2005). For many years, ELI and Sweetland occupied different sites several blocks apart in downtown Ann Arbor: ELI is located off campus in rented space and is somewhat hard to find, whereas Sweetland occupied a suite of offices on the first floor of a prominent campus building. Thus, these two units' locations have not provided shared space for the cross-campus institutes and centers that provide common areas in which faculty work together and network informally, as described by Kezar. In addition, as is typical for what Kezar calls "department silos," each unit has its own sense of identity and mission that may preclude coming together to create joint programs, for instance, or to share space. Still, new institutional structures will bring the units closer together, at least geographically. The construction of North Quad, a dorm and classroom building just two blocks from ELI to which the Sweetland moved in the fall of 2010, may facilitate additional interaction between the two units. Housing the School of Information, the Department of Screen Arts and Cultures, Communication Studies, the Language Resource Center (used by ELI faculty and students), and the Sweetland, North Quad has been designed to include common areas, where "lively interactions among students and faculty spill seamlessly from classrooms to hallways to faculty offices to living quarters—all under the same roof" (http://www.aec.bf. umich.edu/projects/ NorthQuad/index.html). With food services and commons areas, as well as high-tech classrooms and meeting spaces, North Quad may attract faculty from ELI and elsewhere and provide physical space for the kind of informal networking and sharing of ideas that forms the bedrock of any collaboration.

As this chapter goes to press, the authors continue to work together analyzing instructor discourse in Writing Workshop with native and non-native English-speaking students; the coding of the Chinese and Korean Generation 1.5 and international essays also continues apace. However, for a better understanding of ESL writers to have more meaningful effects, it is imperative to attract the interest and cooperation of faculty from a much wider range of departments. With their own networks and spheres of influence, these faculty, armed with a deeper understanding of the myriad challenges that ESL writers face, could advocate and work for greater integration of ESL students within their discipline-specific discourse communities. At the administrative level, the university must continue to work to understand the diversity of ESL students in order to provide appropriate forms of instruction. For the university's mission of a diverse campus to become a reality, accommodation must be mutual: it should not be enough to teach ESL students how to write in an American way and how to live in an American world; American students must also learn about the worlds that international and U.S.-resident ESL students inhabit and the various discourse communities in which they participate. Classes and workshops where U.S.-resident ESL, international, and NES students meet specifically to talk about language and cultural issues with faculty and administrators would encourage such reciprocal relationships and create a local, international community on the university campus. As the history of ELI and Sweetland's recent work together suggests, only with more face-to-face conversations among students, faculty, and administrators, will communication—and, indeed, effective collaboration—be possible.

REFERENCES

Brooks, J. (1991). Minimalist tutoring: Making the student do all the work. *Writing Lab Newsletter, 15*(6), 1–4.

Friederich, P. (2006). Assessing the needs of linguistically diverse first-year students: Bringing together and telling apart international ESL, resident ESL and monolingual basic writers. *Writing Program Administration, 29*(1/2), 15–35.

Gillespie, P., & Lerner, N. (2004). *The Allyn and Bacon guide to peer tutoring.* New York: Pearson.

Harklau, L., Siegal, M., & Losey, K. (1999). Linguistically diverse students and college writing: What is equitable and appropriate? In L. Harklau, K. Losey, & M. Siegal (Eds.), *Generation 1.5 meets college composition: Issues in the teaching of writing to U.S.-educated learners of ESL* (pp. 1–14). Mahwah, NJ: Lawrence Erlbaum Associates.

Harris, M. (2008). Cultural conflicts in the writing center: Expectations and assumptions of ESL students. In C. Murphy & S. Sherwood (Eds.), *The St. Martin's sourcebook for writing tutors* (pp. 206–218). Boston: Bedford/St. Martin's.

Kezar, A. (2005). Moving from I to we. *Change: The Magazine of Higher Learning, 37*(6), 50–57.

Reid, J. M. (1997, Summer). Which non-native speaker? Differences between international students and U.S. resident (language minority) students. *New Directions in Language Learning, 70*, 17–27.

Roberge, M. (2002). California's Generation 1.5 immigrants: What experiences, characteristics, and needs do they bring to our English classes? *CATESOL Journal, 14*(1), 107–129.

Rumbaut, R. G., & Ima, K. (1988). The adaptation of Southeast Asian refugee youth: A comparative study. *Final report to the U.S. Department of Health and Human Services.* Office of Refugee Resettlement. Washington, DC: U.S. Department of Health and Human Services. San Diego: San Diego State University. (ERIC Document Reproduction Service ED 299372)

Shamoon, L. K., & Burns, D. H. (1995). A critique of pure tutoring. *Writing Center Journal, 15*(2), 134–151.

Singhal, M. (2004). Academic writing and Generation 1.5: Pedagogical goals and instructional issues in the college composition classroom. *The Reading Matrix, 4*(3), 1–13.

Thonus, T. (2003). Serving Generation 1.5 learners in the university writing center. *TESOL Journal, 12*(1), 17–24.

THE EMERGENCE OF CENTERS FOR WRITING EXCELLENCE

Emily Isaacs

Centers for Writing Excellence (CWEs) are more than just writing centers with new names, although the use of the word "excellence" is deliberate and useful. CWEs and other similarly formulated comprehensive writing centers are created with the assumption that a writing center can and should be deeply valuable to *all* students and faculty on their campuses, and to the field of writing studies more broadly as well. This list of beneficiaries sounds familiar, of course, but in their sheer largeness of vision and expectation, CWEs are markedly different from either English department "basement" writing centers or small Learning Center-annexed writing centers that have still dominated the national higher education landscape despite significant progress over the last fifty years (Ferruci & DeRosa, 2006, pp. 25–26).

CWEs are deliberate in their mission of becoming truly valuable to all: to all students by targeting the highest succeeding students such as graduate students, honors students, and upper level students; to university faculty by providing *targeted, desired, and concrete* support in teaching writing across the disciplines; to studies in writing and higher education through production of original research; and to the entire institution through sponsorship and support for an intellectual culture—a culture of writing—in the university and in the community that the university serves. In short, CWEs are the opposite of modest—in budget and demand for university space, time, and resources, but also in what they dare to promise.

What could be the flagship institution in this wave of writing centers is Miami University at Ohio's Roger and Joyce Howe Center for Writing Excellence, about which the president of Miami University, David Hodge, declared, "This magnificent initiative will measurably improve the writing skills of virtually every Miami student and assure that every student appreciates that being a strong writer brings many valuable personal and professional benefits" (*Giving Tribute*, 2006). While we might all recognize some aspect of this declaration as typically presidential, it's nonetheless important to emphasize the goal of improving—not touching—the skills of "virtually every Miami student" and the presence of two atypical but very public supporters of this writing center—the president of the institution and Roger Howe, a senior executive from the commercial banking corporate world.

CWEs—a term that is not used by all of this class of high-profile, ambitious, comprehensive writing centers, but one that well describes the group—come about because of investment from stakeholders who have not been involved in writing center support before. These investors include graduate and research faculty not typically interested in writing centers; by developing programs, initiatives, and locations that are designed to meet the particular needs of faculty in the disciplines—instruction in poster presentations, support for writing research grants, for example—CWEs gain support from deans and faculty outside of English. Other potential investors are presidents, chancellors, development officers who see in the writing center not a Band-aid for the problem of weak students, but rather a vehicle to advance the institution's status. Of particular note is the relatively new category in *U.S. News and World Reports'* "America's Best Colleges" that identifies schools that have "stellar" programs in writing in the disciplines (*America's Best Colleges 2008*, 2008). Senior administrators also see in CWEs a means to address retention problems through engaging students intellectually (Light, 2001); and, less cynically, a way to promote and support meaningful teaching and learning at a time when research pressures on faculty have arguably decreased faculty attention to individual student learning (Grose, 2007). Finally, with luck and skill on the part of the director and development office, important stakeholders for CWEs can be alumni and other donors from the business community who do not have to be persuaded of the value of writing and for whom impacting the entire campus is immediately attractive. As any university development officer will tell you, gifts come most easily for projects that are perceived as broadly valuable, relevant to the non-academic as well as the academic world, and that have the potential of permanency, like a named building or position. "Writing" fulfills the former quite easily, and "Center" fulfills the latter equally so.

WHY "EXCELLENCE"?

For all of these populations just discussed, the term "excellence" is appealing. Clearly excellence is language imported from the corporate world: an internet search for "excellence" brings up, among others, *Excellence*, a magazine for Porsche owners, a handful of associations for excellence in manufacturing, and various self-help organizations designed to achieve both vague and specific excellence. Further, "excellence" is just as clearly not the language of humanities professors. For many of us, the first reaction is an eye-roll; "excellence" is vague yet superior, just the kind of corporate-speak that many of us lampoon in our composition classes when we teach advertisement analysis. As English professors, we can readily imagine the parodies possible—earning this or that badge, certificate, or medal of excellence for just about anything not worth studying. Beyond these gut reactions is the association with the use of excellence elsewhere on campus, primarily in areas far from the humanities, in the business and engineering schools and in student support services—all very much outside the culture of English. I want to echo Adler-Kassner (2008), Eodice (2003), Ritter (2006), and Schwalm (2001) in arguing that writing people can and should give up their fear of *appearing* un-English, un-academic or anti-intellectual in choosing to use the language of the dominant culture (and yes, that is often corporate culture) because often it's the very language that will allow us to reach much-needed and desired public *and* student audiences.

Nonetheless, it's appropriate to take up the most serious critique of excellence, one that I was reminded of by a colleague on WCenter (Orange, 2008) who, in response to a query I had sent about the CWEs, offered up an extensive quote from the second chapter of Bill Readings' (1996) book, *The University in Ruins*. Readings' central argument is that the modern university is without bearings and purpose, no longer bound toward teaching the national culture as has been the case since the Enlightenment (p. 5). Echoing others (Downing, Hulbert, & Mathieu, 2002; Ohmann, 2003) who argue that public universities have become corporations, Readings sees the terms as emblematic of the current crisis of purpose in higher education. He critiques universities for adopting "techno-bureaucratic notion[s] of excellence" (p. 13), which are purposely and problematically "non ideological" (p. 14). Most interestingly, Readings (1996) argues that the term excellence "deflects attention from the questions of what quality and pertinence might be, who actually are the judges of a relevant or a good University, and by what authority they become those judges" (p. 32). In some ways, I think Readings is right: excellence does serve as a kind of mask, covering discussion of what good writing might be by asserting that only "excellent" writing is valued.

In fact, that "writing excellence" can mean so many different things for many people, yet at the same time suggest, in its forthright assertion of supremacy, that there is only one kind of writing valued, that of excellent writing, is what makes it most useful for a writing administrator.[1] Most of us have observed that people outside of the writing disciplines are unfamiliar with the idea of genres, that genres have different criteria for excellence, and that the skilled writer of one genre is frequently unable to easily bridge to the next genre. In other words, while we in writing studies have come to realize the plurality of writing, for the vast public that uses the term, in and outside of academia, there is simply good writing and bad writing. The term "writing excellence" capitalizes on that perception, without doubt. While as Kelly Ritter (2006) notes, "Composition, unlike other disciplines, is perpetually at the mercy of cultural conceptions of literacy" (p. 45), writing administrators, always engaged in public work, must work to use cultural conceptions to the advantage of the students who will benefit from their work. Clearly, for some (Bosquet, 2004; Readings, 1996, among others), working with dominant beliefs and working with those in power who primarily support dominant beliefs, is to get in bed with the devil. However, I believe a diverse group of people who believe strongly in the importance of writing can come together, through a CWE initiative, and, once there, have the conversations that will reveal differences in writing values and criteria. It seems to me that it's important to do more than critique those outside of the academia: we need to engage with them.

Jeanne Simpson (2006) and David Schwalm (2001) have called on writing administrators to accept and use the language of upper-level administrators, an argument that Adler-Kassner (2008) extends on when she asks Writing Program Administrators (WPAs) to join her in working locally and nationally to "think consciously about developing messages" (p. 142) that counter prevailing stories about students and schools' failures in writing and writing instruction. Adler-Kassner, drawing on political and community organizing principles, asks us to change our language, to drop colons and academic speak, and instead to explain issues with an awareness that many we need to speak to have little or no insider knowledge of higher education and writing instruction. Drawing on the work of these advocates for employing and valuing outsider language, I am arguing that the language of

---

[1] I use the term "writing administrator" deliberately as a term that potentially includes writing center director and writing program administrator as others (Ianetta, Bergmann, Fitzgerald, Haviland, Ledbuska, & Wislocki, 2006) have argued. I think today's writing center directors and writing program administrators have much more in common than they have ever had. Although each has their own specialization, both draw on the same core beliefs and knowledge about writing, both are faculty-administrators, and both are at the threshold of stepping out of narrowly defined programs—traditional first-year writing programs or writing centers—nd into broader, more central work in promoting and supporting literacy throughout higher education.

excellence attempts to speak the language of administrators, potential donors, non-humanities faculty, and the general public.

But is there a danger in adopting the language of administrators and corporate America? For Melissa Ianetta, quoted at length from a WCenter email in *The Everyday Writing Center* (Geller, Eodice, Condon, Carroll, & Boquet, 2007), although necessary at times, "using the terminology of administration changes the message" (p. 118). Principally, for Ianetta, using administrative language can change the message and "obscure what we do well" (p. 118). Much of the richness and complexity of what we and students do well is lost, she suggests, when we adopt others' language. Going well beyond Ianetta's warning, Geller and her co-writers of *The Everyday Writing Center* express deep concern about administrative language use, seeing it as co-option (my term). For them, advising writing administrators to provide administrators what they want, as Simpson and Schwalm do, is dangerous and a little immoral, more or less by definition. They write:

> We commonly hear the claim in our field, for example, that the most effective tool we have to create necessary and productive relationships with those we report to on the organizational chart is our rhetorical skill. We agree that many writing center directors are skilled rhetoricians, yet we are troubled by the assimilationist idea of this approach in the same ways that we are troubled by the all-too-familiar axiom about our role in bringing student writers to an understanding of or accommodation to the discourse of the academy. (2007, p. 116)

Yet in this book-length text, what exactly is dangerous about using administrative language, or, by extension, corporate language never really becomes clear. It seems that some find using the language of administration "assimilationist" (Geller et al., 2007, p. 116) perhaps because it's "non-ideological" (Readings, 1996, p. 14), or perhaps using such language is dangerous simply because it's not the academic language that we have worked so hard to master and in which we have invested our very sense of identity?

Some of what critics of the excellence movement and critics of writing center directors and administrators who work collaboratively with upper administrators are concerned about is valid, however, particularly as articulated by Adler-Kassner (2008). There is a reasonable concern that, in the drive for funding, we may exploit rhetoric and public perceptions about writing and learning that ultimately cement notions of a vast and increasingly illiterate population that needs to be either kept out of school or scared straight or some equivalent. Linda Adler-Kassner (2008), in *The Activist WPA*, asks that we avoid "justifying[ing] requests for support for student writing by citing what students cannot do" (p. 142) because while this method may lead to short-term gains (funding and support), this strategy will further the view of a nation of ever-more failing writers. This is an important point that architects of new centers and programs need to negotiate as they work to gain funding and help the public better understand the current state of student writing in higher education. In fact, a CWE can be instrumental in the effort to move beyond the negative rhetoric of Johnny Can't Write, perpetuated so well through many of our nation's more celebrated educational acts and texts (e.g., *A Nation at Risk, a Test of Leadership*, NCLB, etc.). A CWE that invites in individuals from outside the community who hold dominant views of literacy can be transformative simply by celebrating rather than castigating student writing. By using our professorial and academic clout, we can be part of defining writing excellence, and thereby be part of what Adler-Kassner (2008) describes as an effort to create "an overall change in the stories told about writers that circulate" (p. 155) at our universities and in the culture more broadly. Directors of CWEs, and others of the same philosophy, in their willingness to talk about writing outside our circles, as difficult as that can be, are giving up the tradition and ideology that leads many writing administrators to avoid working with others outside their communities, preferring to view the world outside as antagonistic, holding onto what Eodice (2003) calls a "margin/containment trope" that has become "embedded in our lore to such a degree as to become *doxa*—we pass along these beliefs and their resulting practices to the detriment of future generations of writing center leaders" (p. 117).

CHALLENGES TO CHANGE

As I call for writing administrators to join me in considering the possibility of a CWE on their respective campuses, I do so with some sense that writing center history, like history of literacy crises, is not a straight line of progress, and that this movement to redefine and redirect ourselves toward excellence (and against focus on remediation and supporting first-year writing) is less new than promotional materials might suggest.

Boquet (1999), Carino (1996), and Lerner (2001, 2004, 2006), among others, have worked hard to debunk some popular and dangerous, if often immediately self-satisfying, tropes about the history of writing centers and writing center work. One myth, debunked by Lerner in several historical essays, is that in the old days the writing center was all about remediation and working with the "deficient" student-writer, whereas now, with the rise of the independent field of writing study scholarship, we understand the writing center as a progressive institution that seeks to develop the abilities of all writers, as these writers themselves define the goals and skills of writing. In reading excerpts of reports from across several decades, one can't help but notice that we keep re-announcing ourselves as more than re-mediators and servants of first-year writing. Clearly these re-makings have proven difficult, in large part, because much growth in writing center history comes from perceptions of deficiency that force writing centers in to "a defensive stance" (Boquet, 1999, p. 472) and make changing this remediation and service image difficult. As Lerner (2006) notes, "It is remarkable how little these conditions have changed in the hundred years since laboratory methods in writing were offered" (p. 10).

The myth of progress is persistent because it is satisfying to current writing center directors; it suggests that our field is on the upswing when we, conveniently, are involved in it. Further, as Lerner (2001) writes in another article, "The sense of newness and its concomitant instability and urgency serve well the notion that writing center directors must be ever vigilant to ensure their survival" (p. 25). In fact, as readers will recall, Brannon and North's landmark work in identifying the writing center movement as a "new" movement in 1980 (Lerner, 2001, p. 25) was an attempt to separate writing center work from remediation and images of deficient writers. Yet still, thirty years later, in most administrators' eyes, as well as in the eyes of the public, the writing center does exist primarily for "remediation." We have gained and lost funding from shifting attitudes about the importance of educating and supporting students perceived to need remediation, and there has been little that we have been able to do about it. So thus while I am embracing the call for CWEs that strike out to reverse the image of the writing center as solely a site for remediation and an adjunct to first-year writing, I fully recognize the difficulty of this task given the historical record and the reality that it has been easier for us, up to this point at least, to gain funding for a "literacy crisis" than for celebrations of writing that "provide alternative conceptions—and alternative frames—for discussion about writing and writers (Adler-Kassner, 2008, pp. 184–185) or what I will call a literacy opportunity.

A second trope that writing administrators need to break out of is the idea that they must be accommodating and, most importantly, modest. This myth is deeply rooted, to say the least. To look again to Neal Lerner's historical work, we see early on in the history of writing centers that under-funding is accompanied by not only a lot of industry but also relatively little complaint. Writing about the University of Illinois-Champaign's Writing Clinic, directed by Albert Tillman, "the lowest paid member of the English faculty" from 1949 to 1982, Lerner (2001) observes, "the Illinois Clinic took advantage of the fact that it was a small, low-profile, relatively inexpensive operation. . . . English Departments and most universities are essentially conservative places: when entities such as writing clinics are established, particularly if they continue to play a certain rhetorical or political role and they do not take up too many resources, they will tend to stick around for a long time" (pp. 20–21).

It is this very history of gratitude without complaint that caused Jeanne Simpson (2006) to advise us that "Nothing is gained with passivity and meekness" (p. 202). I suspect our tendency toward meekness comes from reasoning that if we're small we won't be worth cutting. But small operations are routinely cut—when a dean has to cut 3 percent out of her budget, a $15,000 writing center budget removal may solve half of her problem, with few angry individuals with whom to contend. Our contemporary scholarship and practitioner conversation, as one can most quickly observe by participating on the WCenter list for a few weeks, indicates that many of us have taken Tillman's approach of trying to survive by presenting ourselves as a very small budget line item. The fear of being cut back, re-categorized, or removed keeps us with our heads down, asking simply to be left alone to do our work with our tutors and students. We go to our own community for comfort, and to share our strategies for stretching budgets, our methods for darting irritating questions from ignorant colleagues, and our last-minute responses to administrators' questions and demands.

Importantly, this tendency toward accommodation and modesty has been well earned from a long history of marginalization, first within English departments and then within composition studies—"marginalized by the marginalized" (Carino, 2001, p. 7). Writing center administrators themselves feel marginalized and comparatively devalued, along with writing program administrators—despite efforts by the MLA and WPA—because they are still often seen as inferior simply due to the common and seemingly persistent view of administrative work as "service" and something other (lesser) than the intellectual work of teaching and scholarship (Marshall, 2001, p. 75).

Yet still, what is striking about the rhetoric of writing center administrators as opposed to say athletic directors—recall your university newspaper accounts—is how different these leaders are in their talk about the money they need to do the job for which they have been hired, their needs from the institution and the community, and their central and long-lasting value to these institutions. In promoting CWEs, I am actually arguing for a self-image upgrade—stop thinking like a writing center director who is lucky to have anything and start thinking like the athletic director who expects a hell of a lot more.

WHAT IS A CENTER FOR WRITING EXCELLENCE?

My enthusiasm for CWEs comes from my work chairing a taskforce aimed at re-building a small English department writing center that was "accidentally" cut, and from studying the success of writing centers at diverse universities across the United States. The result of this study was a proposal that was accepted by the administration of my New Jersey state university, and which has been significantly enacted. Here is a list of the features that I see in strong writing centers and CWEs that aim to be broad and comprehensive and also play a role "in systemic and institutional transformations" (Geller, Eodice, Condon, Carroll, & Boquet, 2007, p. 117), or, in my language, in transforming the culture of writing at their institutions.

MISSION FOR A CENTER
FOR WRITING EXCELLENCE

Transform the Culture: A writing center that is focused on excellence and responding to the needs of the *entire* student body can change the way all students—remedial, average, honors, graduate—perceive the value of writing and their own abilities to develop as writers. The key for creating universal concern for writing is to transform the culture: students need to believe that writing matters in every discipline and at every level. At a university with a strong culture of writing, students see writing as central to all the work that they do: to understanding anthropological concepts in their general education courses; to making a case for admission to law school; to writing a persuasive proposal in their capstone Marketing course; to presenting original research at a national conference in Audiology. A CWE—an idea as much as a place—is flexible and dynamic, responding to immediate needs and long-term institutional changes, and ultimately central in establishing, maintaining, or elevating the intellectual climate on campus.

Range of Writing Services: A CWE expands on the core work of one-on-one tutoring to a broad range of activities that build upon one another, enabling the CWE to affect every student on campus. It provides:

- One-on-one tutoring in the center
- A strong OWL for
    - One-on-one tutoring
    - Live "chat" for quick questions
    - Documentation and writing guides
- An attractive, interactive, and resource-rich website—for students, faculty, and other constituencies—that links directly from the main institutional site.
- A university common book program. The CWE, with links to first-year writing and the rest of the academic departments, is the ideal sponsor for a common book.
- Public readings of contemporary writers

- Public readings and celebrations of university writers—basic writers open-mic, student-research conferences, first-year writing faculty readings, etc.
- Workshops or non-credit mini courses that focus on
    - writing tasks or skills (e.g., resumes, application personal statements, job letters, thesis/dissertation writing workshops, writing presentations, poster presentations)
    - genres in writing (sciences, social sciences, humanities, business, arts, etc.)
    - writing conventions and mechanics (APA or MLA style, editing and proofreading, tips for ESL writers)
- A mobile writing center—CWE staff can visit classes to provide teaching writing support, thus providing a "centerless" CWE experience for large numbers of students (e.g., presenting, modeling, and supporting peer review; leading and responding to brainstorming sessions; teaching editing skills; modeling and teaching discipline-specific writing conventions).
- Writing fellows—development of a program pairing senior writing consultants with selected disciplinary faculty to support writing-intensive, WAC, or WID initiatives or classes.
- Faculty and writing in the disciplines support services
    - Course design consulting—the director provides one-on-one consultation with WAC faculty who aim to design courses with a writing emphasis.
    - Department consulting—consultation for departments on integrating writing into courses or curricula, responding to and evaluating student writing, developing assessment measures, or designing and sequencing writing and research assignments.
    - Peer feedback for faculty scholarship—small writing faculty writing groups to provide intimate and supportive environments to support faculty toward successful scholarship as well as one-on-one feedback from writing faculty and even outside senior scholars brought to campus primarily to review and respond to junior faculty work.
- Research on writing
    - For the purpose of improving instruction and curricula
    - For assessment of teaching and learning
    - For contribution to the field
    - To support the institution's efforts toward retention and student engagement
    - To support the broader community
    - For systematic assessment of the center's work

CENTER FOR WRITING EXCELLENCE STAFF

A CWE is flexible and diverse in its staffing, drawing on a range of traditional and non-traditional personnel to provides its services in and out of the center. These include:

- A faculty director who is able to understand the challenges that faculty and students face, is active in the field, is engaged in the work of teaching or supporting student writing, and is interested in writing and learning across disciplines.
- An associate director to run the day-to-day operations of the CWE.
- An associate director to run the out-of-center operations of the CWE, primarily through writing in the disciplines and/or writing in the community activities.
- An administrative assistant
- A CWE Board chosen for its diversity and representation of diverse stakeholder interests, possibly including local or national representatives.
- Writing consultants
  - Graduate assistants from various disciplines who have taken appropriate coursework in the field and who can model and support best practices for all writing consultants.
  - Non-assistant graduate students
  - Adjunct staff
  - Peer writing consultants who have taken appropriate coursework
  - Undergraduate service learning students drawn from new classes in Education or Writing
- Writing fellows—advanced writing consultants who are given greater independence and responsibility than consultants, often engaged in work outside the CWE.

PLACEMENT AND FUNDING
OF THE CENTER FOR WRITING EXCELLENCE

Administrative location. Administrative location of the CWE is crucial to success. While much depends on local context, a CWE is most likely to be successful if it is perceived by users—students most importantly, but also the rest of the campus community and ultimately the larger community it seeks to serve—as a *university* center. The CWE director and budget should therefore be independent of an academic or other department, reporting directly to a high-level administrator such as the provost. Further, although clearly there are successful centers that do not follow this approach, given that the CWE needs faculty interest and engagement to be effective in affecting the lives of *every* student, the CWE should be tied to the academic side of campus. Many faculty will not see a center located in student support services as a place where they can get support for their teaching and writing.

Physical Location. My former colleague, Paul Butler, has argued persuasively that a CWE must have a striking, light-infused, centrally located space, configured variably for public readings, private tutoring, technologically driven mini-lessons, with office space for staff and a range of reading, writing and thinking spaces for the many people who visit the center (Isaacs, 2006). Crucial to this arrangement is location—ideal locations include the library, the most-used academic building, or a student center.

Funding. While some private and well-funded public universities are successful in gathering the large funds necessary for a CWE, funding from existing sources is possible; raising this budget, however, will mean decreasing or eliminating that of some other programs in the institution (Simpson, 2006), something administrators are reasonably hesitant to do. Other sources will be needed to provide additional funds.

- **Student Fees.** Although I have located no references to raising money through fees in any scholarly article, I have identified a dozen universities, mostly public, that support writing centers through some sort of fee—attached to a writing-intensive course, as a semester fee, for non-graduation credit courses. Of these I favor a small, universal, and clearly identified "Center for Writing Excellence" fee. This approach is upfront—students and parents are made aware of the CWE and the CWE is held appropriately accountable.
- **Development Money.** Development money is ideal, and while never a sure thing, attempting to support aspects of the CWE through a donor may be successful. A significant number of "named" writing centers already exist as testament to the real possibilities of raising this money in this way.[2]

---

[2] A partial list of named writing centers includes: Farnham Writing Center (Colby College), Roth Writing Center (Connecticut College), Stone Writing Center (Del Mar College),Nesbit-Johnston Writing Center (Hamilton College), Zuckerman Writing Center (LA Valley College), Normal H. Ott Memorial Writing Center [2]

- **Grant Money.** Available for particular aspects of a CWE mission—for support of community needs or to seed a new program; for faculty development or teacher education.

EXEMPLARY CENTERS FOR WRITING EXCELLENCE

Many centers across the country run programs that exceed expectations, making significant strides in changing the culture of writing at their institutions. Here are highlights of a few such centers.

At Miami University's Roger and Joyce Howe Center for Writing Excellence website (Miami University), a web reader will see a broad range of services: personal consultations, short classes, online resources—for undergraduate and graduate student writers. Faculty and teaching assistants (TAs) are offered individual assistance, workshops, online resources, and $5,000 grants for faculty projects to improve instruction in writing. Beyond these extensive services are efforts to celebrate, value, and learn from writers. On the day I visited the website, the top of the page read "Miami Students Blog from Ghana," and readers were invited to read this impressive piece of student writing. As well, the website also announces readings, writing contests, and recent winners of some of these contests. As the current director Paul Anderson (2008) explains, a "constant theme" of the Howe Center's advertising is the emphasis on serving "even the most accomplished" students.

Notably, Miami's CWE was originally established to support "faculty and departments wanting to improve and increase the amount of writing provided in their courses" (Anderson, 2008), and it has an extensive faculty-development program of workshops, grants, and other support services. The success of these initiatives is broadcast on the website: Under "News" is an announcement of Miami University's most recent *U.S. News and World Report* ranking, and in the linked page, readers learn that Miami received notice as 1 of 28 schools with "stellar programs in 'Writing Across the Disciplines' " (Miami University). Notably, in its mission statement, Miami's CWE identifies tutoring students last; the first two of four goals are to work with faculty to develop their abilities in teaching writing, and the third goal is "foster a culture of writing in which students welcome the writing instruction they receive in their courses, seek additional opportunities to write outside of class, and strive continuously to improve their writing

(Marquette), The Joyce and Roger Howe Center for Writing Excellence (Miami University), Marian E. Wright Writing Center (University of Michigan-Flint), The Gayle Morris Sweetland Writing Center (University of Michigan), Hume Writing Center (Stanford), and William L. Adams Center for Writing (Texas Christian University).

skills" (Miami University). Miami has a robust staff that includes a tenured faculty director and two tenured assistant directors, three classified staff members, and a slew of tutors of various types; additionally, the director and staff are guided by an advisory committee of faculty, program directors, and at least one dean, and, finally, a "National Advisory Board" composed of Chris Anson, Andrea Lunsford, Martha Townsend, Kathleen Yancey, and Art Young. Not surprisingly, the physical Howe Center is also extremely impressive; located in the library, it boasts a very large, open space, available to students 24 hours a day. As Anderson (2008) explains, "The open space gives us a bigger footprint, a larger physical space, and it enables the library to host us without giving more space than is appropriate." Funded through the endowment and general university funds, the Howe Center budget will likely exceed $2 million by 2010.

Temple University's Writing Center, directed by Lori Salem, who is the Writing Center Director and Assistant Vice Provost, steps outside of traditional writing center purview in that it is the administrative home for Temple's writing-intensive course program, which offers 250 w-courses each semester, taught by faculty in the disciplines. As well, Temple's program has three guiding principles that I find exemplary and that Salem articulates as follows: (1) "to promote a progressive atmosphere . . . in which the value and complexity of writing and teaching writing are valued"; (2) "that services and supports the need to be diversified to meet the needs of different 'niche' groups among students and faculty"; and (3) that services are better and more useful when data about all services are collected and analyzed not only so that these services can be improved, but so that the writing center can "collaborate with central admin on large-scale assessment projects" (Salem, 2008). Following these principles has enabled the Temple Writing Center to support faculty in the writing-intensive (WI) courses deeply and individually, and likewise to go beyond one-on-one tutoring in a generic way to, for example, develop specialized services for dissertators in the forms of writing groups, dissertation seminars, and "dissertation bootcamp." This center's close to half a million dollar budget comes almost entirely out of the provost's office. Notably, Lori's position is not faculty, but administrative, and the center is located in the center of the university in the learning center that also houses the library. This impressive writing center has broad impact, exemplified by a truly stunning as well as comprehensive website (Temple University Writing Center). It has also achieved "relative stability," and I would say excellence, despite several changes in central administration during those years, in large part because Lori Salem, not a faculty rotating director, has been director for twelve years, building an increasingly important center that is in itself an academic program as well as a center for student and faculty services.

The CWE at West Virginia University appears to be separate from the university's writing center, although both remain in the English department. The writing center offers traditional in-center one-on-one tutoring that focuses on the writer, not the product (*West Virginia University Writing Center*, 2008). In contrast, West Virginia's CWE, which "supports faculty, students, and staff in the improvement of writing and the teaching of writing at West Virginia University" (*West Virginia University Center for Writing Excellence*, 2008), is primarily an institutional home for academic writing programs. The CWE oversees the English department's required writing curriculum, conducts assessment and research on writing and the teaching of writing for the institution and beyond, while also supporting *three* academic writing programs—in creative writing, professional writing, and distance writing—and a Center for Literacy Computing, which "rethinks literacy studies for the digital age" (*West Virginia University Center for Writing Excellence*, 2008). The director, Laura Brady (2006), explains that the CWE grew out of an institutional prompt for the English department to engage in intense self-study and planning, which led the full department to realize that the majority of courses offered by the department were writing courses, although writing faculty held minority stake in the department's direction and emphasis. For Brady (2006), it is not enough to simply recognize the need for change, but that we must accept change as a permanent condition: "Just as writing instructors help students become aware of different revision strategies for different purposes, so a department must develop program-change strategies to keep its revisions purposeful rather than random, substantive rather than superficial" (p. 31). Continually in transformation, the CWE at West Virginia is prominent and appears well funded, representing atypical growth for an English department, with new curricula and programs as well as prominence for writing of various kinds.

The website for the CWE at Ohio University foregrounds WAC and faculty services, comparing itself with "other faculty development units on campus" and declaring itself first as "dedicated to enriching student learning and faculty teaching through writing" (Ohio University CWE). Directed by Sherrie Gradin, who is also a faculty member in English, the CWE is an umbrella organization that, beyond its emphasis on WAC, focuses on "writing-to-learn." It also houses the Ohio University Appalachian Writing Project, a junior writing in the disciplines university requirement, and a traditional writing center that provides one-on-one tutoring as well as other student writing support programming. This CWE, located in a new floor of the library as part of the "Faculty Commons" area, along with the Center for Teaching and Learning (Ohio university, 2008) is funded through the provost's office with a $250,000 budget (Gradin & Stewart, 2008) and includes the director, who is also a tenured and full professor of English, and a full-time coordinator to run the student writing center. Notably, a web browser will first see the work that the CWE does with faculty and staff in pursuit of the CWE mission: "to create and support a comprehensive writing-across-the-curriculum initiative and strengthen engagement with writing on all levels and in all disciplines" (Ohio University CWE). To my mind, this de-emphasis of the CWE from traditional and expected writing center work with students, and basic or struggling writers in particular, serves to elevate the writing center's importance and increase its reach; by working with faculty on revising curriculum and pedagogical practices toward writing, this writing center impact is potentially much stronger than if it presented itself as working solely with students.

The CWE at Penn State University, directed by Jon Olsen, home of *The Dangling Modifier* and recent host of the National Conference on Peer Tutoring in Writing, is intriguing as much for its work beyond the institution as within. Although the website's most immediate links are to the separate undergraduate and graduate writing centers and a substantial WAC program, boasting the support of development of close to 100 additional Writing Intensive (WI) courses, bringing the institutions total number of "WI" courses to well over 300, the CWE has also begun a project entitled "The Public Writing Initiative" (Center for Writing Excellence, 2008). Students in professional writing classes, under the oversight of CWE writing fellows, work with local organizations to create professional quality documents. The website highlights one project "that uses a commissioned writing assignment from the Public Issues Forum (PIF)" "to prepare issue books to guide non-partisan deliberation of local civic issues among community members" (Penn State CWE, 2008). This program, adopted and perhaps adapted from a previously existing Technical Writing initiative, highlights what appears to be Olson's drive toward creating "public scholarship"—ways for Penn State University students to engage with the public, learning marketplace or life skills, and also contributing meaningfully to communities outside of the university. This approach toward the CWE, like Ohio's national writing project connection, enables a CWE to be valuable to stakeholders and community members outside of the university.

At the University of Kansas (KU), Terese Thonus, new director of the KU Writing Center, describes a "roost" model that addresses the need to provide broad and comprehensive writing center services by providing writing tutoring services all over campus (Thonus, 2008). At KU, the emphasis is on student services, and each year the Center tutors significantly more students by opening "Writer's Roosts" in libraries, residence halls, and other student-centered locations according to student request (2007, KU Writing Center Annual Report). Located in Student Services and with a reporting line to a vice provost, this non-faculty director model approach provides a yearly budget of over a quarter of a million dollars and emphasizes student services.

An interesting CWE that is still emerging is Florida Atlantic University's "University Center for Excellence in Writing" (*University*

Center for Excellence in Writing, 2003–2004), which describes itself as "devoted to the support and promotion of writing for all members of the FAU community." Additionally, at Montclair State University, where I work, the Center for Writing Excellence is up and running. Just in its second year of operation, central funding has enabled the faculty director to hire the staff needed to be a prominent and important force on campus. Yet to be determined is both its ultimate direction and its ability to actually become a vehicle for positively impacting the intellectual culture on campus, deepening and broadening the experience all students—and other community members—have with the intellectual power of writing.

CONCLUSION

In 1999, Elizabeth Boquet concluded "Our Little Secret" with a call for writing centers and writing center research to go beyond concerns for best ways to tutor, how to use new technologies, and the like. Instead, she asked that we embrace "off-task" possibilities to allow writing centers to go past the scope of what they are intended to do. She writes, "What is most challenging to me about my work in the writing center [is] the excessive institutional possibilities that the writing center represents. The way in which a writing center exceeds its space, despite the university's best effort to contain it" (p. 478). A CWE enables writing directors to inspire faculty, students, administrators, and community members to do just this—to be excessive in their influence, to make the best writers better, *and* to effect all writers on campus. Only a CWE isn't working despite the administration, it is working deliberately and openly with it. What was once off-task is, for a CWE, most definitely on-task.

REFERENCES

Adler-Kassner, L. (2008). *The activist WPA: Changing stories about writing and writers.* Salt Lake City: Utah State University Press.

Anderson, P. (2008, August 10). Writing center questionnaire (E. Isaacs, Interviewer).

America's best colleges 2008. (2008, July 15). Retrieved July 15, 2008, from http://colleges.usnews.rankingsandreviews.com.

Boquet, E. (1999). "Our little secret": A history of writing centers pre- to post-open admissions. *College Composition and Communication, 50*(3), 463–482.

Bosquet, M. (2004). Composition as management science. In M. E. Bosquet (Ed.), *Tenured bosses and disposable teachers: Writing instruction in the managerial university* (pp. 11–15). Carbondale: Southern Illinois University Press.

Brady, L. (2006). A greenhouse for writing program change. *WPA, 29*(3), 27–43.

Carino, P. (1996). Open admissions and the construction of writing center history: A tale of three models. *Writing Center Journal, 17*(1), 30–48.

Carino, P. (2001). Writing centers and writing programs. In J. Nelson & K. Evertz (Eds.), *The politics of writing centers* (pp. 1–14). Portsmouth, NH: Boynton/Cook.

Center for writing excellence at the Pennsylvania state university. (2008, May 26). Retrieved July 14, 2008, from http://www.psu.edu/dept/cew/.

Downing, D., Hulbert, C. M., & Mathieu, P. (2002). *Beyond English, Inc: Curricular reform in a global economy.* Portsmouth, NH: Boynton/Cook.

Eodice, M. (2003). Breathing lessons, or collaboration is. In M. A. Pemberton & J. Kinkean (Eds.), *The center will hold: Critical perspectives on writing center scholarship* (pp. 114–129). Salt Lake City: Utah State University Press.

Executive Vice President and Provost Faculty Senate Reports Academic Year 2007-2008. Ohio University. (2008). Retrieved July 14, 2008, http://www.ohio.edu/provost/upload/EVPP%20Faculty%20Senate%20Reports%20AY07-08.pdf.

Ferruci, S., & DeRosa, S. (2006). Writing a sustainable history: Mapping writing center ethos. In C. Murphy & B. L. Stay (Eds.), *The writing center director's resource book* (pp. 21–32). Mahwah, NJ: Lawrence Erlbaum Associates.

Geller, A. E., Eodice, M., Condon, F., Carroll, M., & Boquet, E. H. (2007). *The everyday writing center: A community of practice.* Salt Lake City: Utah State University Press.

Giving tribute: Writing center inspires learning. (2006, Fall). Retrieved July 1, 2008, from http://www.forloveandhonor.org.

Gradin, S., & Stewart, C. (2008, July 30). Writing center questionnaire (E. Isaacs, Interviewer).

Grose, T. K. (2007, January). 21st century professor. *ASEE PRISM, 16*(5), 1–9.

Ianetta, M., Bergmann, L., Fitzgerald, L., Haviland, C. P., Ledbuska, L., & Wislocki, M. (2006). Polylog: Are writing center directors writing program administrators? *Composition Studies, 34*(2), 11–42.

Isaacs, E. (2006, May). *Developing a culture of writing at MSU: The center for writing excellence.* In-house proposal. Montclair State University, Montclair, NJ.

KU writing center annual report. (2007). Retrieved July 1, 2008, from http://www.writing.ku.edu/.

Lerner, N. (2001). Searching for Robert Moore. *Writing Center Journal, 22*(1), 9–32.

Lerner, N. (2004). Writing centers fifty years later. *The Writing Lab Newsletter,* 1–5.

Lerner, N. (2006). Time warp: Historical representations of writing center directors. In C. Murphy & B. L. Stay (Eds.), *The writing center director's resource book* (pp. 3–11). Mahwah, NJ: Lawrence Erlbaum Associates.

Light, R. (2001). *Making the most of college: Students speak their mind.* Cambridge, MA: Harvard University Press.

Marshall, M. (2001). Sites for (invisible) intellectual work. In J. Nelson & K. Evertz (Eds.), *The politics of writing centers* (pp. 74–84). Portsmouth, NH: Boynton/Cook.

Ohio university center for writing excellence. (n.d.). Retrieved July 14, 2008, from http://www.ohio.edu/writing.

Ohmann, R. (2003). *Politics of knowledge: The commercialization of the university, the professions, and print culture.* Middleton, CT: Wesleyan University Press.

Orange, T. M. (2008, June 25). Re:[wcenter] Survey on comprehensive writing centers (Email to WCenter ListServ).

Readings, B. (1996). *The university in ruins.* Cambridge, MA: Harvard University Press.

Ritter, K. (2006). Extra-institutional agency and the public value of the WPA. *WPA, 29*(3), 45–64.

Roger and Joyce Howe center for writing excellence. (n.d). Retrieved July 24, 2008, from http://www.units.muohio.edu/writingcenter.

Salem, L. (2008, July 16). Writing center questionnaire (E. Isaacs, Interviewer).

Schwalm, D. (2001). The writing program administrator in context: Where am I? and can I still behave like a faculty member? In I. Ward & W. Carpenter (Eds.), *The Allyn and Bacon sourcebook for writing program administrators* (pp. 9–22). New York: Longman.

Simpson, J. (2006). Managing encounters with central administration. In C. Murphy & B. L. Stay (Eds.), *The writing center director's resource book* (pp. 199–214). Mahwah, NJ: Lawrence Erlbaum Associates.

Temple university writing center. (R. Buchanan, Producer). (n.d.). Retrieved July 24, 2008, from http://www.temple.edu/writingctr.

Thonus, T. (2008, July 17). Writing center questionnaire (E. Isaacs, Interviewer).

University center for excellence in writing. (2003–2004). Retrieved July 14, 2008, from http://www.fau.edu/UCEW/.

West Virginia university center for writing excellence. (2008, March 30). Retrieved July 14, 2008, from http://english.wvu.edu/centers_and_projects/cwe/.

West Virginia university writing center. (2008, January 30). Retrieved July 14, 2008, from http://english.wvu.edu/centers_and_projects/wcenter/the_center.

CENTERS FOR WRITING EXCELLENCE AND THE CONSTRUCTION OF CIVIC RELATIONSHIPS

Robert T. Koch, Jr.

The local community is a vital constituency for every university. Rooney (2006) identifies four forces that have helped universities and communities recognize the potentially symbiotic opportunities of their relationships: the community service and service learning movement, increased dialogue in the public policy and governance of both parties, recognition of the economic impact and value of the university, and opportunities for innovative alliances, especially in knowledge sector growth and development. In academia, these two potential partners are often referred to as "town and gown." The label "town" signifies any size community in which an academic institution resides, while the university, or "gown," derives its moniker from the traditional commencement regalia worn by faculty and graduates. The extent to which town and gown recognize and attend to Rooney's forces often determines the amount and strength of goodwill between them. Steinkamp (1998) describes several examples in which these parties have collaborated to enact real local advancement, in effect attending to the aforementioned forces. These collaborations include developing common goals, increasing economic impact, revitalizing communities and redeveloping neighborhoods, and engaging in civic planning. Both Rooney and Steinkamp note the high value both town and gown place on knowledge sector developments, which require high-level critical thinking, oral and written communication.

Because writing centers attend to campus needs for both process *and* product, creating better writers *and* advising in the creation of better specific texts, they often play an indirect role in developing the knowledge and communication skills of participants in town–gown relationships. This is especially true with regional universities and smaller colleges, where the town's business, political, and spiritual leaders are often the gown's alumni, employees, and business partners. More significantly, the relatively recent development of centers for writing excellence open the possibility for direct impact in the community itself—through workshops and support for local literacy initiatives—that can elevate a college or university's standing and forge an important connection with the community, especially when these initiatives accomplish both university and community goals.

A plausible argument can be made that there have been three seismic shifts in writing centers over the past eighty or so years since the writing labs of the 1920s. The first and largest shift might be termed the Enrollment Shift. It coincides with the period of transformation in American higher education that began with the 1945 GI Bill and lasted through the establishment of Open Admissions policies in the 1960s and 1970s. In significantly changing the demographics of who could attend college and how prepared or unprepared they could be, the government forced colleges and universities to reconceive their purposes, programs, and support systems. This massive upheaval created an environment that enabled the transformation of writing center identity, purpose, and pedagogy (Boquet, 1999; Carino, 1996; Lerner, 2006). These policies heightened the identity crisis of the writing laboratory: Would it provide remedial service for underprepared students or service for all students? This identity crisis provided impetus for writing laboratories to challenge their limited function as writing program supplements and forge ahead with the larger purpose of serving the whole student body (Carino, 1995, 2001).

The second shift, or Technology Shift, began in the 1980s, hit its peak in the 1990s, and continues today. This shift involved the integration of digital technologies, including online and distance learning asynchronous and synchronous tutorial support. It also involved the creation of OWLs as tutorial sites and clearinghouses of writing process, higher order concern, and lower order concern knowledge. This shift performed a similar feat as the first: it required writing centers to reassess their pedagogy and identity. For example, Coogan (1999) offers a book-length exploration of the asynchronous e-mail tutorial, including an examination of the practice as a dialogic activity and, as such, its impact on composition. Blythe (1996) compares and contrasts OWL pros and cons, accounting for questions of pedagogy, space, and funding that could cause conflicts among students, faculty, and administration. Issues of pedagogy, administration, and the subsequent impact of OWL technologies on writing center identity are developed and argued throughout Inman and Sewell's (2000) *Taking Flight with OWLs: Examining Electronic Writing Center Work*, as well as in the technology section of Murphy and Stay's (2006) *The Writing Center Director's Resource Book*. Both sets of editors recognize the significance of technology on the writing center community. Murphy and Stay write, "The future of writing centers will definitely contain—if not be defined by—technology" (p. xv). More specifically, and nodding back to the Enrollment Shift, Inman and Sewell note that, "Writing center practitioners have long discussed their roles in relation to their supporting institutions; now, they are challenged to explore—even reinvent—their roles as computer technologies transform centers and institutions" (p. xix).

The third and most recent shift, what I call the CWE Shift, is the re-conceptualization of some writing centers into centers for writing excellence. Writing center directors who consider this option, whether by free will or at committee or administrative request, must re-conceive writing center identity, purpose, and perhaps eventually pedagogy, expanding the roles of their writing centers on campus and, more frequently, off-campus as well. In "The Disappearing Writing Center within the Disappearing Academy: The Challenges and Consequences of Outsourcing in the Twenty-First Century," Murphy and Law (2001) recognize the future of the university as one of "multiple identities, roles, and purposes within business, technology, and industry" that will have "social relationships and partnerships as its core principle of action and identity" (p. 139). As a consequence, they assert that writing centers will need to "move away from traditional and classical concepts of the academy . . . toward the politics and policies of the entrepreneurial university" (p.141), which is itself a "complex of partnerships between academics and industry" (p. 141). In other words, it is entirely believable and arguable that the current transformation of the university, and the ever greater role it plays within local and regional community leadership, development, economics, and industry, may and likely will necessitate a transformation of writing centers. Enter the center for writing excellence (CWE).

CWEs may seem like an argument of semantics. For example, Isaacs provides a well-developed discussion and overview of CWEs in this volume, but she has also greeted this label with skepticism in "After the Fall: Rebuilding a Writing Center" (Isaacs, 2008). However, a re-consideration of writing center names through history reveals that such changes are a standard disciplinary vehicle for promoting evolving identities. First, there was the classroom *laboratory method* of the 1920s and 1930s, which served as an alternative to memorization and the lecture hall. This then became a location external to the classroom, a *writing lab*, which the field renamed *writing clinic* (Lerner, 2006). The name clinic evokes images of the compositionally infirmed and injured, perhaps suffering from lead poisoning from their pencils or carpal tunnel from typing. Furthermore, neither laboratory nor clinic are particularly good terms to use when seeking either internal or external funding. As McQueeney (2001) notes, "when the [grant] writers substituted lab or clinic to identify the [funding] request, the comment was that no funding was available for remedial purposes" (p. 18).

For the most part, the names writing laboratory and writing clinic seem to have given way to *writing centers* and, less frequently, *writing studios.* While the studio carries with it a more romantic notion of the starving artist at work, the term writing center has become the popular label for that place on campus that helps students with their writing. Yet even under this name, writing centers have not shaken the popularly held notion that they are places where remedial writers go to get help or where students go to "get writing fixed," as one student told me. What should be obvious here is that, historically, the writing center discipline has often changed names in an effort to define or clarify its perceived responsibilities. This may be one of those times.

The label Center for Writing Excellence carries four advantages, all embedded in the word *excellence.* First, as my co-editor on this collection has told me several times, "no one in their right mind is going to dispute whether or not they want writing excellence on a college campus." The term negates some possibility of open or public attacks that may come from administrators and faculty who do not understand the center's purpose. Second, it provides an opportunity to engage in a discussion of writing culture with those who question the name change. These conversations provide an opportunity to open dialogue and build partnerships around the campus and in the community. Third, the term "excellence" offers some resistance to the connotation of remediation (Isaacs, 2008) and suggests bigger ideas and opportunities—such as establishing or re-energizing a literacy culture on campus and/or in the community. After all, for much of the public, the university is considered the expert and should therefore demonstrate intellectual excellence. The fourth, and final, advantage is that donors may be more fond of giving to a center for writing excellence than to a writing center. In an interview with campus grant experts, it was reaffirmed that most "donors simply don't want their name associated with remediation; they want their legacy attached to excellence."

So are CWEs simply writing centers by another name? That depends on the program. Despite the above advantages, changing a name only really works if the product is changed as well. A writing center that calls itself a center for writing excellence but which doesn't actually expand its services in some substantial and visible manner—some way that gets "excellence" into the university and public mindset—is most likely to suffer an eventual relapse of the old stigma of remediation. After all, what is essential to consider here is the opportunity the new title affords the center: the chance to rebuild identity by considering a broader range of audiences, purposes, and activities, from faculty professional development, adjunct training, and course development assistance to public writing consultations, readings, and community workshops. The programs a center enacts, however, should be natural functions of university and community needs. The following descriptions of the UNA Center for Writing Excellence history, context, and community programs illustrate how easily a CWE can have a direct impact on a community.

WRITING CENTERS
AT UNIVERSITY OF NORTH ALABAMA: A HISTORY

Prior to 2004, there was no writing center at the University of North Alabama (UNA). Whether for political or financial reasons, its creation had been requested repeatedly for many years but had never been approved. Finally, in spring 2004, a dozen English faculty members took matters into their own hands, serving at least one office hour per week in a volunteer center located at the back of a classroom—an origin story familiar to many writing center community members. During the first two years, attendance in the center was limited when compared to the student population of the university (7,000). The faculty volunteer hour had to be weighed against committee work, research, conferences, and other responsibilities that most academics would grant higher priority status. In addition, there was little writing center advertising across the university. With limited staffing and record-keeping and without formal advertising, the center functioned mostly for a single demographic: students in the Liberal Arts English courses.

Then in spring 2007, the English department received sudden approval to hire a director for a university writing center. This hire would be a member of the English faculty, but in his capacity as director would answer to an upper level administrator. According to the call for applications:

> Primary responsibilities will be as director of the University Writing Center, with some opportunity for teaching first-year composition or developmental writing courses. Responsibilities will include training and supervising peer tutors, developing WAC workshops for faculty, and coordinating programs with student developmental services. The successful candidate is expected to demonstrate excellence in planning and organizing skills and proficiency using Microsoft Office. Classroom teaching and tutoring experience are desired.

In this advertisement, we can detect the previous discussion of name and identity. The ad describes a *university* writing center, but the faculty member is limited to Liberal Arts and remedial courses, as well as developmental services. Let me be clear: I am not trying to belittle remediation or argue against its importance; I am trying to underscore the belief that remediation should not be the exclusive purpose of a university writing center or a center for writing excellence. More importantly, in the brief history of the UNA Center for Writing Excellence, the above position announcement is an important identity marker because it sparked a need to immediately clarify and more specifically outline what the position would actually be and what the center would actually do. This clarification and outline could only be achieved through a needs assessment, but while that assessment was being conducted, the services listed in the job description would need to be immediately implemented.

Simpson (2006) writes that, "Encounters between writing centers and central administration can be frustrating and scary, especially if the writing center director doesn't know much (anything?) about administrators except that they apparently wield great power (p. 200). One cure for this initial problem is to discover administrators' goals. Aligning the center with the administration's needs and goals cannot hurt the chances for continued or additional funding and support. One place to find this information is in the university's strategic plan. And so, in my first month of employment, I secured a print copy of the plan and highlighted every goal, strategy, or initiative that might impact, or be impacted by, my new position and our new center. The plan contained strong support for both the university writing center and Professional Development in Writing Across the Curriculum and Writing in the Disciplines. However, I also realized that a CWE—as a specific office engaging in community outreach and larger issues of campus and community literacy—might be a possibility, especially when I read the last of the plan's five major goals:

- Goal: "To Enhance and Support Regional Development and Outreach" (University of North Alabama, 2007, p. 7)
- Description: "UNA serves the surrounding community as an intellectual nucleus and strives to maintain a sense of cohesiveness with that community by working collaboratively, disseminating information, providing intellectual, social, civic, and cultural experiences, and offering assistance to businesses and schools. The growth of UNA and its community is dependent on reciprocal interactions to address the needs of the region through continuous environmental assessments and action oriented responses." (University of North Alabama , 2007, p. 7)

Though the goal provided an opening for outreach, my bare-bones budget would limit what I could accomplish. Rather than develop grander plans for speakers and high-profile experts, I chose a low-budget option supported by yet another goal and strategy:

- Goal: "Build and Maintain a Student Centered University" (University of North Alabama, 2007, p. 5)
- Strategy: Provide an overall co-curricular experience that gives students an opportunity to develop as productive citizens outside the classroom while providing support for academic success. (University of North Alabama, 2007, p. 5)

I believed that this goal and this strategy justify the use of trained peer tutor volunteers in workshops and presentations off-campus, where they can build professional experience while giving back to the community. Both my administration and, just as vitally important, my tutors agreed.

Although I didn't realize it at the time, I was following Isaac's (2008) six strategies for creating a CWE. I had initial stakeholders: the administration, the English department, and the students. However, based on the job description and the strategic plan, there were other stakeholders: faculty in other disciplines who would participate in WAC/WID or who would send their students to the center, online faculty and students, and probably community members. Having identified my on-campus stakeholders, I conducted research, prioritizing my constituents using tutorial demographics and evaluations. My findings revealed that most writing center business during the first semester of operation came from four locations: Liberal Arts Writing, the Colleges of Business and Nursing, and the Geography department. I began informally visiting these faculty members, conversing with them to discover their needs—both for their students and in their own professional development. The Geography department proved to be an exception to this plan; the chair had sought me out to integrate the center into their already vibrant undergraduate research community.

Meanwhile, I also learned about community needs. A billboard campaign clued me in to a high local public school dropout rate—a major problem. At the same time, my partner had taken a position in the town's brand-new public library: a community showpiece led by a dynamic director. This new information provided two opportunities to build relationships with community stakeholders by creating programs with the public school and public library. After a few conversations with a high school teacher and the public library director, I had multiple constituencies—both on and off campus. These stakeholders add value to the center far more than if I just limited it, or had been limited, to serving a single campus demographic. We are now a visible part of the community, not an isolated, insulated academic support unit of the university.

Funding is an obstacle today more than ever. Like many writing centers, there wasn't much money in my initial writing center budget, but in this case I was blessed with a number of advantages. First, I had an excited and supportive administration that wanted to see this new writing center succeed regardless of its name. Second, I had the benefit of good data collection and evaluation, from which I could show marked growth in tutorials and workshop services each semester, as well as anecdotal approval from students and faculty. Finally, as I described earlier, my programs were designed to operate on a shoestring budget with peer tutor volunteers. Given the budget challenges at the time, my supervisor, Dr. Priscilla Holland, the Assistant Vice President for Academic Support Services and Academic Affairs, asked for both what I wanted and what I needed. She allocated something in between, a show of strong support for the Center.

Finally, I had tremendous input into the location and name of the facility. We located the CWE in a New Deal-era stone cottage located in the geographic center of campus. Every day, students walk past the front door to go among residence halls, academic classes, and the student union. It is practically impossible to walk through the campus and not notice the building. As for the University Writing Center, it became a program within the CWE. The net result of my first year of writing center work at UNA was the creation of the Center and its three programs: the University Writing Center, which offered tutorials and workshops; Faculty Professional Development Workshops in WAC & WID; and Community Programs, which sought programming contact with Florence High School and Florence-Lauderdale Public Library.

THE FLORENCE HIGH SCHOOL
WRITING CENTER

In the course of my first year at UNA, I discovered that one of our adjuncts, Mrs. Dorlea Rickard, was also the head teacher of the English department at Florence High School. One afternoon I approached her about possible joint programming. Our ideas quickly turned toward starting a high school writing center, one that would be open during the lunch hour and, if successful, would be offered after school. It would be housed in the high school library and be staffed by high school AP and Honors English students. In the spring, Dorlea and I secured support from the high school administration, and I made a sales pitch to the high school faculty at their final staff meeting. Over the summer, I adapted a training manual from resources available on the IWCA website, and that fall we opened the center in the school library with a staff of 11 peer tutors. Thursday afternoon training sessions were conducted by either myself or my colleague, Dr. Kelly Latchaw, and we were assisted by one of the UNA CWE tutors, Mr. Ash Taylor, who was a graduate English major.

This program carries with it several advantages beyond providing peer writing tutorial support for high school students:

- It helps high school tutors develop their writing skills and process awareness.
- It encourages high school tutors to put their writing and tutoring skills to work in a volunteer capacity.
- It forged a recruitment relationship between FHS and UNA, hopefully encouraging more students to attend our university upon graduation. At least one high school tutor has already verbally committed to UNA and requested that I keep him in mind for employment in our Center.
- It provided Kelly and me with an opportunity for professional development and service that could count towards tenure and promotion. For Ash, the experience could be useful to inform his teaching practices and will likely appeal to prospective employers.
- It helped the high school faculty and administration find a connection to university faculty, and it established a positive relationship where previously none had existed.

In addition to these benefits, some potential opportunities now exist. The FHS Writing Center could become a site where UNA English Education majors tutor to complete some of their required observation hours. Kelly's involvement in this community program is especially important because she teaches the Theories of Composition course, which requires these hours. Ideally, this joint venture will also help lower the dropout rate. Of course there is no measurement for this opportunity, but all the involved parties— the Florence School District and Florence High School administrations, the English teachers, the peer tutors, and the university faculty—agree that our presence will not hurt the cause and may help those students whose frustrations with literacy may lead them to give up on school. Having peers who can provide support and comfort is at least a step in the right direction.

There are obstacles and challenges to this endeavor as well, some easily overcome, some not so easily solved. Scheduling both the center hours and the training is one of the less challenging obstacles. Trust, however, is an issue that is less easily resolved. In this case, trust is required between the high school faculty and the peer tutors, as well as among the high school administration, faculty, and university faculty. These relationships are vital, as their strength may impact relationship building at the institutional level as well. While peer tutors work to understand their teachers' assignments and expectations, which are not always easy to grasp, the teachers are also being challenged to trust the students as peer tutors—a very different role from what has traditionally been the case. If it is difficult for some university professors to place such trust in peer tutors, it must certainly also be difficult for some high school teachers.

The difference in the perception of our purpose between school administrators and faculty may create other issues of trust. At present, the school administration is pleased with the relatively inexpensive support we provide for writing in their school. However, we do not have any gauge, beyond the positive opinions of the English department, as to how the rest of the high school faculty view our presence. Are we seen as interlopers or intruders? If the prevailing opinion is that writing centers are remedial sites, what might this mean to the high school faculty's opinion of the English department? Most importantly, what would the continued success or sudden failure of the high school writing center mean to the school and university relationship? Issues like these require regular conversation and consideration.

FLORENCE-LAUDERDALE PUBLIC LIBRARY WRITING WORKSHOPS

When I approached her in spring 2008, Mrs. Nancy Sanford, Director of the Florence-Lauderdale Public Library, was excited to hear that the UNA Center for Writing Excellence wanted to partner with them in a writing or literacy activity. As with Dorlea at Florence High School, I was careful not to assert my own ideas but instead asked what kind of project they could use that could help us forge a relationship. Nancy explained to me that the library was going to do a community One Book Program that fall, using John Grogan's *Marley and Me* as the common text; she wondered if we could offer a writing workshop tied to the book. The result of this discussion was a six-week memoir writing workshop, which met for two hours each Saturday, from 10 am until 12 noon, in the library's Genealogy Room. Rather than conduct all the meetings on my own, I again turned to the CWE tutors for help. I recruited Ms. Jessica Lanier, an Elementary Education major; Mr. Ash Taylor, the Graduate English major who helped at Florence High School; and Mr. Trey Canida, a UNA graduate who had majored in English. Our content included discussions of purpose, character development, setting, plot, and dialogue, and each class involved work-shopping and peer review in small groups. My three tutors each provided a lesson plan on these issues and responded to our participants' texts. Twenty community members participated in the workshop, all of them middle aged or senior citizens, and another 20 people were placed on a waiting list. A write-up of the program was published in our school paper, the *Flor-Ala*.

Beyond the community service opportunity for my tutors, our involvement with the public library yielded several benefits, not all of which were expected. We wished to spark community members' interest in writing. Most of our participants gained confidence in their ability to share the stories of their lives, ranging from plantation life to surviving the holocaust to traveling across Ireland. As we worked together those six weeks, they began to ask about our lives on campus, creating a learning opportunity across generations. Several participants who were UNA alumni shared stories about their time at the university. Their contributions have been integrated into our website's history of the stone lodge, the Center's home. Most touching, perhaps, is a comment I received from one individual who told me that, after staying away from the campus and the university for several years, he was glad to see us getting involved in the community, and to see that the university had made a commitment to literacy in the community. His words exemplify the invaluable goodwill that programs such as ours can build on behalf of the university.

Early in the program, I heard at least one of my university colleagues grumble about the selection of Grogan's text for the program, arguing that it did not pose any significant academic challenge. As a writing center director participating in the community, I have to remind myself that this work isn't necessarily about academic rigor. The library staff chose the book based on its appeal to their diverse patrons. As participants in their program, it was our responsibility to provide a product that would serve their patrons' needs. We were so successful at this endeavor that we agreed to do three more writing workshops in 2009: one each in spring, summer, and fall. The spring workshop works with an audience of new writers, the summer workshop is intended for high school writers, and the fall will focus on senior citizens.

This new opportunity for additional workshops has created its own set of challenges as well. With limited funding, I have begun more actively seeking grants to cover our materials expenses. I must also secure peer tutor volunteers for summer. There is also the danger that people will not show up for the program. For this spring's workshop, fifteen people signed up. Ten appeared on the first day. We have never had more than six in the two subsequent meetings. If the program is judged strictly on numbers, than this term's workshop is not as successful as the fall workshop. If it is judged on the impact we make on others' lives, then this semester is just as successful as the previous, perhaps even more, because of the increased time and care we can give each participant. However, as long as the cost does not outweigh the benefit, and as long as the director of the library supports the workshop series, the relationship will continue to be productive for the community.

GROWING CONSIDERATIONS

In addition to the benefits of community relationship building and additional programming opportunities, getting involved in the community has helped me identify new literacy partners. A freelance writer whom I met at a social gathering will be assisting in the instruction for the 2009 writing workshops. Furthermore, through a staff member at the library, I met a woman who works for the Northwest Alabama Reading Aides, a United Way Program that helps non-native speakers develop their literacy skills enough to enter college. Standing next to the buffet table at our common friend's Christmas party, we agreed to work on a transition program to help non-native speakers move from their basic literacy program into the university. While we don't yet know any of the particulars of this program, it demonstrates that a successful and visible commitment to the community can breed further opportunities to make a difference both off and on campus.

Yet this new and increased awareness breeds challenges, too. By all accounts, the UNA Center for Writing Excellence has been a success for its first two years. However, the stakes grow higher with each success. Earlier, I discussed the danger of a relapse in identity that might occur without a substantive and visible change in purpose. In addition to the problem of relapse, centers for writing excellence also risk the danger of being viewed as a panacea: a catch-all problem-solving entity for the entire campus, or worse, the entire local community, even when the problems do not involve writing, reading, or literacy. Directors of centers for writing excellence need to be supportive of their constituents, be selective in their programming choices, and, above all, must know the limitations of their resources: physical, financial, and human. What new initiatives and relationships are possible? What resources can be allocated to develop them? Without additional resources to allocate, I had no choice but to forward my contact at Northwest Alabama Reading Aides to colleagues who might be able to create successful relationships: in this case, a colleague who has focused on adult literacy in the past and the new Vice Provost of International Programs. The drain on limited resources affects other areas as well: program marketing and time to develop instructional materials among them.

In addition to issues of resource allocation, the danger of turf warfare can accompany these new relationships. Has the center grown too fast and too quickly, and, in the process, upset university or community traditionalists? Will someone be slighted if the resources aren't available? In our coverage of creative writing and reading, do we risk upsetting local or university creative writers or reading teachers who might otherwise have started such workshops or activities? I like to consult with other potentially interested parties, at least at the university, before engaging in such community programs. For example, I checked with my colleagues who regularly teach creative writing, and when they did not express an ability to participate in the public library workshops, I felt more secure in making the proposal without causing an issue with my on-campus stakeholders. Issues such as these must be considered with each program, and a re-evaluation of the CWE, its mission, and its programs as they relate to the university strategic plan should be an annual activity.

Regardless of the label, a precedent has already been established for writing center and local community relationship building, although direct relationships with community constituents seem to be few and far between. The online journal *Praxis: A Writing Center Journal* has offered two issues (fall 2004 and fall 2006) that offer descriptions and explanations of the work writing centers are doing off-campus, from supporting high school and community writing centers to participating in pen-pal projects and community tutorials and workshops. On the surface, there may appear to be no difference between operating these programs out of a writing center as opposed to a CWE. However, the expressly stated purposes of each might play a role in what programs can be conducted, especially because most writing centers have an exclusively campus-oriented mission. Additionally, the potential exists for significant difference in the administrative and financial support each receives. Earlier, I pointed out that funding is harder to secure for writing centers than for centers for writing excellence by virtue of the identities each seems to carry. Whereas the first is perceived, rightly or wrongly, as remedial and generally operates exclusively within the college or university, the second is perceived as multifunctional, providing support for students, faculty, and the community. Where community programs in the first may seem extra-curricular to the primary function of tutorial support, the multi-functionality of the second—the fact that its goal is to promote the university's literacy agenda on and off campus—makes it much harder to question whether such community programs should be discontinued in a budget crisis. Certainly, there is no guarantee that extending literacy into the community will ensure funding and security in the midst of an economic recession, but strong relationships with community stakeholders, relationships that are sanctioned and encouraged by the administration, cannot hurt the cause.

REFERENCES

Blythe, S. (1996). Why OWLS? Value, risk, and evolution. *Kairos 1*(1). Retrieved from http://english.ttu.edu/kairos/1.1/owls/blythe/owl.html

Boquet, E. H. (1999). "Our little secret": A history of writing centers, pre- to post-open admissions. *College Composition and Communication, 50*(3), 463–482.

Carino, P. (1995). Early writing centers: Toward a history. *Writing Center Journal, 15*(2), 103–115.

Carino, P. (1996). Open admissions and the construction of writing center history: A tale of three models. *Writing Center Journal, 17*(1), 30–48.

Carino, P. (2001). Writing centers and writing paradigms. In J. Nelson & K. Evertz (Eds.), *The politics of writing centers* (pp. 1–14). Portsmouth, NH: Boynton-Cook/Heinemann.

Coogan, D. (1999). *Electronic writing centers.* Stamford, CT: Ablex.

Inman, J. A., & Sewell, D. N. (2000). *Taking flight with OWLs: Examining electronic writing center work.* Mahwah, NJ: Lawrence Erlbaum Associates.

Isaacs, E. (2008). After the fall: Rebuilding a writing center. *The Writing Lab Newsletter, 33*(3), 5–8.

Lerner, N. (2006). Time warp: Historical representations of writing center directors. In C. Murphy & B. L. Stay (Eds.), *The writing center director's sourcebook* (pp. 3–12). Mahwah, NJ: Lawrence Erlbaum Associates.

McQueeney, P. (2001). What's in a name. In J. Nelson & K. Evertz (Eds.), *The politics of writing centers* (pp. 15–22). Portsmouth, NH: Boynton-Cook/Heinemann.

Murphy, C., & Law, J. (2001). The disappearing writing center within the disappearing academy: The challenges and consequences of outsourcing in the twenty-first century (pp. 133–146). In J. Nelson & K. Evertz (Eds.), *The politics of writing centers.* Portsmouth, NH: Boynton-Cook/Heinemann.

Murphy, C., & Stay, B. L. (2006). *The writing center director's resource book.* Mahwah, NJ: Lawrence Erlbaum Associates.

Rooney, J. D. (2006). Town-gown: A new meaning for a new economy In B. Holland & J. Meeropol (Eds.), *A more perfect vision: The future of campus engagement.* Providence, RI: Campus Compact. Retrieved from http://www.compact.org/20th/papers

Simpson, J. (2006). Managing encounters with central administration. In C. Murphy & B. L. Stay (Eds.), *The writing center director's resource book* (pp. 199–214). Mahwah, NJ: Lawrence Erlbaum Associates.

Steinkamp, J. (1998). Reshaping town-gown relations. *Connection: New England's Journal of Higher Education & Economic Development, 13*(1), 24–27.

University of North Alabama. (2007). *University of North Alabama Strategic Plan 2007-2012.* Florence, AL: University of North Alabama Press. Retrieved from http://www.una.edu/research/Strategic%20Plan/StrategicPlanapprovedJune2007.pdf

WRITING CENTERS AS NEXUS OF TRANSFORMATION: STRENGTHENING EDUCATION AND INSTITUTIONAL RELATIONSHIPS THROUGH CONCURRENT ENROLLMENT PARTNERSHIPS

Laura Bowles
Joanna Castner Post

Concurrent enrollment (CE), sometimes called dual enrollment, is a partnership between a university and a high school that provides university credit for high school courses. Supporters hope that CE will create productive ties between the high school and the university that will strengthen education in both spheres. The purpose of this chapter is not to argue for or against CE but to highlight ways that writing center practitioners can accomplish several of their oldest and dearest goals, as well as explain writing center work effectively to upper administration given the current scene of expanding CE partnerships. CE programs provide an opportunity, in other words, to expand our reach and work with more students earlier in their intellectual development, while also strengthening institutional relationships through our support of a university initiative.

In a CE partnership, college faculty ideally train and mentor high school teachers as they teach their regular high school classes that will also count as their university counterparts. For example, the junior-level high school English course may count dually for high school credit and the first-semester college composition course. The level of university content and pedagogical practice integrated into the regular high school courses varies according to the success of the partnership and the philosophy of the faculty and administration on both sides. There may be little to no revision to a high school algebra course, but university faculty may believe a high school English course needs significant revamping to be comparable to a college English or writing course. Indeed, when there is faculty resistance to CE, it often comes from English and writing departments. One objection is that literacy is not a skill that is learned once; it is an art, craft, and social practice that one develops over a lifetime. As a result, students need more not fewer literacy experiences. Another concern is that college-level reading and writing are substantively different than in high school, and faculty training for high school teaching is much different than training for institutions of higher education.

The University of Central Arkansas (UCA) Writing Center became the administrative body in the Writing Department to take on much of the oversight of the CE program. The program developed all at once, coming into being with no chance for planning ahead of its arrival. The then department Chair, David Harvey, asked the two of us and another colleague, Jennifer Deering, to form a triad to work with CE. Joanna was to be the Writing Center Director and Jennifer and Laura the Assistant Directors. In addition to taking on the regular duties of the writing center, we would create university orientations and professional development workshops for our new high school colleagues as well as our regular writing faculty. We would also work with a newly hired UCA liaison to the high schools, Vicki Simmons, to institute the activities only recently laid out by Arkansas state law and the National Association of Concurrent Enrollment Partners (NACEP) to govern the way CE partnerships should be managed. NACEP is a professional organization that accredits CE partnerships; some states, like Arkansas, require such accreditation. For the first year of CE in our department, Vicki traveled to the high schools to talk to the teachers, bring them standard syllabi, and observe the classes, and the three of us learned about the laws governing CE, held workshops and orientations to help bring our new colleagues into the college composition and university communities, and began tutoring one CE partner class through our online writing center. This tutoring partnership has now extended through another semester.

In the second year of CE in our department, the 2007–2008 academic year, Vicki took a new job with Academic Outreach, the for-profit arm of the university that recruits high schools for CE partnerships, and Laura took her place as liaison to the high school teachers. We have come to see the writing center as the perfect site for constructive collaborations and institutional relationship-building of several kinds:

- working with high school students to enter/construct productive engagement with academic discourse and university communities

- strengthening relationships with upper administration by using the familiar-to-them language of CE ideals to highlight the importance of writing center work
- developing relationships with high school colleagues
- fostering collaborations between high school and university colleagues to co-construct this new context that is teaching college composition in high schools

We have only just begun to realize the possibilities of these collaborations and relationships. In the next sections, we explain a bit more about the ideals that CE proponents hold and where we see crucial roles for writing center work in support of these ideals. Importantly, we believe that each role represents an opportunity for writing centers to expand their reach, explain their importance, and further longstanding goals.

Opportunity 1: Help high school students, especially those from underrepresented groups, enter/construct academic discourse and university communities.

Constructing Academic Discourse Communities

CE advocates hope that the partnerships will inspire students, especially students belonging to populations that traditionally have lower graduation rates, to stay in high school and then graduate from college. The lower minority college graduation rate is significant but improving. The Spellings Commission report on higher education includes these statistics: "While about one-third of whites have obtained bachelor's degrees by age 25–29, for example, just 18 percent of blacks and ten percent of Latinos in the same age cohort have earned degrees by that time" (U.S. Department of Education, 2006, p. 1).

But the National Center for Education Statistics reports good news:

> Between 1995–96 and 2005–06, the number of associate's degrees earned by minority students grew at a faster rate than for White students and accounted for over 60 percent of the increase in the total number of associate's degrees awarded. While the number of bachelor's degrees earned by White students rose by 19 percent, the number of bachelor's degrees earned by minority students rose by 64 percent and accounted for 44 percent of the total increase during this period (indicator 26). (Schneider, 2008)

CE proponents hope high school/university partnerships will continue to bring up these numbers by helping underrepresented populations understand what it means to do college-level work and, through positive experiences with such work in high school, develop the desire to finish a postsecondary education. There is some evidence that this plan will work: According to the Education Commission of the States, 25 percent of students who earn nine or more concurrent enrollment credits not only complete college but also continue on to graduate school (*Dual/Concurrent*, 2008). What isn't clear from these statistics is whether these students are from populations already graduating from college.

We believe that the ideal CE goal of bringing to college and graduating more students from underrepresented groups could remain unrealized without significant support of those students. Retention and education researcher Vincent Tinto (2005) writes that retention research has advanced quite a bit and can argue with some authority that academic preparedness, strong personal identification with a university, and active academic and social engagement together correlate strongly with retention (p. ix). Alan Seidman (2005), an educational researcher who founded the *Journal of College Student Retention: Research, Theory, and Practice* and the Center for the Study of College Student Retention Web site, translated this research into a usable formula for universities: Retention = Early Identification + (Early + Intensive + Continuous) Intervention (p. 296).

Intervention that is significantly intensive and continuous, though, is not typically available through traditional reading and writing courses at either the high school or college level. Writing centers, of course, provide just this kind of help. Many writing center practitioners have positioned themselves on the margins of mainstream disciplines and courses as literacy experts who can help students, especially students historically underrepresented at the university, thrive (Barron & Grimm, 2002; Bokser, 2005; Howard, 2004; Newmann, 2003). In other words, writing center practitioners are already set up through longstanding theories and practices to support the students whom CE proponents would most like to reach. For most writing center scholars, helping students from such groups thrive does not mean that we will bring them into dominant discourse communities uncritically, but that we would like to be sites of transformation where students from all backgrounds can talk about their ideas, discoveries, and writing in personal ways that affirm their intelligence, creativity, and unique place in the academy.

At first we were skeptical about this particular CE goal: how could CE do anything but widen the gap between those populations that typically attend the university and underrepresented groups when most universities have entrance requirements for CE courses that could keep them out? CE looked like an initiative that replicated the AP system already in place.

However, we are hearing from some of our partner schools that serve larger populations of underrepresented groups that the presence of CE programs brings to mind the possibility of a higher education. Bright students who have nevertheless not seen themselves as "AP material" get to their senior year and become willing to try on a university education due to free CE offerings in their high schools. It is true that not everyone will be able to meet the entrance requirements, but writing center work would not have to be limited to students in CE programs. We can also reach out to those students interested in preparing for CE classes.

For CE programs to accomplish the high-level goals that are their ideals and, indeed, the goals of all educators, university and high school faculty will have to mentor and scaffold students' literacy development collaboratively in rigorous and continuous ways to appropriate the Seidman language on retention. Some CE students will need help to engage the dialogues of dominant academic discourse communities, and all CE students will need help as they negotiate and construct an experience that includes their high school cultures and the new university cultures. Just a few of the issues we can help students navigate are the particulars of writing for standardized tests as compared to writing for literature and the conventions different from both inherent in essays required in college-level composition courses. We can develop on-site and online workshops on numerous activities such as using university library databases and effectively engaging with voices from a variety of disciplines. Many writing centers, including our own, ask tutors-in-training to develop YouTube videos on various subjects. This might be a good medium to use for such workshops if they have to be developed online for students some distance from the university.

Through the online component of the UCA Writing Center, we have been able to work with the high school students from one CE partner school for two semesters. We were happy to begin this work so quickly. Our CE program only started in earnest in 2006, and at the end of 2008 we are only now able to say that we have productive, positive relationships with our high school colleagues. Developing collaborative relationships across institution types takes time. University and high school contexts really are very different—in effect, we have had to learn one another's institution type and discipline-specific languages, even though we are working with English and writing teachers.

Our online writing center has two parts, an online scheduling and reporting application called WCOnline from RichCo., and a student paper exchange and discussion through Google e-mail asynchronously or MSN Messenger in real-time. Much of the work we do with CE students may have to be online because they are quite geographically dispersed. Our pilot work last year went well; the teacher reported a great deal of student satisfaction with the interaction with the tutors. This work was actually a pilot on several fronts: it was also the first semester and year of the online component to the writing center.

All of the students chose the e-mail option for tutoring, and much of the interaction stopped upon their receipt of the first feedback the first semester. Although we will have to continue ways to foster dialogue, the second semester of our work with this partner school included much more interaction as most of the students e-mailed back with questions and second and third drafts. We plan to visit all the partner schools at least once this semester to talk about the possibilities of writing center work with the students and teachers, and then also to investigate ways to promote the more interactive real-time technologies. We are intrigued by the ways that students are using technologies at UCA. E-mail is actually not very popular; it seems to be the way students communicate with older people, such as their professors and parents. This may be why the high school students chose that medium over real-time chat when working with us, but when communicating with one another, they seem to prefer text messaging and Facebook. Although we have an official Facebook presence, as well as several unofficial Facebook sites, we haven't yet developed ways to use it or text messaging to interact substantively about writing with our students.

One of our most serious challenges is the lack of technology in some schools, especially some rural schools and poorer schools in larger cities. The CE students we saw in the writing center this past year were from one of the wealthier schools in the area, and the students there have good access to technology in their homes. A lack of technology is a hurdle not only for communicating with us, but also for conducting research for writing projects. Providing adequate access to technology in the schools has to be one of our first priorities, and it will most likely not be solved without grant money. Helping schools get adequate technology is an enormous opportunity for writing center practitioners to help strengthen education and reach out to students. In another wrinkle, in some schools where most of the students are middle to upper middle class and have good access to technology at home, their teachers do not have computer classroom space to show students how to use the online writing center; plus, many of these same teachers are not interested in using technology to support education, nor do they have the training to understand how it might work. As a result, they are not interested in advocating online writing center use in their classrooms.

Another challenge we are gearing up to face is the overload of our writing center facilities. Already, as a result of our efforts all over campus to publicize our work to support CE initiatives and promote the work we are doing on campus, we have forged productive ties to professors in almost every college and department, as well as to all of our Student Services groups. These connections have paid off enormously in student numbers. In the spring of 2008, we had 682 one-to-one sessions, and in the fall of 2008, we had an astonishing growth to 2,355 sessions. The addition of many more high school partnerships and students will be overwhelming. We see this as a positive hurdle to face, though, and we are eager to keep reaching out to as many students as we can. The ripples we are making on campus have also helped us create closer ties to the Dean of our college, the Dean of Undergraduate Studies, and our Provost.

Constructing University Communities

Another way that we see writing center work with high school students as crucial to the ideal success of CE partnerships is in the early identification piece of student retention. Again, Seidman's (2005) often-used formula for student retention drawn from recent retention studies is Retention = Early Identification + (Early + Intensive + Continuous) Intervention (p. 296). Early identification here refers to two areas, personal and academic. Writing center culture blends these two areas quite effectively (Wingate, 2001). Retention research shows that students who are not able to engage both personally and academically in satisfying ways tend to drop out of the university altogether or switch to another institution. So students must create fulfilling personal relationships and participate in interesting and fun extracurricular activities, and they must connect to the academics of the university in real ways. Writing center culture does both. Our writing center, for example, is staffed by as many as 18 bright undergraduates and two to three graduate assistants. Most of them are involved in all sorts of academic, creative projects that they love to talk about. Many of them work on the student newspaper and the student literary journal. All of them see themselves as writers and share their personal work with one another both formally and informally.

One tutor started an online group for all tutors so they could share their work. Several of the tutors created multiple writing center workshop series for all students on campus covering topics of their own interest, such as how to get published, how to write for science fiction markets, and what it means to be a writer. One of our graduate assistants started a writing center book club. Another tutor got a group together and started a writing center conversation group held every Friday for a large, dynamic group of Japanese students. He wrote a grant and won it to fund the project. This group on their own took the Japanese students to the beach for spring break — collective writing center vacations are typical, in fact.

Our writing center has just begun to connect high school students to this dynamic group. We did so through our online writing center, and a few high school students from our town came to some of the tutors' workshop series. But we need to find ways for students in the high schools to participate more fully in this culture. Some ideas we've had so far are promoting more interactive, real-time tutorial sessions, making the workshop series available online through YouTube, and then creating real-time discussion groups, including tutors and high school students, and taking tutors with us when we visit high school classes to talk about the ways they can make use of the writing center.

In short, to create real ties to high school students that will work to bring in and graduate underrepresented groups and strengthen education in both spheres, university faculty will have to do more than administer the program and mentor the high school teachers. The students will need ongoing, rigorous, and personal support. Writing center practitioners specialize in just these activities.

Opportunity 2: Strengthen relationships with upper administration by using the familiar-to-them language of CE ideals to highlight the importance of writing center work.

We all know that recruitment and retention are important to every university, and CE is viewed at UCA, and most likely at other universities, as a way to secure and retain students from a surrounding region. The role that writing center support can play in these efforts can only help writing center practitioners forge better relationships with upper administration. UCA's CE program was extremely modest before 2006. But when the President of the university realized that two- and four-year institutions in the state were crossing regional boundaries to offer general education courses to populations traditionally UCA-bound, our CE program was developed quickly over the course of about a year and a half. Based on Seidman's formula, it is easy to see why administrators at a university would hope that students in their high school CE programs will finish their degrees at their institution. In a CE program, a university reaches students much earlier, sometimes in the sophomore year of high school, works to prepare them more rigorously for university-level work, and does so for the remainder of the student's high school career. The program at UCA went from 50 students at one high school linked to two departments to 800 students at seven high schools involving eleven departments over that year and a half growth spurt.

Recently, a few writing center scholars have voiced concern that the kind of critical, theoretical discourse we use to talk to one another is off-putting and obscure to colleagues in other disciplines as well as administrators (Gardner & Ramsey, 2005). These scholars call for the development of a different kind of discourse we can use to explain what we do and why it is important to those who hold the purse-strings in upper administration, as well as colleagues in other disciplines who might send us their students if they understood our work better. We agree. Further, we should develop more ways to show how writing center work supports some mainstream university initiatives rather than positioning ourselves on the margins so completely that our work isn't considered immediately as connected and key to all literacy programs that arise on campus.

In these regards, reaching out to students and teachers in CE programs through writing centers provides the perfect opportunity to showcase the strengths and possibilities of our work to administrators and colleagues campus-wide, strengthening our institutional relationships in the process. Further, CE programs present the opportunity to work toward one of our most cherished goals: providing occasions for dialogues about writing that can help students from underrepresented groups engage the academy in effective, creative, culturally affirmative ways. CE rhetoric is familiar language that already resonates with upper administration. We can use it as we explain how we can contribute to CE initiatives, and, importantly, how this is the kind of work we do for all of our students.

To get the word out about what the UCA Writing Center is doing to support CE teachers and students and how these activities can translate to others on campus, we have sent campus e-mails, met with numerous administrators and other university services groups, and conducted workshops that invite people to collaborate with us on ideas for ways the writing center can work with them. We would say that the Dean of our college is extremely supportive of all that we've accomplished through the writing center this past year. He has sent us many encouraging e-mails and asked us often whether he can do anything to help us. We have also made ourselves far more visible and understandable to a variety of student services on campus through our work with CE partnerships. The department on campus that administers transitional reading, writing, and math courses has asked whether we would send several tutors to them three nights a week this next academic year, and at-risk advisors are sending us many of their students now.

Opportunity 3: Foster collaborations between high school and university colleagues and work with high school colleagues to co-construct this new context that is teaching college composition in high schools.

*Foster Collaborations Between High School
and University Colleagues*

Concurrent enrollment also provides a unique opportunity to forge relationships between secondary and post-secondary educational institutions. We complain that students are not prepared for college writing, but this is not due to a deficit in the students or in the high school teachers. The cause for this lack of preparation lies within the assessment programs that have been implemented in secondary schools. A new report shows that "states have created unnecessary and detrimental barriers between high school and college" because "high school assessments often stress different knowledge and skills than do college entrance and placement requirements. Similarly, the coursework between high school and college is not connected" (Venezia, Kirst, & Antonio, 2003, p. 10). Perhaps nowhere in the academy is this more pronounced than in English studies. Advances in understanding how people write have not, by and large, made it to the high school English classrooms. And even if a high school teacher embraces contemporary composition scholarship, high school administrators tend to see English as a place for current-traditional pedagogy, with any other approaches being strictly supplemental.

In the past year, the writing center at UCA has become involved with our CE program, possibly by default, as the team of directors happened to be three people who were interested in reaching out to students and faculty and building communication channels. To that end, we began a series of conversations with the CE faculty who are located at the area high schools and our own faculty to talk about issues such as norming, assessing student work, and building effective assignments. We were also privileged to be able to listen to the high school teachers talk about their challenges with their own curriculum mandated by the state, as well as the difficulties of integrating our expectations into what they already do. The high school teachers talked about timed writings, literature, tests, Advanced Placement, and benchmark tests. Because the reputation of their schools, and their own reputations, is based on high-stakes testing, getting ready for those tests is important. And, oddly enough, the students who do well on the benchmark tests are not necessarily the best writers, but instead the students who write formulaically. In other words, teaching the kind of writing valued in a college writing classroom can hurt a student's chances of doing well on the state benchmark test.

Each state sets requirements that each public school must follow. In Arkansas, these are called "frameworks," but each state that we have looked at calls them something different. The Arkansas frameworks are divided into different knowledge areas and different skills areas. In the average classroom, these are taught primarily using literature, often selections from the "canon" delivered in ponderous textbook anthologies that have changed little in the past fifty years. The frameworks, themselves, do not predicate this emphasis on literature. Strands outlined in the frameworks include: Oral and Visual Communication, Writing, Reading, and Inquiring/Researching. These strands are comprised of multiple standards: Oral and Visual Communication includes Speaking, Listening, and Media Literacy; Writing includes Process, Purposes, Topics, Forms and Audiences, Conventions, and Craftsmanship; Reading includes Comprehension, Variety of Texts, Vocabulary, Word Study, and Fluency; and Inquiring/Researching includes Research/Inquiry Process. Most of these frameworks can be adequately addressed in a typical composition classroom, with the exception of some specific types of literature required under Variety of Texts. Despite the flexibility offered under the frameworks, the benchmark tests require students to answer multiple-choice grammar questions as well as to respond to a writing prompt.

The varied demands on high school teachers can be ameliorated to a degree through the writing center. The writing center, as a non-threatening, collaborative, and vibrant community, can aid high school teachers first by responding to drafts. We respond to student work using terminology that they understand, but we emphasize skills and features that are valued in the university. In addition, because we send a report to the teachers using the values and terminology of the university, we draw them into the university discourse community as well. In this way, the writing center is co-constructive, strengthening both high school and college writing. The writing center's place on the margins can bring people in from both sides and give both a role in conversation. When information is offered by the writing center, it is not as likely to be seen as threatening as it would be if offered by the WPA. The writing center brings to the table experience in teaching college composition as a collaborator rather than a supervisor. The WPA cannot escape the authority that she carries, and any conversations with her cannot completely ignore her authority. Because the writing center lacks supervisory capacity, it offers support from the ranks.

Work With High School Colleagues to Co-construct this New Context that Is Teaching College Composition in High Schools

Scholars, educators, and education advocacy groups who are optimistic about CE partnerships hope they will create mutually informing dialogues so that high school teachers and students will be able to hone in on knowledge and practice that will prepare them better for university coursework (*Achieve*; Farris, 2006; Kirst & Venezia, 2001; *NextStep*, 2007). Indeed, Christine Farris (2006), after a long process of developing CE partnerships between Indiana University and 90 high schools in Indiana, Michigan, and Ohio, writes:

> . . . [M]y reasons for working with a program that is technically outside my job description have to do with the bridging of the high school and college English—a connection I have come to believe affects nearly everything we do and hope for as teachers of writing. (p. 105)

In mentoring high school teachers, Farris encountered a persistent belief that academic writing must be impersonal and overall correct. The high school teachers had not experienced writing in the academy as engaged or as a process of discovery. As a result, Farris reworked her own composition assignments to highlight even more these aspects of college writing and integrated this focus into her high school teacher training in rich, multi-layered ways.

What is happening, then, is a collaboration between university and high school that is mutually enriching. Farris strengthened her own courses and teacher training, and the high school teachers were able to talk to their students about college writing in more current, accurate ways. At the University of Central Arkansas (UCA), we have certainly found ourselves in the Writing Department having extended and productive conversations about what it is we do as a result of our collaborations with high school teachers. We are in the midst of rethinking the role of our first-semester course and how it transitions to the second semester. These conversations have also led to a faculty study group on ways to rework the writing major given the move of many of our first-semester composition courses to the high schools. Inspired by an argument by David A. Jolliffe and Bernard Phelan (2006), we would like to develop a range of interesting and challenging courses for CE graduates to transfer into. Jolliffe and Phelan argue that AP credit should not replace college writing; it should instead provide the opportunity for university faculty to create more courses at different levels that will facilitate students' lifelong literacy development. We're drawing a parallel between this argument about AP courses and CE courses, especially given that CE and AP courses are often locally merged in high schools.

CONCLUSION

Interestingly, it was the UCA Writing Center's position on the margins of the Writing Department that gave it the flexibility needed to respond quickly to the immediately ramped-up CE program. But in our appropriation of the language of CE ideals, we were able to talk to multiple university and high school stakeholders in ways they already understood, and in the process, our work in the university has moved much more toward the center of literacy education here. Just a little over a year has passed, so we will have to do much more to keep writing center work as visible as it was last year. However, we see a great deal of potential given the ubiquity of CE programs for our work here and for writing centers nationwide for strengthening education and institutional relationships.

REFERENCES

Achieve, Inc. Retrieved February 2, 2007, from http://www.achieve.org/

Barron, N., & Grimm, N. (2002). Addressing racial diversity in a writing center: Stories and lessons from two beginners. *The Writing Center Journal, 22*(2), 55–83.

Bokser, J. A. (2005). Pedagogies of belonging: Listening to students and peers. *The Writing Center Journal, 25*(1), 43–60.

Dual/concurrent enrollment: Quick facts, (2006, March). Education Commission of the States. Retrieved June 6, 2007, from http://www.ecs.org/html/Issue Section.asp?issueid=214&s=Quick+Facts

Farris, C. (2006). The space between: Dual-credit programs as brokering, community building, and professionalization. In K. B. Yancey (Ed.), *Delivering college composition: The fifth canon* (pp. 104–114). Portsmouth, NH: Boynton/Cook.

Gardner, P. J., & Ramsey, W. M. (2005). The polyvalent mission of writing centers. *The Writing Center Journal, 25*(1), 25–42.

Howard, R. M. (2004). Deriving backwriting from writing back. *The Writing Center Journal, 24*(2), 3–18.

Jolliffe, D. A., & Phelan, B. (2006). Advanced placement, not advanced exemption: Challenges for high schools, colleges, and universities. In K. B. Yancey (Ed.), *Delivering college composition: The fifth canon* (pp. 89–103). Portsmouth, NH: Boynton/Cook.

Kirst, M., & Venezia, A. (2001). Bridging the great divide between secondary schools and postsecondary education. *Phi Delta Kappan, 83*(1), 92–97.

Newmann, B. M. (2003). Centering in the borderlands: Lessons from Hispanic student writers. *The Writing Center Journal, 23*(2), 43–62.

Next step for Arkansas' future. Retrieved February 2, 2007, from http://www.next steparkansas.org/parents/parents_home.html

Schneider, M. (2008). *The condition of education.* National Center for Education Statistics. Retrieved July 1, 2008, from http://nces.ed.gov/programs/coe/state-ment/s7.asp

Seidman, A. (2005). Where we go from here. In A. Seidman (Ed.), *College student retention: Formula for student success* (pp. 295–316). Westport, CT: American Council on Education Praeger.

Tinto, V. (2005). Foreword. In A. Seidman (Ed.), *College student retention: Formula for student success* (pp. ix–x). Westport, CT: American Council on Education Praeger.

U.S. Department of Education. (2006, September). *A test of leadership: Charting the future of U.S. higher education* (Report No. ED-06-C0-0013). Retrieved July 1, 2008, from http://www.ed.gov/about/bdscomm/list/hiedfuture/reports/pre-pub-report.pdf

Venezia, A., Kirst, M., & Antonio, A. (2003). *Betraying the college dream: How disconnected K-12 and postsecondary education systems undermine student aspirations.* Final Policy Report from Stanford University's Bridge Project.

Wingate, M. (2001). Writing centers as sites of academic culture. *The Writing Center Journal, 21*(2), 7–20.

GETTING BEYOND MEDIOCRITY: THE SECONDARY SCHOOL WRITING CENTER AS CHANGE AGENT

Pamela B. Childers

Writing centers don't settle for the status quo. By their very nature, writing centers and their directors want to move beyond mediocrity. Look at their purpose or mission statements, which all say something about "improving," "risk taking," "excellence," or a combination of these terms. In the unstable environment of many secondary schools, a writing center becomes a safe place for students to succeed because it offers challenge with no grades involved; it creates an environment where students are free to take intellectual risks with their writing; and it encourages all to excel by improving attitudes toward writing and the writing process. However, not every institution has the same freedoms and constraints in pursuing these goals. Vygotsky (1978) and his Zone of Proximal Development aside, adolescents in secondary schools are minors, and teachers are legally responsible for the well-being of these young people in a structured environment that seldom allows the freedoms that a writing center might usually offer. Discipline, socio-economic concerns, safety issues, statewide testing, and federal mandates offer secondary schools many challenges that can be met in a writing center; however, financial and other sorts of problems may limit what directors can do to get beyond mediocrity and act as agents of change.

As many rhetoricians follow the work of key writing scholars, so do secondary writing center directors. For instance, the works of Janet Emig, Donald Murray, Peter Elbow, and Kenneth Bruffee, to name a few, have impacted secondary school writing centers (Childers, Fels, & Jordan, 2004). And, these centers must provide a service to all, including in many cases English Language Learning (ELL), literacy intervention, and Deaf and Hard of Hearing (DHH) students.

In these times of economic challenges that impact both public and independent secondary schools, it is difficult for writing centers to do more than tutor with staff limitations, class overloads, and pressure to keep only those programs that will improve standardized test scores. Secondary school directors want to advance their own intellectual studies and try to fit everything into a school day with the challenges of NCLB, colleagues who don't really understand what they are trying to do, and their own class loads. A writing center can step up to the plate and make changes to improve teaching and learning. Secondary teachers who direct writing centers must do their own homework in the form of research, be creative in finding resources, and present themselves and their centers as the one way to make a difference. As Melissa Turner (2006) states, "Writing centers offer many benefits: response to the writing of all students including those at risk, reinforcement of writing as a process, intellectual and attitudinal growth in tutors and students alike, resources for faculty in all content areas, and favorable publicity for the school" (p. 45). In years of regional accreditation audits, for example, administrators frequently showcase a writing center because it offers students individual learning opportunities across disciplines, but students have to use that center in order for the showcase to work. A secondary writing center "has to be a place of safety, a place of exploration and discovery, a place of risk taking without fear of judgment" (Jordan, Snow, Frankel, & Severns, 2002, p. II.4.2). In order to create and sustain such a center, the school and center must have clear mission statements. Then, the writing center director and staff must fulfill those statements through collaboration with students, faculty, administration and staff, alumni, parents, community, nearby institutions, and professional organizations.

MISSION STATEMENTS

By looking at the mission statements of a sampling of secondary school writing centers, one notes that some statements may mention tutoring, but most go beyond that in either long or short mission statements. Here are a few examples:

Warsaw Community High School Writing Center, Warsaw, IN

The Writing Center is to help writers learn to use language more effectively, to produce clear writing appropriate to their purposes and audiences, and to develop positive attitudes about writing and about themselves as writers (Scroggs, 2008).

Mercy Reading and Writing Center, Mercy High School, Burlingame, CA

The website refers to the center as "Creating a Community of Literacy" (Wells, 2006).

University High School Reading Writing Center, Orlando, FL

The purpose of the University High School Reading Writing Center is to promote literacy appreciation in all of our students and to encourage literacy staff development in our faculty. We further wish to teach students to become independent thinkers, readers and writers who realize that attention to literacy skills will result in improvement (Spillane, 2005).

Caldwell Writing Center, The McCallie School, Chattanooga, TN

We are here to serve the entire McCallie community. We invite students, faculty, parents, and alumni to become part of the commitment to writing and learning across the curriculum at McCallie (Childers, 2009).

One consistent feature of each of these mission statements is that they don't say "Our mission is to provide one-to-one conferences." Instead, they promote literacy, language appreciation, commitment to writing and learning, and positive attitudes. All of these missions give writing center directors the freedom to be agents of change in a variety of ways and do not limit their work to peer tutoring. Although these writing centers do provide services, creating an active community of learners is clearly a priority.

SURVEY OVERVIEW

In the summer of 2008, I created a survey to determine how different public and independent secondary school writing centers function beyond "tutoring writing." I then announced the survey for secondary school writing center directors on the secondary school writing center listserv (SSWC-L) and WCenter. Respondents to the announcement emailed me, and they were sent a survey (Appendix A) as an attachment to complete and return. Several responded immediately, whereas others needed a follow-up email or reminders to complete the survey.

The survey questions included how secondary school writing center directors collaborated within their institutions (with students, English faculty, other faculty, administrators, staff, alumnae) and outside their institutions (with community, colleagues at other institutions, and professional organizations). I wanted to discover what they were doing beyond tutoring, what they have in common, and what successful secondary writing centers do to get beyond mediocrity as agents of change within and outside their own institutions. Eighteen U.S. secondary school writing center directors responded and completed the survey between August 2008 and January 2009 (Appendix B). I also received seven survey responses from a group of German writing center directors, thanks to Gerd Bräuer's distribution and translation.

Each center is unique, and these busy directors wear multiple hats, which may explain why some are limited in the ways they can collaborate. Of those surveyed, the majority are primarily classroom teachers of English, writing, social studies, or cross-disciplinary courses, while also holding other extra positions, such as writing-across-the-curriculum (WAC) director, K-12 writing administrator, department chair, or dean of students. Many also sponsor student council, the school newspaper, a literary magazine, and/or a forensics club; and some coach athletic teams after school. With full days lacking office hours or little unstructured time in more than eight-hour school days, plus grading and planning time at night, many only find time for research if they are taking graduate courses.

A few lucky directors work at public and independent schools that fund a full-time position in the writing center, which may focus as a literacy center or reading-writing center. Although these names may differ, most of the writing centers in this survey focus on reading and literacy as integral parts of writing. However, the majority have little time left to research and write for publication or presentation at conferences. In fact, with their classes, writing center responsibilities, parent conferences, committee meetings, frequent marking period grading and reporting, and test accountability, I am amazed at all they do, based on both this survey and informal interviews I have conducted with other secondary school writing center directors over the last 25 years.

To ease some of the burden, many have established some kind of relationship with nearby colleges and universities, and a few of these directors are actually college/university teachers who direct a nearby secondary school writing center. These relationships inspire directors to go beyond settling for the status quo at their own institutions. Through the International Writing Centers Association (IWCA) and local or regional affiliates, WAC programs and National Writing Project (NWP) sites, secondary school writing center directors have discovered ways to collaborate and share what they have learned with others. For example, several have presented at National Council of Teachers of English (NCTE), NWP, Conference on College

Composition and Communication (CCCC), International Writing Across the Curriculum (IWAC), and IWCA conferences with other secondary school and college/university directors. Others have joined local writing center collaboratives and attended the IWCA Summer Institute.

Whether these schools function on block or regular schedules, finding a time and a place for a writing center may be difficult. For example, Ted Domers and Stacey Carlough at Freire Charter School (Philadelphia) collaborate with students primarily during lunch periods and after school. Others started in a similar manner and found that their centers should be available all day. However, I doubt that any of these directors think of themselves as change agents, but they and their centers seem to be having an impact on students, colleagues, college/university writing centers, and communities. Even if we consider only the impact of secondary-level writing centers on the students who work in them, there is rich evidence that the directors of these centers are real agents of change.

In 2009, I conducted a second survey of my own former writing center consultants (Appendix C) to discover the importance of their writing center experiences at McCallie. With 70 percent of the writing center alumni responding to the survey, they clearly indicated the importance of their writing center experience on their occupation, their writing, and their lives since graduating from McCallie. Of those who graduated between 1995 and 2006, all ranked these three categories as 4, 5, or even a 6 on a scale of 1 to 5. The anecdotes indicate involvement outside of their professional careers that have been influenced positively by their writing center experiences at McCallie. Only the 18 percent who have just completed their first or second year of undergraduate school had more mixed responses of 2 to 5, with a mean of 4. Stories from alumni in the working world or graduate school indicate cases where they have been called upon by CEOs or other executives to write letters or reports that they were praised for and presentations that they felt comfortable giving because of their writing center training (Childers, 2009).

U.S. writing center directors whom I have met or heard from through conferences, phone calls, or emails have mentioned alumni returning to help out, sharing success stories, or seeking advice on writing graduate school or job application essays. In other words, the impact of the writing center experience has been life-changing for students who continue to value feedback on their writing from a trusted professional. If they move to higher education, these students value those writing centers because of their high school experiences. If the students go immediately into the workforce or military, they know the questions to ask and how to interact with others in positive ways. That is, secondary school writing centers change more than student attitudes toward writing, thinking, and learning, at least for the tutors themselves.

COLLABORATION WITH STUDENTS

As is true of many writing centers in higher education, secondary-level centers collaborate with writers and tutors/consultants in a variety of ways. As I was reading over the surveys, Amanda Scroggs of Warsaw High School (IN) sent the following email on the secondary school writing center listserv (SSWC-L):

> I just hosted my first Senior Scholarship Application & Essay Workshop. We had 27 students sign-up and show-up. Word spread and there is now a waiting list of 10 to petition for another writer's workshop. It's a lot of hard work but the rewards of having a high school writing center and student writing tutors outweigh all the struggles. I really appreciate being a part of this community. (Amanda, 2009)

Amanda's message says it all. She did her research to determine a need, and students responded. Yes, it made more work for her to prepare and facilitate the first and future workshops, but her writing center is clearly fulfilling the specific needs of its learning community as stated in the writing center mission statement.

As in higher education, directors and students can together offer workshops in the writing center or specific classrooms. For instance, they take mini-lessons into classrooms across disciplines, as well as reading and writing workshops. This work involves collaborative learning, preparation of material, and review of presentation skills. If subject content is added to this mix, then students and directors are also learning new material across disciplines as well. As a result, secondary directors must consider research on teaching in secondary education that includes multiple disciplines, as well as theory and practice in writing more generally.

States often require public school teachers to renew certification periodically through advanced study, no matter how many degrees the teacher may have. Independent schools offer study grants and other incentives to encourage teachers to remain current in their fields. There is ongoing faculty development in the form of advanced study on the part of these writing center directors. No one I know is directing a writing center to avoid teaching; in fact, many speak of becoming involved with writing centers because they wanted to do more than they or their colleagues could do in the classroom alone.

Students and writing center directors also write collaboratively, generating important feedback for one another as part of writing groups, like Cynthia Dean of Erskine Academy (ME), who collaborates with her students on projects to promote writing. Patty Melei's students at Lemont High School (IL) collaborate through an electronic blog, called the

Speakeasy, where they "share responses from articles in the *Wall Street Journal*, writing magazines and professional journals." They also reflect "on the tutoring process, write papers and share ideas for revision . . . create digital stories in the various disciplines and share them" (Childers, 2009). These kinds of academic exchanges are important in preparing students for writing in college and beyond. They are improving everyone's reading, thinking, and writing.

Having been part of multiple collaborative writing experiences with students, I know the value of exposing them to the critical eyes of editors who give objective feedback. In the Caldwell Writing Center at McCallie School, students and faculty have written articles with me for *Writing Lab Newsletter* (Laughter & Childers,1996; Straka & Childers, 2004), *Southern Discourse* (Baker, Conney, Jones, Mullen, Murnan, & Childers, 2007; Davis & Childers, 2006), and *The Clearing House* (Grant, Murphy, & Stafford, 1997), as well as chapters in writing center books like *Weaving Knowledge Together* (Childers, Laughter, Lowry, & Trumpeter, 1998). These writing opportunities free students to research something that interests them, to reflect on how their writing center experiences have changed them, and to consider how their work has impacted peers, but they also enable students to become part of a professional writing community. One year, I even challenged consultants to submit a research-based persuasive essay for publication in *The Contemporary Reader* (Goshgarian, 2008), a college text; one student had his essay published (Mullens, 2008) and was able to share it with his freshman English professor at University of Virginia the following year.

Directors like Tom Brandt of Berkeley Preparatory School (FL) and I have also collaborated with our students to present their research at conferences such as IWCA, CCCC, or IWAC. Other secondary directors do the same. Tom's students presented a self study and research on OWL programs. In fact, I observed his students interacting with writing center leaders in a similar way to my own students' interactions at an IWAC conference. These workshops and presentations at professional conferences prepare students for later opportunities in academia, so the inspiration and high standards of professionalism set by their directors do make a difference.

Many of the respondents to the survey mentioned collaborating with students on weekly staff meetings, mentoring other students, sponsoring student readings and music presentations, preparing lessons and promotional material, supervising OWLs, and training new tutors/consultants. There are also multiple national competitions in writing that these directors and students advertise and promote as part of their work. In schools with boarding students, directors work with tutors in the dorms or libraries to offer workshops on writing college application essays or academic papers, for example. In elementary and middle schools, Ellen Kolba and Sheila Crowell at Montclair Public Schools (NJ) collaborate with students and teachers in grades 4–9 to train students to become peer responders, and Karen Boozer at Fairhill School (TX) works with special needs students in grades 4–12. In Germany, directors collaborate with students in grades 4–9 as they train to become effective peer responders to students in grades 1–6.

Most of these responses parallel the work that college writing center directors do beyond tutoring; yet there is still not an equally substantial body of work that discusses this work among secondary-level writing center directors. There are, however, multiple sources for strategic planning, dealing with politics, technology, and other issues. A select bibliography created for secondary school writing center directors (Appendix D) names only some of the many existing sources. There are many others forthcoming, which is inspiring.

COLLABORATION WITH FACULTY

When I asked about work with English departments, the respondents gave diverse answers. While some report periodically to the English department, work together with/on curriculum, instructional practices, and mission statements, and plan development and revision of assignments, rubrics, and mini lessons; they mostly focus on ways to improve writing. Some departments collaborate with the writing center on writing college application essays and teaching the research paper. However, several respondents commented, "Our English department is dysfunctional," "My department is just not interested in the writing process," and "Very little collaboration—not because I haven't tried." Each writing center director determines how he/she will collaborate with faculty. At McCallie, as part of our work with the English department, the writing center director and members of the department created *Guidelines for Parents* to help them work with their children on writing (Childers, 2009). John Brassil, English department chair and writing center director at Mt. Ararat High School (ME), presents another positive model. Brassil has supported the writing center by involving only those English teachers committed to conference teaching to collaborate with student volunteers.

Meanwhile, frustrations with English colleagues parallel those of directors of WAC programs. Both often find faculty in other disciplines, primarily science and history departments, who collaborate or even team teach with the writing center director to develop student writing in the areas of research, writing to learn, writing to communicate, and writing for social action, for example. There are many teacher-led initiatives in schools that involve the writing center, including faculty development study groups, development of literacy instruction strategies, practical collaborations with faculty in all disciplines on writing effective student comments and providing teachers resources in the form of professional books, journals, and handouts or web links on writing, writing across the curriculum, research, and teaching.

Some of the more creative efforts toward these kinds of collaborations are interesting. Amanda Scroggs holds a "Book Shower," asking teachers to donate new or used style manuals, writing guides, or reference books. Carol Blosser, at Regent School of Austin (TX), an interdisciplinary K-12 school, is developing the writing curriculum that will be an essential part of the school's mission. Jeanette Jordan of Glenbrook North (IL) works with faculty across disciplines to complete a publication of their work each year, focusing on some aspect of the writing process within specific disciplines. All respondents felt that a significant segment of their faculty saw the writing center as an important resource that opens the door to meeting unique challenges and providing means of improvement.

COLLABORATION WITH ADMINISTRATORS AND STAFF

There are so many variables in working with administrators, especially because secondary school writing centers and their directors cannot have the autonomy that many college/university center directors do. Yes, those in higher education have to show how they encourage retention of students and serve students and faculty effectively; however, they do not also have to deal with issues of discipline, close adult supervision, schedules that require students to be accounted for every minute of the school day, and parents. Administrators make the rules that determine how the writing center functions within the institution, so it is essential to have an administrator who listens, understands the idea of a writing center, and wants to work with the writing center director. Because the demographics and mission of institutions differ, writing center directors must encourage such collaborations with administrators and work with them on unique local professional development opportunities, curriculum development and district or statewide writing assessments, possibilities for grant funds, and ways the writing center can respond to literacy issues and intervention programs. Secondary-level writing center directors serve on school improvement planning committees, work with individual department chairs, and one has even trained administrators to work in the writing center.

But writing center directors work with other areas of administration such as college counseling, guidance, career counseling, admissions, development, and public relations, too. They also work with the school staff on graduate school papers, application essays, cover letters, resumes, articles for publication, and sometimes personal matters that require maintaining the privacy and integrity of the collaboration. Most have encountered at least one situation where they were helping a staff member apply for another job or respond to a report by a supervisor. As one director said, "I don't want to step on toes," but that is one of the dances that writing center directors have to do. Many college writing center directors encounter similar situations.

COLLABORATION WITH PARENTS AND ALUMNI

The ease of email engenders another dance, the one with parents. Writing center directors offer parents evening seminars on how to support their child's writing and how to help their child through the college application process, for example. Through the PTA, parents and secondary school writing center directors collaborate on ways to improve the services of the writing center and in coauthoring articles for the parents' newsletter. Some have parent volunteers in their writing centers, and many respond to parents online or by phone to collaborate on parents' own projects. For instance, a parent called the Caldwell Writing Center at McCallie from another state to ask for help in writing a grant to start a writing center in her local public library. I was able to offer some suggestions, collaborate with her on her plans, and refer her to a nearby university writing center director for further collaborations. At McCallie, we also created anthologies for the first two anniversaries of 9-11, asking parents as well as students, faculty, and alumni to contribute short essays, poems, or personal experiences, which were then published online. Other schools have their own collaborative projects through which they involve parents in fundraising activities to support the writing center or a special event for the writing center staff, such as attendance or presentation at a nearby conference or transportation to attend a reading.

Parents are wonderful collaborators, but there are no better collaborators than former students. Many of the survey respondents shared tales of former students who are now teaching nearby, who have returned to provide workshops in the writing center, or who volunteer their own papers as models of "successful" college application essays or research papers. Many directors get email updates from alumni who volunteer helpful information and resources. One former student came back to recommend a book for one of the courses I teach, and we adopted it the next year. Others tell of meeting the writing center director at their college/university and discovering that what they were doing in their secondary school writing center applied directly to their work in higher education.

One collaborative effort involved a presentation with a university writing center director, Tommy Tobin, one of my former students now at Stanford University, my current students, and writing center director Dilek

Tokay of Sabanci University, Istanbul (Tobin, Alexander, & Boyd, 2008). Since that Austin meeting in 2008, Tommy has now visited Dilek in Turkey and has written a draft of an article based on the research for their joint presentation.

COLLABORATION WITH COMMUNITY

For writing center directors, the term community has many meanings, but in this section it refers to the school district and local community. Directors spoke of outreach with economically disadvantaged students in a private middle school and workshops on writing for the township's ELL Parent Center, for instance. Ellen Kolba explained how the writing center is "a good will ambassador for the district because the bulk of our coaches come from the community." Others talk of collaborations involving guest speakers who are poets and journalists living nearby, working with arts commissions and public libraries, and even a Moose Lodge making a donation toward furniture for their writers' circle discussion groups. Nancy Wilson of San Marcos High School (TX) tells of how they went to the Hays County Juvenile Center to work with high school students preparing for their GED and ended up leading creative writing workshops on two different campuses because of student interest. Writing center directors can almost always think of more ways to work with the community. As one director said, "I would love to do far more with the community, but my schedule and time do not allow it" (Childers, 2009).

COLLABORATION WITH OTHER INSTITUTIONS

Several years ago I researched collaborations between secondary and higher education with writing across the disciplines. That study revealed many programs that have started, failed, stopped due to lack of funding, or succeeded and grown. The survey suggests that a number of collaborations among secondary schools and between secondary schools and higher education are already in place. As one director said, "Service to others is part of our mission." Some directors, such as Sandy Davis of North Cobb High School (GA), made contact with directors at nearby institutions Agnes Scott College, Georgia State University, and The McCallie School. Others offer support to nearby schools starting writing centers, and several are part of collaboratives that they have formed for exchange among schools, support for ideas, suggestions for professional reading, and encouragement. The Tennessee Writing Center Collaborative, the Chicagoland Organization of Writing, Literacy, and Learning Centers, and the group connected to the

Center for the Study of Teaching and Writing at Ohio State all exist for this purpose. In some cases, high school and college directors team teach courses on the teaching of writing, prepare joint presentations, and collaborate on articles, chapters, or books.

From Maine to Florida, Texas to California, there are collaborations going on to instruct, host pre-service teachers, offer workshops and presentations at conferences or staff development programs, and partner with elementary, secondary, undergraduate, and graduate school programs. John Brassil and I served on the Northeastern University Advisory Board for the Institute on Writing and Teaching for several years, while Ted Domers and Stacey Carlough worked with the University of Pennsylvania Graduate School of Education Ethnography Forum. Patty Melie has done a pilot study with the College of DuPage to examine whether they are preparing students for college writing, and most of the directors have visited or at least spoken online with many college and university writing center directors. Many of the secondary school directors answering the survey have also started or completed advanced degrees in writing because of their writing center experiences, collaborated with others to encourage their advanced studies and to publish their work, and inspired college students who want to start a writing center when they begin teaching on the secondary level (Childers, 2009).

Finally, I have to mention the great inspiration of Gerd Bräuer at the University of Education in Freiburg, Germany. As host of the 2008 European Writing Centers Association (EWCA) Conference and past chair, he has developed a system of reading and writing centers in Germany (Bräuer, 2006) that continues to impact students in primary school through university. The directors are partners in the region as model schools for *Scriptorium*. Coached by Bräuer, they have steering groups and in-house training for faculty colleagues and volunteer parents. They invite local writers to do workshops and work on a regular school newspaper. This program is a comprehensive collaboration between the university and area schools.

COLLABORATION WITH PROFESSIONAL ORGANIZATIONS

Most respondents to the survey demonstrate that they have become involved in the writing center community as well as other professional organizations. They have either participated in or facilitated a workshop at a regional conference affiliated with IWCA or a smaller region such as University of Maine, Chicagoland, or other groups within a regional affiliate. The majority have also attended conferences and become members of IWCA, almost half have attended or led an IWCA Summer Institute (there is a secondary leader every year), and three presented at the 2008 EWCA conference. Most also belong to NCTE, while some belong to IRA, NWP, and WPA. A few make presentations during and attend CCCC, and most participate online at WCenter and SSWC-L. Most also have their own websites that enable them to share links with colleagues, and their websites are listed with IWCA (www.writingcenters.org). This involvement with national and international organizations might seem routine to those in higher education, but for most secondary people, such a commitment requires their own financial and time arrangements in busy, long days and nights. Secondary teachers may have as many as six or seven classes a day and multiple lesson plans, if they are not scheduled all day for the writing center. For those who only teach a few classes, their time outside the classroom is devoted to being in the writing center. Most do not have "office hours," have to schedule their personal appointments after the 8–4 school day, and still handle extracurricular assignments as well.

In order to attend regional, national, or international conferences of professional organizations, most either get no funding or limited funding that requires a report when they return, and they have to work out plans for coverage of all their classes and the writing center. They cannot cancel classes because students must be supervised during the entire school day. In other words, these writing center directors must find time to do research, submit proposals, make all arrangements for coverage if their proposal is accepted, create their presentation, attend the conference, take notes at other sessions toward their report on the value of the conference, and then return to straighten out all that has happened while they were away. They also carry papers to grade at conferences, just as their colleagues in higher education do.

Yes, there are similarities between secondary directors and those in higher education. Through collaboration, these professional colleagues may go beyond mediocrity in many ways. Those partnerships are key because those in higher education may keep up on current research to share with their secondary colleagues. Both can collaborate on ways that help students make the transition from high school to college-level writing. As I mentioned at the beginning of this chapter, writing center directors do not settle for the status quo. Secondary school writing center directors who made time in their busy schedules to respond go beyond mediocrity in their work before and after tutoring.

Should we consider them agents of change? When pushed to answer such questions, they readily offer multiple examples of what they do to change the status quo. However, as one of these people who shamelessly finds secondary school writing center work a lifelong commitment, I must challenge my colleagues to continue to take intellectual risks, to spend time looking at where we came from (familiarity with the major writing center works of the past), to examine the present as it evolves before our very eyes, and to predict the future based on what we know. There are so many important collaborations that we all need to know about, so just as we ask our students to journal, research, and reflect, we must do the same by continuing to publish and share what we have learned as well.

ACKNOWLEDGMENTS

I would like to thank Writing Fellows Arun Augustine and Phil McGill for collaborating with me on this chapter.

REFERENCES

Baker, W., Conney, A., Jones, B., Mullens, D., Murnan, S., & Childers, P. (2007, Summer). Independent studies in writing based in the writing center. *Southern Discourse: Publication of the Southeastern Writing Center Association, 10*(3), 6–7.

Bräuer, G. (2006, November/December). The U.S. writing center model for high schools goes to Germany: And what is coming back? *The Clearing House, 80*(2), 95–100.

Bruffee, K. A. (1978). The Brooklyn plan: Attaining intellectual growth through peer-group tutoring. *Liberal Education, 64,* 447–468.

Childers, P. (2009). Caldwell Writing Center. *The McCallie School.* Retrieved from http://www.mccallie.org/podium/default.aspx?t=103888&rc=0

Childers, P. (2009, March). *Caldwell writing center survey.* Unpublished manuscript, Chattanooga, TN.

Childers, P., Fels, D., & Jordan, J. (2004, Fall). The secondary school writing center: A place to build confident, competent writers. *Praxis, 2*(2). Retrieved from http://projects.uwc.utexas.edu/praxis/?q=node/91.

Childers, P. B., Laughter, J., Lowry, M., & Trumpeter, S. (1998). Developing a community in a secondary school writing center. In C. Haviland, T. Wolf et al. (Eds.), *Weaving knowledge together: Writing Centers and collaboration* (pp. 28–57). Emmitsburg, MD: NWCA Press.

Davis III, M. H., & Childers, P. (2006). Practicing what you preach: A collaborative column. *Southern Discourse: Publication of the Southeastern Writing Center Association,* 6–7.

Elbow, P. (1973). *Writing without teachers.* New York: Oxford University Press.

Elbow, P. (1981). *Writing with power.* New York: Oxford University Press.

Elbow, P. (1983). Embracing contraries in the teaching process. *College English, 45,* 327–339.

Emig, J. (1971). *The composing processes of twelfth graders.* Urbana, IL: National Council of Teachers of English.

Goshgarian, G. (2008). *The contemporary reader* (9th ed.). New York: Pearson Longman.

Grant, T., Murphy, A., Stafford, B., with Childers, P. (1997, November/December). Peer tutors and students work with assessment. *The Clearing House, 71*(2), 103–105.

Jordan, J., Snow, S., Frankel, P., & Severns, K. (2002). The high school writing center: An identity of its own. In B. B. Silk (Ed.), *The Writing Center resource manual.* Emmitsburg, MD: National Writing Center Press.

Laughter, J., & Childers, P. (1996, January) Collaboration and college application essays: Two writing center perspectives. *The Writing Lab Newsletter,* pp. 4–5.

Mullens, D. (2008). Overexposure of violence in our society. In G. Goshgarian (Ed.), *The contemporary reader* (9th ed., pp. 233–238). New York: Pearson Longman.

Murray, D. M. (1979). The listening eye: Reflections on the writing conference. *College English, 41,* 13–18.

Murray, D. M. (1980). *Expecting the unexpected.* Portsmouth, NH: Boynton/Cook.

Murray, D. M. (1982). *Learning by teaching.* Upper Montclair, NJ: Boynton/Cook.

Murray, D. M. (1985). *A writer teaches writing* (2nd ed.). Boston: Houghton Mifflin.

Scroggs, A, (2008, April 12). Mission statement. *I write, therefore I am* [Web log message]. Retrieved from http://wchsthewritingcenter.blogspot.com/

Scroggs, A. (2009). Re: Survey: Collaboration in secondary school writing centers [Electronic mailing list message]. Retrieved from listserv@lists.psu.edu

Spillane, L. A. (2005). *University high school reading writing center.* Retrieved from http://www.laspillane.org/philos.html

Straka, J., & Childers, P. (2004, June). Developing lifelong language skills in a writing center. *The Writing Lab Newsletter,* pp. 5–6.

Tobin, T., Alexander, R., & Boyd, N. (2008, May). *Secondary or university WAC-based writing centers: What's the difference?* Presentation at the International Writing Across the Curriculum Conference, Austin, TX.

Turner, M. (2006, November/December). Writing centers: Being proactive in the education crisis. *The Clearing House, 80*(2), 45–47.

Vygotsky, L. S. (1978). *Mind and society: The development of higher psychological processes.* Cambridge, MA: Harvard University Press.

Wells, J. (2006). *Mercy reading and writing center: Creating a community of literacy.* Retrieved from http://mrwc.squarespace.com/

APPENDIX A
Survey

Collaboration in Secondary School Writing Centers

Name: _____ Title: _____

School Name: _____

Address: _____

Email address: _____

Website address (if applicable): _____

As a secondary school writing center director, please indicate how you collaborate with each of the following groups. Please fill out this form and return to pam.childers@gmail.com as an attachment. Thank you for your assistance.
Students -

Faculty
    English
    Other Disciplines
Administrators
Staff (e.g., Guidance, Admissions, Public Relations)

Alums
Community

Colleagues at Other Institutions

IWCA
Regional WCAs
Other Professional Organizations
Others – Please Explain

APPENDIX B
Survey Respondents

Blosser, Carol - Humanities Instructor, K-12 Writing Coordinator, Writing Center Director, Regents School of Austin (TX) – cblosser@regents-austin.com

Boozer, Karen - Writing Center Director and English Teacher, Fairhill School, Dallas (TX) – kboozer@fairhill.org

Brandt, Tom – Director of the Writing Center, Berkeley Preparatory School, Tampa (FL) – brandtom@berkeleyprep.org

Brassil, John – English Department Chair, Mt. Ararat High School, Topsham (ME) – brassilj@link75.org

Brooks, Ellen Olson – Director The Ryan Patrick Keshbaugh Center for Writing and Creative Learning, The Fayetteville Academy (NC) – brooksel@mindspring.com

Carlough, Stacey – 11th Grade English Teacher, Freire Charter School, Philadelphia (PA) – staceycarlough@freirecharterschool.org

Childers, Pamela B. – Caldwell Chair of Composition, Writing Center Director, Teacher, The McCallie School, Chattanooga (TN) – pchilder@mccallie.org

Davis, Sandra – English Teacher, North Cobb High School, Kennesaw (GA) – Sandra.Davis@cobbk12.org

Dean, Cynthia – Writing Center Directory/Literacy Coach/English teacher, Erskine Academy, So. China (ME) – cindy@umit.maine.edu

Domers, Ted – 12th Grade Social Studies Teacher, Freire Charter School, Philadelphia (PA) – ted@freirecharterschool.org

Jacoby-Burns, Jyll – Lead instructor/coordinator, Center for Writing & Reasoning, Cape Fear Academy, Wilmington (NC) – jjacobyburns@cape-fearacademy.org

Jeter, Andrew – Literacy Center Coordinator, Niles West high School, Skokie (IL) – andjet@niles219.org

Jordan, Jeanette – Writing Coordinator and Assistant Dean, Glenbrook North High School, Northbrook (IL) – jljordan@glenbrook.k12.il.us

Kolba, Ellen – Founding Director, The Writers' Room Program, The Montclair Public Schools, Montclair (NJ) – emkolba@aol.com

Melei, Patricia – Writing Center Director, Lemont High School, Lemont (IL) – patty@lemont.k12.il.us

Metzenbacher, Gary – Instructional Information Services, East High School, Columbus (OH) – garymetz@hotmail.com

Newton, Jeff – Writing Center Director, Culver Academies, Culver (IN) – newtonj@culver.org

Scroggs, Amanda – English Teacher, Warsaw Community High School, Warsaw (IN) – ascroggs@warsaw.k12.in.us

Wilson, Nancy Effinger – Writing Center Director, San Marcos High School, San Marcos (TX) – nw05@txstate.edu

German Respondents - Contact Gerd Bräuer, University of Education, Freiburg (Bräuer@ph-freiburg.de) for the following respondents:

Adami, Martina – Realgymnasium Bozen/Bolzano
Caspan, Stephen – Gesamtschule Mettlach-Orscholz
Feist, Jurgen – Gymnasium Neubeckum
Kolling, Mrs. – Gesamtschule Hardt, Mochengladbach
Reimann, Ulrich – A.-Schweitzen-Grundschule
Roth, Ursula – Schloss-Schule Durlach
Zimmer, Barbara – Gesamtschule Neunkirchen

APPENDIX C
Caltwell Writing Center Survey

Demographic Information

Your name: _____ (optional)

Your email address: _____ (optional)

Today's date: _____ What is your age?: _____ When did you graduate?: _____

What was (were) your major interests? _____

What additional education have you pursued since graduation from McCallie? Please specify degree(s) and institution(s). If you are currently a graduate student, please specify institution and degree.

How many *semesters or years* did you work with the Writing Center _____

Did you take a credit-bearing course such as peer tutoring, an independent study in writing, or writing fellows program? Yes _____ No _____

What other forms of writing development did you participate in (please check all that apply)?
____ none
____ preparation for college, scholarship or job interviews
____ work on writing for AP Exams
____ regional or national conferences
____ special evening or weekend functions related to writing
____ social events (lunches, dinners or other outings)
____ other (please specify)

What occupation(s) have you pursued since graduation?

Reflections on your Caldwell Writing Center Experience:

1. What are the most significant abilities, values, or skills that you developed in your work with the writing center? Please list them.

2. Of the abilities, values, or skills that you listed above, would you illustrate those that strike you as most meaningful by sharing an episode or event that took place during your time in the writing center?

3. Did those abilities, values, or skills that you developed seem to be a factor in your choice of job or graduate work? Would you elaborate?

4. Did these qualities seem to play a role in your interviewing, in the hiring process, or in acceptance to college and/or graduate school? How do you come to that conclusion?

5. Do any of the qualities you listed in question one play a role in your social or family relationships? Can you give an example?

6. In your occupations(s), have you used the qualities you developed through your work in the writing center, if at all? Would you elaborate? Give an example?

   Would you rank the importance for your occupation of the skills, qualities, or values you developed through your writing center work?

5	4	3	2	1
Highly important				Unimportant

7. To what extent do you think your own writing has been influenced by your experience in a writing center? Please explain.

   To what extent has your writing been influenced by your training and/or work in the writing center?

5	4	3	2	1
Very influenced				Not influenced

8. What have you learned from working with the writing of others? Please elaborate or provide an example.

9. Were there any downsides to your experience in the writing center? Please elaborate.

10. Would you please rate the importance your writing center training and experience as you developed after McCallie?

5	4	3	2	1
Highly important				Unimportant

Please explain your rating.

Thank you for taking the time and effort to respond to this survey. I will keep you informed about the results.

Pamela B. Childers, EdD
March 6, 2009
*Based on the research model of Kail, Gillespie, and Hughes (2007)

APPENDIX D
Resources Specifically Targeted to K-12 Writing Centers

Baker, Wills, Anthony Conney, Brandall Jones, David Mullens, Sean Murnan, and Pamela Childers." Independent Studies in Writing Based in the Writing Center." *Southern Discourse: Publication of the Southeastern Writing Center Association* 10.3 (Summer 2007): 6-7.

Childers, Pamela B. "Bottom Up or Top Down: A Case Study of Two Secondary School Writing Centers." *The Writing Center Director's Resource Book.* Mahwah, NJ: Lawrence Erlbaum, 2006.

____ . "College/High School Connections." *The Writing Lab Newsletter,* May-June1992, 1+.

____ , ed. *The Clearing House.* Special Issue on Secondary School Writing Centers 80.2 (Nov/Dec. 2006).

____ . "Designing a Strategic Plan for a Writing Center." *The Writing Center Director's Resource Book.* Mahwah, NJ: Lawrence Erlbaum, 2006.

____ . "The Evolution of Secondary School Writing Centers." *Kansas English* 90.2 (2006):83-91.

____ . "High School-College Collaborations: Making Them Work." *Across the Disciplines* Feb. 2007 *http://wac.colostate.edu/atd.*

____ . "The Talk I Didn't Give at the Watson Conference." *Writing at the Center: Proceedings of the 2004 Thomas R.Watson Conference Louisville, Kentucky.* Eds. Jo Ann Griffin, Carol Mattingly, and Michele Eodice. Emmitsburg, MD: IWCA Press, 2007.

____ . "What Students Have Taught Me About Writing." *Exploring Language,* 11th ed. Ed. Gary Goshgarian. New York: Harper Collins, 2007.

____ . "Writing Center or Experimental Center for Faculty Research, Discovery and Risk Taking?" *Writing Centers and Writing Across the Curriculum Programs: Building Interdisciplinary Partnerships.* Robert W. Barnett and Jacob S. Blumner, eds. Westport, CT: Greenwood Press, 1999.

____ , Dawn Fels and Jeanette Jordan. "The Secondary School Writing Center: A Place to Build Confident, Competent Writers." *Praxis.* Vol. 2 Issue 2 Fall 2004. http://projects.uwc.utexas.edu/praxis/?q=node/91.

____ , Jeanette Jordan and James K. Upton. "Virtual High School Writing Centers: A Spectrum of Possibilities." *Wiring the Writing Center.* Eric H. Hobson, ed. Logan, UT: Utah State Press, 1998.

____ , Jud Laughter, Michael Lowry and Steve Trumpeter. "Developing a Community in a Secondary School Writing Center." *Weaving Knowledge Together: Writing Centers and Collaboration.* Eds. Carol Peterson Haviland, Maria Notarangelo, Lene Whitley-Putz, and Thia Wolf. Emmitsburg, MD: NWCA Press, 1998.

____ . and Jim Upton. "Political Issues in Secondary School Writing Centers." *The Politics of Writing Centers.* Jane Nelson and Kathy Evertz, eds. Westport, CT: Greenwood Press, 2001.

Farrell, Pamela. *The High School Writing Center: Establishing and Maintaining One.* Urbana, IL: NCTE, 1989.

Gardner, Clint and Pamela Childers. "Differences That Draw Us Together." *Southern Discourse: Publication of the Southeastern Writing Center Association* 10.2 (Spring 2007): 6-7.

Geller, Anne Ellen, Michele Eodice, Frankie Condon, Meg Carroll, and Elizabeth Bouquet. *Everyday Writing Center: A Community of Practice.* Logan, UT: Utah State UP, 2006.

Grant, Tripp, Andrew Murphy, and Ben Stafford with Pamela Childers. "Peer Tutors and Students Work with Assessment." *The Clearing House,* 71.2 (Nov./Dec. 1997), 103-105.

Jordan, Jeanette. "Change from Within: The Power of a Homegrown Writing Center." *The Clearing House.* Special Issue. 80.2 (Nov./Dec. 2006): 52-55.

Kent, Richard. *A Guide to Creating Student-Staffed Writing Centers, Grades 6-12.* New York: Peter Lang, 2006.

McAndrew, Donald A. and Thomas J. Reigstad. *Tutoring Writing: A Practical Guide for Conferences.* Portsmouth, NH: Boynton/Cook, 2001.

Mullin, Joan and Pamela Farrell-Childers. "The Natural Connection: The WAC Program and the High School Writing Center." *The Clearing House,* Sept./Oct. 1995, 24-26.

Mullin, Joan A. and Ray Wallace, eds. *Intersections: Theory-Practice in the Writing Center.* Urbana, IL: NCTE, 1994.

Murphy, Christina and Steve Sherwood. *St. Martin's Sourcebook for Writing Tutors.* 3rd ed. Boston: Bedford/St. Martin's, 2008.

Murray, Donald. *Write to Learn.* New York: Holt, Rinehart Winston, 1984.

Murray, Donald. *A Writer Teaches Writing.* 2nd ed. Boston: Houghton Mifflin, 1985.

Robinson, Wayne. *Writing Across Borders.* Corvallis, OR: Oregon State Press, 2005.

Silk, Bobbie, ed. *The Writing Center Resource Manual.* Emmitsburg, MD: NWCA Press, 1998.

Silva, Peggy. "Launching a High School Writing Center." *Praxis.* Vol. 2 Issue 2 Fall 2004. *http://projects.uwc.utexas.edu/praxis/?q=node/40.*

Straka, Jan and Pamela Childers. "Developing Lifelong Language Skills in a Writing Center." *The Writing Lab Newsletter* June 2004, 5-6.

Tipper, Meg. "Real Men Don't Do Writing Centers." *The Writing Center Journal* 19. 2 (1999).

Turner, Melissa. "Writing Centers: Being Proactive in the Education Crisis." *The Clearing House.* Special Issue. 80.2 (Nov./Dec. 2006): 45-48.

Wells, Jennifer. "'It Sounds Like Me': Using Creative Nonfiction to Teach College Admissions Essays." *English Journal* 98.1 (Sept. 2008): 47-52.

Additional Resources
for Secondary School Writing Centers

Barnett, Bob and Jacob Blumner. *WAC and Faculty Development in Writing Centers.* Westport, CT: Greenwood Press, 1999.

Bishop, Wendy. *Teaching Lives.* Logan, UT: Utah State University Press, 1997.

Black, Laurel Johnson. *Between Talk and Teaching: Reconsidering the Writing Conference*. Logan, UT: Utah State University Press, 1998.

Brannon, Lil, Melinda Knight and Vara Nemerow-Turk. *Writers Writing*. Upper Montclair NJ: Boynton/Cook, 1982

Briggs, Lynn Craigue, and Meg Woolbright, eds. *Stories from the Center: Connecting Narrative and Theory in the Writing Center*. Urbana, IL: NCTE, 2000.

Childers, Pamela, Eric Hobson, and Joan Mullin. *ARTiculating: Teaching Writing in a Visual World*. Portsmouth, NH: Boynton/Cook, 1998

Duke, Charles R. and Rebecca Sanchez. *Assessing Writing Across the Curriculum*. Durham, NC: Carolina Academic Press, 2001.

Elbow, Peter. *Writing with Power*. Rev. ed. New York: Oxford UP, 1998.

Farrell-Childers, Pamela, Anne Ruggles Gere and Art Young. *Programs and Practices: Writing Across the Secondary School Curriculum*. Portsmouth, NH: Boynton-Cook, 1994.

Harris, Jeanette and Joyce Kinkead, eds. *The Writing Center Journal* 11.1. (Fall/Winter 1990).

Harris, Muriel. *Tutoring Writing: A Sourcebook for Writing Labs*. Urbana, IL: NCTE, 1982.

North, Stephen. "The Idea of a Writing Center." *College English* 46:5 (1984): 433-36.

____. "Revisiting 'The Idea of a Writing Center.'" *The Writing Center Journal* 15.1 (Fall 1994): 7-19.

Kinkead, Joyce, and Michael Pemberton. *The Center Will Hold*. Logan, UT: Utah State UP, 2003.

Murphy, Christina and Joe Law, eds. *Landmark Essays on Writing Centers*. Davis, CA: Hermagoras, 1995.

Nelson, Jane and Kathy Evertz. *The Politics of Writing Centers*. Portsmouth, NH: Boynton/Cook, 2001.

Romano, Tom. *Clearing the Way: Working with Teenage Writers*. Portsmouth NH: Heinemann, 1987.

Ryan, Leigh and Lisa Zimmerelli. *The Bedford Guide for Writing Tutors*. 2th ed. Boston: Bedford, 2006.

Shapiro, Susan R. and Deborah A. Marinelli. *College Transition: A Critical Thinking Approach*. Houghton Mifflin, 2001.

Shea, Renee H., Lawrence Scanlon, and Robin Dissin Aufses. *The Language of Composition: Reading, Writing, Rhetoric*. Boston: Bedford/St. Martin's, 2008.

Tchudi, Stephen, ed. *Alternatives to Grading Student Writing*. Urbana, IL: NCTE, 1997.

White, Edward M. *Assigning, Responding, Evaluating: A Writing Teacher's Guide*. 4th ed. Boston: Bedford/St. Martin's, 2007.

Note: Prepared by Jeanette Jordan and Pamela Childers for IWCA Workshops and Presentations

c h a p t e r **13**

MAKING FRIENDS WITH WEB 2.0: WRITING CENTERS AND SOCIAL NETWORKING SITES

Jackie Grutsch McKinney

Client: I know, I have already met you.

Me: Oh, really, I am sorry I don't remember meeting you. Have I tutored you before? (I was sure I hadn't.)

Client: No, we have never met in real life. I met you on the internet...on facebook last night.

The look on my face was probably priceless. Then, the session got started as normally as I could, while in shock. The next time I logged onto Facebook I made my account more limited and private. Not that I had anything to hide or info on display that I did not want people knowing... I am not that dumb. But, I just did not want clients having the ability to see my pictures/wall/"know me" coming into a session. What they think of me could alter their expectations of a session.[1]

---

[1]Quotations in italics in this chapter are from email correspondences with tutors on their use of Facebook and are used with their consent. I have maintained their texts as written.

When writing center scholars began writing about technology and online writing centers, one adjective seemed to sneak into several accounts even when the writers were advocating the use of technologies: *dehumanizing*. Harris and Pemberton (1995), for example, wrote, "but there are losses as well in this faceless, disembodied world, as the lack of personal contact may seem to dehumanize a setting that writing centers have traditionally viewed as personal and warm" (p. 156; see also Carlson & Apperson-Williams, 2007; Hobson, 1998; Russell, 1999). Technology was seen as a barrier in the tutor–writer relationship. In online tutoring, the relationship became tutor–technology–writer. Moreover, the underlying fear, as Lerner (1998) reminds us, is that the human on our end, the tutor, would eventually be dropped from the equation, and writers would be left interacting with technology alone. Because technology has been seen in these ways, as either interference in our relationships with clients or as the first sign of our eventual demise, writing centers have had an ambivalent relationship with emerging technologies.

Enter Web 2.0 which promises connectivity at each turn. New era websites like YouTube, Flickr, Facebook, Twitter, and MySpace allow users to add content and connect with other users. Blogs and microblogs allow for easy web authoring and instant status updates from computers or cell phones, giving users frequently updated news from friends, family, acquaintances, and whomever else they want to follow. Wikis reveal collaborative writing in action (and the public's ambivalence about this). Webcams built into laptops and monitors enable video chats, vlogging, and VoIP calling like Skype. None of this sort of deeply *human* technology was widely available or possible when scholars began to speculate on the possibilities of the Internet for writing centers.

One of these new era technologies—social networking sites (SNS)—has attracted considerable attention from writing center professionals, perhaps, because the express purpose for such sites is to foster relationships. On the surface, it solves the dehumanizing technology problem: it may still be a disembodied technological land, but it isn't faceless. Moreover, these sites are wildly popular with the students in high school and college who work at and use writing centers; in fact, most teenagers and young adults mediate the majority of their relationships through this sort of technology. Yet, despite the seemingly wide experimentation with SNS in writing center work and the popularity of these sites, there has been little written about these sites in writing center research.[2]

In this chapter, I argue that our existing relationships are being complicated by SNS (before, after, and during tutorials as the opening tutor quota-

---

[2]Though I've seen presentations on SNS at conferences, I haven't found anything in print specifically about social networking sites and writing centers.

tion suggests), and we ought to at least think through the possibilities and pitfalls of this new technological land that we already occupy. To this end, the chapter is arranged around three central questions: What can an SNS do that our webpage can't?, How are writing centers currently using SNS?, and What issues might arise from participation in SNS? By and large, I focus on Facebook only because of its popularity—estimates are that 85 percent to 90 percent of American college students have profiles on Facebook (Hewitt & Forte, 2006)—yet there are hundreds of SNS, and usage on any particular site will certainly ebb and flow in the coming years.[3] Nonetheless, much of what I write here, I hope, would be important to consider in adoption of other Web 2.0 sites into writing center work.

WHAT CAN AN SNS DO THAT OUR WEBPAGE CAN'T?

A former tutor actually introduced me to facebook during downtime in the Writing Center, and she became my first friend. In my four years as a tutor, I've become friends with every tutor I've worked with that is on facebook. I even created a group a couple years ago for tutors that has around 30 former and current tutors on it—many of which I have maintained contact with as a direct result of facebook. The director of the WC is in the group as well.

The first thing one might wonder about is whether having a presence on an SNS would be much different than having a website. After all, most writing centers have had websites for years. There are, however, traits that set SNS apart from more traditional sites, though the line is blurring to be sure.

According to boyd (2007), a leading researcher of SNS, all SNS have at least three features in common: profiles, friends, and comments (p. 4). A profile is a multimodal articulation of identity where users may declare their favorite things such as books, movies, TV shows, or bands; may provide demographic and directory information; may post pictures, audio, and videos; may have an answer to personality quizzes like "what kind of chocolate are you?"; may have games in progress with other users; or may have

---

[3]Tufekci (2008) found that 85.4 percent of surveyed college students at one institution had a profile on an SNS. An ongoing study at the University of Leicester found that 55 percent of first-year students join Facebook before entering the university and another 43 percent joined after arriving on campus—for a total of 98 percent participation among their first-year students. My estimate comes from Hewitt and Forte (2006), who suggest that nationally 85 percent to 90 percent of college students are on Facebook.

digital bumper stickers, flair, or gifts from other users posted on the page among many other possibilities. Depending on the SNS and the user's purposes, their digital identities might be consistent with their non-digital identities, or not. Some sites give more user control over the design, layout, and colors; profiles are generally just a single web page, so longer, more active profile pages require scrolling.

A profile page, in short, is what one finds if one looks for someone on an SNS. To say, "I found you on MySpace last night," means that the profile page was found. boyd (2007) calls the profile page a "digital body" for it projects, in absence of an actual body, information necessary for communication of an identity (see also Williams, 2008). Finding someone, incidentally, is somewhat under the control of the profile composer. Users are generally given options for varying levels of privacy, deciding how others can find them by a search within the site. Some SNS profiles are searchable with a general web search; others are not. For most SNS, one must create a profile before one can enter the site and explore the network.

The second defining feature of SNS, according to boyd (2007), is friending. Upon joining a site, a user is prompted to connect with other users to assert relationships publicly. In MySpace and Facebook, these relationships are called "friends," so this act is known as "friending." Many sites require that, once you assert someone as a friend, the other person has to verify this. Tufekci (2008) cautions not to be thrown by the term; an SNS friend is not necessarily an actual friend because, in many cases, users accept invitations from anyone and may not even know the person. But boyd's (2007) research reveals that the majority of MySpace users, at least, do not use the network to meet strangers; instead, it is a way to connect with people known in the user's non-digital life. For this reason, she emphasizes that social network sites' primary use is not networking but maintaining a personal network.

boyd's (2007) third defining feature, commenting, allows users to add content on others' profile pages. In MySpace and Facebook, this feature is called "comments" and "the wall," respectively, and is used as a stage for public conversations. Often, in Facebook, the wall is used to respond to a user's status message, a short line or two about what the user is doing or feeling. Each time a user writes on someone's wall, the comments are attributed to the user and linked back to the user's profile.

In addition to profile pages, friends, and commenting, SNS differ in other ways from traditional writing center websites. For one, publishing to an SNS takes minimal technological skills. If one can email or fill out a web-based form, one can be competent with web authoring on SNS. It is all web-based, so there's no need for special software programs or advanced competencies. Further, Facebook in particular, for the majority of American universities and colleges, has a built-in student user base who knows the site address and how to navigate the site—this much can't be said, necessarily, for more traditional writing center websites. Finally, connectivity among users is automatically generated by the site. Any additions, changes, news, comments, and so forth are automatically reported to friends. Though it's true that traditional websites can have RSS feeds, these feeds require users to subscribe to pages to receive updates.

In a nutshell, SNS can enmesh writing centers into a very popular, interconnected network, though most writing centers would probably maintain a more traditional site too because there are limits to SNS. For one, users get, in essence, one page in a format and style largely controlled by the site. Beyond these limitations, some institutions have policies restricting official campus entities' digital participation off the institutional grid. Though it is possible for a writing center to create and operate their own SNS, if institutional authorities approve, they would have to populate it with users to benefit from any of the aforementioned attributes. Online tutoring via SNS would be possible through chat or private messaging, but there's no easy way to schedule sessions or share texts. So, if a writing center uses a more traditional website for housing multiple pages of information, for having a presence on the institutional site, or for meeting students for online appointments, it won't find that the SNS can replace that.

HOW ARE WRITING CENTERS
CURRENTLY USING SNS?

On occasion, after discussing a client with fellow tutors and not being certain which client is being spoken about, I or we have facebooked them just to see the client's face. On one occasion, a tutee caressed [a tutor's] hand during a session and spoke very strangely. We looked him up after the session primarily to see if he had a creepy profile—I can't recall what we found. I try not to facebook clients often, just because it feels unprofessional.

The obvious next question is—if it's not a replacement for a website, what can it do? Why are so many writing centers signing up? Searching different sites, I found that there are hundreds of hits for "writing center" on both MySpace and Facebook. Likewise, there are hundreds of "writing center" pictures on Flickr and almost one-hundred "writing center" videos on YouTube. However, digging any deeper into these search results, one finds things quickly get less countable and straightforward. I could see from the search results in Facebook, for example, that some centers have a profile, one or more groups, and what's called a page—so results had to be scrutinized for duplicates.[4] I also found a number of hits on all sites that had the words "writing center" in the title (e.g., "David is a much better Writing Center Tutor than Rebekah . . . and she smells"), but clearly were not an official SNS presence of a writing center.

Being able to count a writing center as using Facebook, for example, was dependent on whether it was searchable. If it wasn't a public listing, I certainly could not count it. Additionally, I didn't count a site as "*x* writing center is using Facebook" if someone affiliated with a center posted something about the center, but it was not an officially a sanctioned writing center activity (see Table 13.1).

Keyword searching only reveals those sites that would be in box A or C—those uses that were searchable. I did find many official sites (Box A); in all, there are probably a hundred or so writing centers on Facebook in some capacity. As of June 2008, none of these Facebook sites had more than one-hundred friends, members, or fans; many had little to no visible activity on their mini-feed, discussion board, or wall; most seem composed of mostly tutors and writing center staffs; and the main function of most is as a portal to other writing center sites such as an institutional web page.

The most popular of these sanctioned, searchable writing center spots on Facebook are groups created for tutors or tutor alumni to connect; Texas A&M and Coe College have good examples of these. Directors and other writing center professionals are increasingly using Facebook to connect with one another either by friending colleagues individually or by joining Facebook groups for writing center professionals like Writing Center Café and WCenter or more general professional groups like CCCCs and *Kairos*.

TABLE 13.1. Types of Writing Center SNS Uses

A. SEARCHABLE, SANCTIONED	B. NOT SEARCHABLE, SANCTIONED
C. SEARCHABLE, UNOFFICIAL	D. NOT SEARCHABLE, UNOFFICIAL

---

[4]Facebook's terms of service require that users (who are given profile pages) be actual people. Users can create "groups" to link users or promote services or businesses on "pages" maintained by users. In practice, many centers and other non-human entities sign on as users because of the increased functionality being a user over having a group or page.

To my knowledge, no niche SNS exclusively for writing center professionals has been launched, nor has any writing center moved to host and populate their own SNS.

As I mentioned, I also found many uses of SNS that would fit in Box C. Those were groups, videos, or photographs which mention "writing center" in the title and thus are easily found by keyword searching. Yet these sites are for fun, making fun, camaraderie, and for letting off steam; sometimes they have little to do with the writing center. For example, the YouTube "writing center" video with the second most views, over 1,800, is "Funny Fish in Pratt writing center." It is a twenty-six second video of a tropical fish tank highlighting one fish that seems to be fighting with its own reflection.

Importantly, the uses in Boxes B and D will not show up in public search results, so I cannot say how *all* writing centers are using SNS. The searchability depends on the user; some users mark profiles or groups as visible only to particular networks. If one is a member of that network as an employee or student of a university, then they can see the profile. For the rest of the public, it is not visible. One might decide to limit the visibility of a writing center profile if it is just for staff members and not a means to advertise the center. Moreover, a public group or profile (a Box A listing) might still have uses that would not be searchable. Private messaging—a capability in most SNS—is an example of this. The biggest surprise to me was discovering how tutors and students engage in those activities that would fall into Box D—those activities that are unofficial and not visible. Notably, tutors and students check out each other's profiles on Facebook as described in the quotation at the beginning of this section, using Facebook as a student directory. On most SNS, there is no trail of pages one views. Friending and commenting are more visible, yet not searchable.

One feature on Facebook that writing centers are not by and large using now, yet that might prove helpful, is the events function. Users can send invitations to other users for a workshop or event and confirm attendees for the event in advance. At the writing center I direct, we have started a page for our center on Facebook and invite clients and faculty to become fans. As fans, we can invite them en masse to events, send them updates from the center, or just enjoy the fact that all of their sites tell the world that they are "fans" of ours. Of course, the viral nature of Facebook is akin to word of mouth marketing. It could, potentially, bring new business if that is what you are after, but the coverage is spotty. Therefore, it's not a replacement for other marketing ventures, like giving bookmarks to the entire first-year class at orientation.

WHAT ISSUES MIGHT ARISE
FROM PARTICIPATION IN SNS?

We did have one incident where a client looked up a tutor and complained to the director because the tutor said she believed in one thing during the session (to play devil's advocate) and then her facebook page said something different.

Many of the tutors, including myself, have had unbecoming photos on facebook — though I've weeded most of them out. I know of tutors who are under age that have photos of them drinking — not always posted by them but by others.

When writing center employees participate on SNS in either sanctioned or unofficial ways, directors may be confronted with new kinds of problems. For instance, in late 2006, a query posted on WCenter about Facebook ethics garnered a flurry of attention. A director wrote:

> A consultant comes in to tell me about the public Facebook page of another staff member. The consultant is bothered because this person listed his/her work in the Writing Center with a description along the lines of, "i helps people lern too right goud." In the words of the offended party, "That's not cool." (Traywick, 2006)

I find this scenario provocative. It is not the worst possible Facebook situation, yet it touches on three of the central concerns I have, and from the WCenter responses, it is fair to say others do, too, about the use of SNS in writing center work: digital collisions, decentralization, and surveillance.

Digital Collisions

In describing how teenagers use MySpace, boyd (2007) asks, "How can they be simultaneously cool to their peers and acceptable to their parents? For the most part, it is not possible" (p. 17). She goes on to suggest that the very reason that teens take to MySpace is because it is a place to get away from the sorts of performances that parents expect of their teens (boyd, 2007, p. 18). Likewise, it seems that college students—at least originally—took to Facebook because it was a way to connect to other students on their own campuses on a space that was off the institutional grid. They were able to perform in ways that complicated their institutionally expected role of "college student" by administrators, faculty, parents, or residence life staff. In Goffman's (1959) terms, this sort of activity might best be called an underlife behavior, a behavior which complicates or differentiates one from the role expected by the institution.

Fast-forward a couple of years to the present, and it is becoming more likely that administrators, professors, parents, and resident hall staff are on Facebook, too. In fact, the climate has changed to the point where one recent study indicated that the majority of students find faculty presence on Facebook acceptable (Hewitt & Forte, 2006). Still, this change means that students have to consider editing their performances in order to still be cool, yet to also be respected by the larger circle of Facebook users. This gets even more complex for peer tutors who may have used Facebook as a space for underlife behavior of their role as student and tutor—as the tutor in the WCenter post had. Before SNS even entered the picture, Trimbur (1987), among others, noted how difficult the role of peer tutor was for undergraduates: "Peer tutoring invariably precipitates a crisis of loyalty and identity for the undergraduates who join the staff of a writing center" (p. 291). This crisis may be a bit different in the age of SNS, but just as daunting. One SNS scholar suggests that today's students are now having to collapse multiple identity performances:

> Students now find themselves in an environment in which the norm is to publicly articulate one's social networks and some of the interactions therein. Such norms of disclosure are having an effect that is the opposite of some of the early predictions about the impact of the Internet: Instead of being about to experiment with multiple identities, young people often find themselves having to present a constrained, unitary identity to multiple audiences, audiences that might have been separate in the past. (Tufekci, 2008, p. 35)

Whatever we might think about the appropriateness of the tutor's writing cited in the WCenter post, we ought to recognize the difficulty, for students especially, of crafting an online persona on Facebook. The digital collision of several audiences on Facebook make the communication difficult, particularly because Facebook was populated first, and only, by college students. The collision of the many competing roles enacted on Facebook is to be expected.

Decentralized Message

Another characteristic of SNS communication is that it is polyvocal; commenting enables any user who has permission to view a profile to write on that page. Beech (2007) in "Fronting Our Desired Identities" writes about how writing center texts can help rewrite campus sentiment about writing centers. SNS allow for such identity revision, too, yet there are more composers of this image. All users—whether they may be writing center administrators, staff, tutors, clients, faculty, university administrators, or the public at large—can participate in the digital composition of a center's identity on Facebook either directly on a writing center profile or on their own profiles. The age of composing tightly controlled identities is vanishing.

This is also the case in the WCenter scenario. The tutor possibly compromises the reputation of his writing center by writing something on his public and easily searchable profile page. The director's question—What do I do about this?—is one that comes from a history of a largely, centralized control of writing center messages. In the past, what is "out there" about our writing centers was largely what we put out there. We no longer can control that.

Surveillance

The last issue which complicates SNS use is the possibility of surveillance. This is intimately connected to the other two issues: it does not matter if there are digital collisions or multiple messages unless someone sees these. Healy (1995) in "From Place to Space: Perceptual and Administrative Issues in the Online Writing Center" warned how the online writing center could be a panopticon with the director seeing all that the tutors do. With SNS, surveillance by any party—students, tutors, directors, faculty, parents, administrators, or the general public—is possible.

The issue brought up on WCenter was an issue because one tutor observed the writing on another tutor's profile. Likely, the tutor did not go to the other tutor's profile looking for something incriminating to get this tutor in trouble. The tutor was likely engaging in an everyday Facebook activity—just looking at the profile pages of known associates. Thus, surveillance might not be intentional on Facebook, but it is likely that directors will be confronted with issues like the WCenter one when something is found on a tutor profile that offends another or is in other ways "not cool."

One response to the new challenges involved in fostering and maintaining relationships on SNS would be to police employee profiles for any objectionable material, memberships, or friends; to ban the use of SNS in writing centers or anywhere else that tutoring takes place; and to prescribe the privacy settings for employees. Personally, I do not know any writing center administrators who have the time, omnipotence, or will for that sort of surveillance and rule keeping. However, I do think we ought to carve out some time for discussions about how our digital lives overlap with our tutoring lives. I think it is fair and thoughtful to extrapolate with our staffs the possible outcomes of using SNS in writing center work.

Trimbur (1987) suggests that when we train tutors, we have two possible paths. We can make them apprentices or we can encourage them to be peers first. I think the advent of SNS gives us another chance to make this choice. We can insist on the professionalization of tutors or we can let tutors try out different performances and learn from them. If we do the latter, we have to have tolerance of performances that push against the tutor role we have carved out for them, and we have to be ready to defend our position to outsiders who question us about sanctioned and unofficial writing center participation on SNS.

CONCLUDING THOUGHTS

The point of facebook is to provide young adults with a platform to net-work with other people. By creating pages for, say, a writing center, face-book is simply allowing an aspect of the university in which the student attends to network with the general student body. Actually, I think it's great because universities and professors realize how prevalent students use facebook and are taking advantage of the service to meet their own goals.

When Carino (1998) wrote his history of writing centers and comput-ers, he ended with "OWLs, MOOs, and Webs" dated from 1992 to "pres-ent" (p. 185). Yet, it seems to me that the technologies we have now—just a decade later—place us in a new technological era. The promise of connectiv-ity and the user revolution of Web 2.0 applications are more than buzz-words. Things *have* changed. For most of us, technology mediates in most of our relationships; in fact, we may connect with some people in our lives *only* by phone, email, blogs, IM, or SNS. The ambivalence of writing centers towards technology because of the fear of the dehumanizing interference of technology or the replacement of humans with technology seem to be non-issues with these Web 2.0 technologies.

Still, Bythe's (1997) rather well known advice for writing center profes-sionals still holds true. He suggested that when we consider technologies for writing centers, we find a path somewhere between the two extremes of either adopting any technology without a second thought or dismissing a technology outright. This middle path involves, for one, adapting given technologies to our own ends. From what I have observed thus far, it seems we have barely started to imagine the possibilities for writing center use of Web 2.0.

REFERENCES

Beech, J. (2007). Fronting our desired identities: The role of writing center docu-ments in institutional underlife. In W. J. Macauley, Jr. & N. Mauriello (Eds.), *Marginal words, marginal work? Tutoring the academy in the work of writing centers* (pp. 197–120). Cresskill, NJ: Hampton Press.

boyd, d. (2007). Why youth (heart) social network sites: The role of networked publics in teenage social life. In D. Buckingham (Ed.), *Mac Arthur Foundation Series on digital learning—Youth, identity, and digital media volume.* Cambridge, MA: MIT Press. [Electronic version]

Carino, P. (1998). Computers in the writing center: A cautionary history. In E. H. Hobson (Ed.), *Wiring the writing center* (pp. 171–193). Logan: Utah State University Press.

Carlson, D., & Apperson-Williams, E. (2007). The anxieties of distance: Online tutors reflect. In C. Murphy & S. Sherwood (Eds.), *St. Martin's sourcebook for writing tutors* (3rd ed., pp. 285–293). New York: Bedford/St. Martin's.

Goffman, E. (1959). *The presentation of self in everyday life.* Garden City, NJ: Doubleday.

Harris, M., & Pemberton, M. (1995). Online writing labs (OWLs): A taxonomy of options and issues. *Computers and Composition, 12*(2), 145–159.

Healy, D. (1995). From place to space: Perceptual and administrative issues in the online writing center. *Computers and Composition, 12*(2), 183–193.

Hewitt, A., & Forte, A. (2006, November). *Crossing boundaries: Identity management and student/faculty relationships on the Facebook.* Poster session presented at annual Computer Supported Cooperative Work Conference, Banff, Alberta, Canada. Retrieved April 7, 2008, from http://www-static.cc.gatech.edu/~aforte/HewittForteCSCWPoster2006.pdf.

Hobson, E. (1998). Introduction: Straddling the virtual fence. In E. H. Hobson (Ed.), *Wiring the writing center* (pp. ix–xxvi). Logan: Utah State University Press.

Lerner, N. (1998). Drill pads, teaching machines, and programmed texts: Origins of instructional technology in writing centers. In E. H. Hobson (Ed.), *Wiring the writing center* (pp. 119–136). Logan: Utah State University Press.

Russell, S. (1999). Clients who frequent Madam Barnett's emporium. *The Writing Center Journal, 20*(1), 61–72.

Traywick, D. (2006, October 13). *Friday afternoon ethics: Facebook and the WC.* Message posted to http://lyris.ttu.edu/read/?forum=wcenter.

Trimbur, J. (1987). Peer tutoring: A contradiction in terms? *The Writing Center Journal, 7*(2), 21–28.

Tufekci, Z. (2008). Can you see me now? Audience and disclosure regulation in online social network sites. *Bulletin of Science, Technology, and Society, 28,* 20–36.

University of Leicester. (2008, October 14). Facebook is "social glue" for university freshers. *University of Leicester eBulletin.* Retrieved November 5, 2008, from http://www2.le.ac.uk/ebulletin/news/press-releases/2000-2009/2008/10/nparticle.2008-10-14.5899461324

Williams, B. (2008). "What South Park character are you?": Popular culture, literacy, and online performances of identity. *Computers and Composition, 25*(1), 24–39.

APPLYING ACCREDITATION STANDARDS TO HELP DEFINE A WRITING CENTER'S PROGRAMMING AND ITS ON-CAMPUS RELATIONSHIPS

Crystal Bickford

Alan Reinhardt

Standards provided by regional accreditation boards, such as the New England Association of Schools and Colleges, Middle States Association of Colleges and Schools, or Southern Association of Colleges and Schools, often provide fertile ground for writing centers to foster institutional administrative relationships. Writing center directors who examine and apply accreditation standards align themselves with administrative purposes, build administrative relationships, and may help their programming efforts, improve initiatives for students, and increase support for the center. When writing center directors review their accrediting agency's standards and site-visit reports, it is helpful to look for areas within the institutional mission statement and the agency's concerns regarding gaps in services, and to help close these gaps.

In the case of the Nichols College writing center, self-evaluation prior to the on-site accreditation visit had already provided an opportunity to examine the writing center's overall mission, to be certain that the mission reflected the goals of the institution. As a result, the authors became aware of possible disparities between writing center services provided to traditional day students, to non-traditional evening students, and to on-line students. We took advantage of the self-study process that normally foregrounds an accreditation to recognize and modify existing programs, as well as initiate new curricula. The accreditation site visit process became not a prescriptive exercise but rather an opportunity for authentic reflection. That reflection allowed us to transform the self-study process into a realization that the writing center could assume a larger role on campus.

For years, writing center research has recorded concerns about autonomy as opposed to marginalization (Carino, 1995; Harris, 1992; Kinkead, 1996). One of the ways in which writing centers can address these concerns is to review institutional relationships that can aid in collaborative efforts that benefit both school and center. In fact, in her 1991 publication, "Collaboration, Control, and the Idea of a Writing Center," Lunsford discusses the numerous effects that collaboration can foster, including those of encouraging problem finding and problem solving, participating in interdisciplinary thinking, having a "deeper understanding of *others*" (p. 5; italics original), promoting excellence, and advancing active learning. By fostering on-campus relationships with essential administrative offices, a writing center can help recast its mission and overall purpose. At the same time, it can offer programming that echoes and supports the institution's goals as they are often stated in the mission statement.

By encouraging writing center directors to participate in this process, writing centers may gain the ability to develop autonomy and control over their own programming with regard to existing staffing, budgeting, site limitations, and current programming prior to any institutional top-down mandates that may not be in the center's best interests. In other words, the writing center is able to adopt Gladstein's (2007) instructions to ". . . uncover and challenge the assumptions that we and others have about the role of the writing center and how this work and these assumptions tie in with the rest of what occurs at the college" (p. 212). Allowing programming efforts to come from the director, the tutors, and the center as a whole places the center in a position of expertise. Rather than allowing faculty and administration to maintain a stereotyped sense of the campus writing center, the center creates a profound ability to offer a supportive role for faculty and tutors that is then administratively supported. In this sense, the writing center creates its own identity as a result of broadening its internal relationships.

THE WRITING CENTER AT NICHOLS COLLEGE

Like the writing centers that Byron Stay (2006) discusses in "Writing Centers in Small Colleges," the writing center at Nichols College is limited by the college's small population of approximately 1,100 students. However, at the same time, it is afforded many academic opportunities to develop programming for students that enable faculty and administrative relationships. Currently, the writing center conducts approximately 1,000 one-to-one appointments a year; however, in total, it has over 3,500 campus-wide contacts as a result of all of its programming efforts. Stay posits, ". . . because of the close sense of community found at most small institutions, writing center directors there might find it easier to affect the development of the academic programs profoundly" (p. 147). This benefit of linking the writing center with curriculum design has been a major factor in the overwhelming number of student contacts in comparison to the institution's population. Furthermore, as the center has increased these numbers, the administration, in turn, has increased the number of support mechanisms to the writing center in terms of visibility, credibility, and financial stability.

The institution's small size also allows effective programming design because it is less of an overwhelming challenge as opposed to larger institutions. A small institution increases the ability for communication with upper level administration when budgeting and programming initiatives arise often because there are fewer administrative layers between the director and the administrator who ultimately controls the budget. The smaller population also increases the writing center's ability to work with entire departments, either faculty-based or administrative, with more ease. Addressing the concerns of five faculty members in a single department is, obviously, far easier than addressing a department of thirty-five.

However, a smaller population does not guarantee success or a seamless integration of any program. Change starts small, and some of the best change originates with "grass roots" programming. For example, starting a writing consultants program, like the one discussed later in this chapter, was met with resistance from faculty—even though NEASC stated writing across the curriculum as a major concern in one of their reports. When the consultants program was introduced, the faculty voiced numerous concerns regarding demands on their time, lack of classroom benefits, potential student reactions, the time required for course redesigns, and so on. When the program was ultimately piloted a year or so later with a handful of interested faculty members, the "word-of-mouth advertising" generated a popularity that made the program expand well outside of its initial plan. By using existing resources and staff, the program proved successful, tutor–faculty relationships were forged, and, consequently, the administration supported the program's expansion with enthusiasm.

THE ROLE OF THE REGIONAL ACCREDITATION PROCESS FOR WRITING CENTERS

Although regional accreditation agencies have slight variations, the overall reaccreditation process remains the same for all schools. What differs is the process among the schools themselves. Larger schools may approach the process by committee, whereas smaller schools may approach the process through each department body. Regardless of what strategy a college or university uses to approach reaccreditation, it is necessary for a writing center director to contact those central to the institution's process and be active in the overall effort. This results in the writing center being able to participate in self-examination, discussions, report-writing, and the overall school analysis with a stronger voice and control locus.

For all institutions, the first step in the accreditation process is that of self-examination. This step provides an opportunity for the writing center to examine its accomplishments and review the relationships already formed within the school. During this process, writing center directors may want to examine usage statistics, programming attendance (outside of traditional one-to-one tutoring), staffing, faculty inquiries, narratives of successful students, and overall writing center growth. This step encourages the writing center to begin with their successes, not their deficiencies, which will, in turn, encourage the center to build upon its strengths rather than simply address its weaknesses.

The second step, peer review, should encourage the writing center director to participate with faculty and administration in the written report that is submitted to the accrediting agency. At Nichols College, each department head writes his or her section and submits it to a common editor who revises, collates, and assembles the individual reports into a single document. At that point, the entire document is reviewed by the department heads to ensure that no meaning has been lost in the process. Where this process is used, writing center directors should not only make sure that their department is included in the report, but they should also write their own sections of the report and later have access to the entire document. This enables the writing center to learn about the institution's successes, needs, and concerns while the institution learns more about the writing center director's goals and achievements. At Nichols, all reports are made public by placing documents on reserve at the college's library.

The site visit, or the third stage, encourages the writing center director to meet with at least one representative from the accrediting agency, thus ensuring that the writing center is represented as part of the overall institution. At Nichols College, the writing center director met with NEASC twice, first as a member of the faculty and then as a member of the student services group. During these meetings, both strengths and weaknesses of the writing center and writing curriculum were discussed. By tactfully discussing a "wish list" for the writing center, the director was able to express ways in which the center could tie into academic programs. This conversation then encouraged the NEASC committee members to support and encourage implementation of these ideas in their subsequent meetings with upper administration. Rather than viewing NEASC's involvement as a threat, the administration, NEASC, and the writing center director found the dialogue to be an excellent opportunity to have an objective, third-party participant assist the communication process. Once NEASC left, the writing center director and management continued their discussions, using the NEASC visit, standards, and initial notes as anchors to improve current practices and develop further programming.

The fourth step is a waiting period for the institution as the accreditation board generates its report in preparation for the final stage. Within this continuous review stage, a writing center director can address NEASC's concerns by re-examining current or existing programming. By viewing NEASC's relationship as one of assistance, as opposed to a threatening entity, the accreditation agency, the institution, and the writing center can build stronger student-focused writing partnerships. Although it does not eliminate the bureaucratic strata of power, this triangular relationship can "level the playing field" so that all parties are heard and respected.

This regional accreditation process allows writing centers two important opportunities: first, by directly applying specific academic standards, they can examine their own educational curriculum and overall mission; second, in the process of such an examination, centers can strengthen important relationships on campus, thus increasing support, fiscal and otherwise. Marshall (2001) determines that a part of a writing center's success is based on its ability to document and make visible the work that it actually does. However, even when that work is documented, "explicit and hidden institutional practices can still recast the work of writing centers as bureaucratic management detached from the intellectual interests of faculty, or as invisible 'service' " (p. 75). By using the accreditation standards combined with the college's objectives, writing center directors can reduce these implied perceptions and further demonstrate their intellectual abilities. Being a part of the accreditation process allows and encourages writing centers to make its work visible while reducing bureaucratic lines.

WRITING CENTER RELATIONSHIPS
WITH CAMPUS OFFICES

Since the specific attention to NEASC standards six years ago, the writing center has had many opportunities to develop and strengthen institutional relationships with multiple offices, and with the application of specific standards, the center has been successful in its quest to fulfill campus needs in its appeals for financial and other support. Relationships have been built with the office of the President of the College, the office of the Vice President for Academic Affairs and Dean, the office of the chief enrollment officer, the office of the chief student affairs officer, and the office of the Dean of the Division of Graduate and Professional Studies (DGPS). As stakeholders, each of these offices has a specific relationship to the writing center. In particular, these administrative leaders comprise the President's Council at Nichols College, a body that is responsible for the management and direction of all campus programs and services, including the writing center, and that is instrumental in decisions related to program development, budgeting, and overall program support.

Combined, these offices represent a host of potential writing center relationships that can support current initiatives and help plan for future ones. As Boquet and Lerner (2008) point out, "it will take all of us who are invested in literacy education, in all of our settings, to maximize the potential of these exciting new opportunities. Our field can no longer afford, if it ever could, to have forged a separate peace between classroom and nonclassroom teaching. There is no separate but equal" (p. 186). In other words, writing centers, even in their desire for autonomy, cannot develop programs separate from the classrooms, faculty members, and students whom they are designed to support.

Boquet and Lerner (2008) argue, as does NEASC, for campus communities to integrate and find common elements that link academic entities together. During the NEASC accreditation process at Nichols, offices with existing links with the writing center were identified, as were offices where little planning had occurred. In some cases, our relationships are taken for granted. For instance, because the writing center director reports to the Vice-President for Academic Affairs and Dean, consistent conversations had occurred over the years. But because of the long standing relationship, both parties viewed the collaboration as a professional courtesy. However, the NEASC process identified significant less connection with the DGPS. The writing center, with its traditional focus on day students, neglected to expand its services to the increasing evening, on-line, and graduate populations. Generally, our daily survival mode took precedence over the ability to "think outside the box" or, in this case, "think outside the office." Thus, NEASC helped the director to examine individual relationships and to critically reflect about the ways in which they could be strengthened.

Office of the President

Because it acts as the compass for the self-study, the first item accreditation agencies review is the college mission statement. The mission gives each department a direction so that they look for ways to complement one another while meeting their own objectives, and because the mission statement should act as a common institutional bond, it is the president, as the chief representative of the college, who is most closely associated with it. She must be the most influential proponent because she interacts with internal constituents, such as the offices listed earlier, as well as a variety of external constituents including the Board of Trustees, the Alumni Association, and the families of Nichols College students. As such, she needs to be certain that her claims regarding the institution's accomplishments are meeting, if not exceeding, the college's educational objectives as expressed in its mission statement. Therefore, it is important to align the writing center's objectives with those of the College. Because the president's office has the final approval of the mission statement and the College's strategic plan, it has been important for the writing center to develop and foster a sense of communication with this office. Through consistent emails from the center, weekly updates from the dean's office, informal end-of-semester faculty meetings at the president's house, and short articles in the school's newsletter, the writing center makes a consistent effort to make the president's office, as well as the campus community at-large, aware of its many activities and accomplishments.

NEASC (2005), too, sees the importance of a meaningful institutional mission statement: "The mission of the institution defines its distinctive character, addresses the needs of society and identifies the students the institution seeks to serve, and reflects both the institution's traditions and its vision for the future" (p. 3). This first standard is echoed throughout the remaining standards. For example, Standard 4.1 under "The Academic Program" begins with, "The institution's programs are consistent with and serve to fulfill its mission and purposes" (NEASC, 2005, p. 7), and Standard 5.1 under "Faculty" begins with, "Faculty categories...are clearly defined by the institution as is the role of each category in fulfilling the institution's mission and purposes" (p. 14). NEASC's standards clearly underscore the importance of developing and fulfilling an accurate mission statement as an essential ingredient to the College's success.

The importance of a well-written/well-applied mission statement is further emphasized by George Kuh et al. (2005), who discuss the importance of a school's "espoused" mission, that is, the one that is written and shared with the institution's stakeholders, as opposed to a school's "enacted" mission, or the one that ". . . guides the daily actions of those in regular contact with students" (p. 26). The same principle applies to a school's "operating philosophy" (p. 27) or education objectives. Kuh et al. further points out that "institutional philosophies serve as a compass, keeping the institution on track as it makes decisions about resources, curriculum, and educational opportunities" (p. 27). Consequently, it is necessary for the writing center to re-examine its mission statement in order to best align itself with its governing institution as that institution refines both its espoused and enacted mission statements.

In supporting the College's efforts during its self-examination process, the writing center took care to construct an appropriate mission statement of its own that took into account the educational goals of the accrediting body as well as those of the institution. Critical thinking, appropriate programming, and the availability of the center's programming to the community were all taken into consideration in the writing of the mission statement. Following another one of Marshall's (2001) suggestions, "directors' (sic) need to establish the framework within which their work is evaluated" (p. 75). Presenting a mutually beneficial writing center mission statement to the institution encouraged communication between the center and the president's office that in turn not only helped the center solicit additional funding and support but also made clear the terms and criteria on which the center was to be evaluated.

In light of the relationship with the president's office, the writing center has been careful to note and address the school's mission statement. This statement emphasizes that, "The Nichols experience happens in a welcoming environment where students are encouraged to learn and grow under the guidance of mentoring faculty and staff committed to student success" (*Course Catalog*, 2007, p. 5). The writing center administration was quick to identify the school's position on "welcoming environment" and the overarching goal for students to "learn and grow." After examining the writing center's physical structure, the institution appropriated funding for new furniture, and although additional space could not be obtained, the school hired a consultant to help the director make the best use of the existing space so that technology, one-to-one tutoring areas, and tutor meeting spaces could be maximized.

Soon thereafter, the writing center was included in the College's strategic planning initiative, and, thus, the opportunity again arose to reexamine the center's institutional purpose in alignment with the college's mission statement. The writing center's mission statement now emphasizes that its purpose is to "...assist and challenge students in developing skills necessary for successful independent learning. The facilitation of dialogue and instructional assistance is used to support *all* members of the Nichols College Community" (ARC Tutoring, 2008). Furthermore, educational objective 2 encourages students to "construct a variety of critical thinking models that include qualitative and quantitative techniques, and be able to analyze and solve problems using these models in an ethical context" (p. 5). Our writing center, "designed to assist and challenge students in developing skills necessary for successful independent learning" (ARC Tutoring, 2008, para 3) is open to the entire Nichols College and promotes an environment to aid "critical thinking and writing" (para 3).

The change in the writing center's mission statement allowed the espoused and the enacted mission statements to align with one another—

within the writing center and in relation to learning and student success. This governing statement is also helpful in preparing tutors because it helps the director train the tutors so that a nurturing environment and a sense of mentoring guidance are stressed above the goal of earning higher grades on course assignments. "Learning" is now the essential element for the writing center and its staff, as it is for Nichols College as a whole. Rather than existing as empty words, the mission statement is brought to life through the efforts of the tutors, measurable outcomes occur, especially those that impact student use of the writing center, and it becomes easier to obtain funding and approval for additional tutors and programs.

The center's regular programming is flexible because the writing center activities are a result of an attempt to provide a variety of support mechanisms. Rather than instituting a single program, our goal has been to use these budget increases to improve programming across the entire writing center spectrum by hiring more tutors, broadening existing programs, and initiating new programs. And because the writing center director has proven her desire and ability to work in the institution's best interest, she is allowed to manage additional monies. This, in turn, allows the writing center to report back to the president's office its success stories, increases in usage statistics, and the tutors' own achievements in professional development, including research presentations and travel.

The Office of the Vice President for Academic Affairs and Dean

This office is one of the primary relationship partners of the Nichols College writing center. Because this dean is the writing center's representative at the President's Council meetings and the immediate supervisor of the writing center director, he is instrumental in approving new program ideas, obtaining funding, and publicly supporting new writing center initiatives that mesh with academic programs and the efforts of faculty members endeavoring to put forth a quality educational experience. Perhaps even more importantly, he is responsible for seeing that members from the different populations and offices are working together to put forth that experience collaboratively.

First, the dean's position coordinates a variety of educational initiatives, perhaps best represented in NEASC Standard 4.3: "Each educational program demonstrates coherence through its goals, structure, and content; policies and procedures for admission and retention; instructional methods and procedures; and the nature, quality, and extent of student learning and achievement" (p. 7). Here, the key word is "coherence," in that the writing center must focus on specific programming, and, equally important, the center must focus on communication about such programming to the institution's general population. This attention to programming, such as supporting improvements in training for the one-to-one and face-to-face tutoring or our in-class workshop programs, helps to ensure that the writing center's activities directly support student retention efforts and new student enrollment initiatives.

The dean's office is also the one most closely linked with the faculty, so for the writing center, the dean is the first-level liaison between the writing center director and the faculty members whom the center is often trying to support. This office is therefore instrumental in marketing, additional budgeting, and guidance in classroom and writing center programming. As such, this relationship needs to have very open lines of communication. The dean needs to be aware of the center's initiatives in order to help promote them with faculty members, while at the same time the writing center director must be in tune with the curriculum and faculty members' concerns and needs.

One of the writing center's strongest initiatives under the above NEASC standard is the development of a writing consultant's program where advanced writing tutors are placed with traditionally non-writing or non-English department faculty members. In this relationship, writing consultants are placed in positions of authority and encouraged to teach mini-lessons, hold in-class workshops, respond to, although not grade, student writing, and advise their faculty members about developing and grading writing assignments, while also maintaining traditional writing tutor responsibilities, such as one-to-one time and office hours. This program was developed as a result of these faculty members expressing concerns about their own writing difficulties, especially when they realized that teaching how to write a research paper was very different than simply assigning a research paper. Thus, the writing consultant's program strengthened communication, trust, and respect among the writing center tutors and the overall faculty population.

Because Nichols College is a small institution, the program's success developed quickly, primarily through word-of-mouth. Currently, the writing center maintains a waiting list for faculty requesting writing consultants, and there is a consistent effort to recruit potential consultants into the program. We credit this growth to each department listening and responding to the needs of others in addition to closely monitoring the program to address concerns as they arise. In fact, the faculty members are so excited about the program, they have made conference presentations with their writing consultants. Most recently, these presentations have been made at both tutoring conferences, such as the New England Peer Tutor Association (NEPTA), and regional faculty conferences, such as the New England Faculty Development Consortium (NEFDC). These joint conference presentations have been some of the most exciting academic events that have occurred at Nichols in recent years, a product of the relationships the writing center has built with the faculty through academic affairs. Rather than have the writing center placed between faculty and administration (Fitzgerald & Stephenson, 2006), thus separating the two entities, the administration helps pave the way for the writing center to work in conjunction with the faculty and foster important, supportive, and long-lasting relationships.

Because of the importance of the faculty–writing center relationship, the director has taken great care to introduce additional programs that support their goals and classroom objectives. In-class workshops, review sessions, independent workshops, and curriculum-based tutoring are just a few of the center's programming initiatives that were designed to provide aid to faculty, and the dean's office has been instrumental in helping the writing center avoid the hazard that "even if documented and evaluated appropriately within the field of composition, explicit and hidden institutional practices can still recast the work of writing centers as bureaucratic management detached from the intellectual interests of faculty, or as invisible 'service'" (Marshall, 2001, p. 75). In each of these programs, the dean's office provided awareness and verbal encouragement to the faculty to utilize the services, thus avoiding the "detachment" that many writing center directors experience.

This relationship, like that with the president's office, also results in fiscal benefit. Because the writing center's successful programming has been developed with specific audience members and goals in mind, the dean's office is instrumental in soliciting funding from the president's office whenever a new program is introduced to the community. Currently, a 7.5 percent budget increase is in place that corresponds with the school's increasing enrollments, and the dean was instrumental in developing the proposal and bringing it to the president for approval.

Additionally, at different times throughout the year, the dean's office often helps multiple offices combine resources so that additional programming can take place that would not otherwise be possible within a single office. For example, it is not unusual for the writing center to help support the campus literary magazine with marketing, editing, and design. Likewise, volunteers from other offices help the writing center with major tasks while hosting a conference or completing work for outside organizations like the New England Peer Tutor Association or the Learning Assistance Association of New England. Without the support of the dean's office, funding and collaboration would be a much greater challenge.

The Office of the Chief Enrollment Officer

The chief enrollment officer is most frequently concerned with issues related to recruitment and retention, a primary concern for many colleges regardless of their overall population. In a study of retention models,

Heywood (1977) identifies one common element among the different theories. In *Assessment in Higher Education,* he notes, "In all these models the entry characteristics of the students are considered to be of considerable importance. The predispositions which students bring to the college experience may have a considerable bearing on their behavior [decision to stay at that institution]" (p. 129). Therefore, the writing center needs to be in contact with the chief enrollment officer on a regular basis so that academic variations that occur among the incoming classes from year to year are addressed and appropriate programming is initiated.

Having strong programs in place that recognize the demographic and psychographic nature of the incoming student is an essential step in recruitment and retention. The writing center, once again, can offer services that are possible within their resources that respond to institutional needs before top-down programming directives are dictated to them. Then, within this process, NEASC standards can also be addressed.

In this case, NEASC Standard 6.7 most closely links the enrollment officer to the writing center by stating, "The institution systematically identifies the characteristics and learning needs of its student population and then makes provision for responding to them" (p. 18). NEASC Standard 6.8 continues with, "In all cases, the institution provides academic support services appropriate to the student body, . . . and provides available and responsive information resources and services . . ." (p. 18). In order to meet these standards, annual admission reports that outline the academic credentials of the incoming class are shared with the writing center. Likewise, the writing center educates the admissions officers and ambassadors about the center's services to help reduce the possibility of misinformation being relayed to new applicants and their parents. By strengthening the relationship between the office of the chief enrollment officer and the writing center director, both parties can promote one another appropriately.

One specific example of programming that resulted from examining the demands of the incoming student population is the development of a program of academic preparation workshops, initiated by the writing tutors themselves rather than by the director or another campus office. Several years ago, a common concern among the writing tutors was an observation that they were spending more time on general study skills, like note-taking, test-taking preparation, and textbook note-taking, as opposed to assisting students with class papers and writing concerns. These observations were also supported by survey results from incoming students during summer orientation. In response to both their and admission's concerns, the tutors designed a series of workshops that addressed these academic concepts. Then, to further support the tutors' concern, the writing center director hired an "academic preparation tutor" through funding from the dean, to whom one-to-one academic tutoring could be referred. Consequently, the successful development of academic preparation workshops led to a new series of workshops on writing that are now also offered in the writing center and as stand-alone activities for the classroom. In the future, these workshops will again be expanded by holding them in the residence halls with the aid of the residential life employees—thus linking a third department and creating a new relationship. This example demonstrates the writing center's provision of "available and responsive information resources and services" outlined by NEASC. At the same time, the tutors both identified students' needs and created a solution that would help the students while becoming more effective at their own jobs. With the addition of the enrollment office, and now residential life, students are supported within multiple areas of the college, and the needs of the overall student population are addressed.

The Office of the Chief Student Affairs Officer

Many writing center directors are concerned with the link between writing centers and the office of student affairs; some directors fear that their operations will become a part of student "activities" rather than an academically linked, self-governing environment. However, many writing center program modifications can be developed when one examines how the standards for student affairs link to academic initiatives.

To increase the partnership between student services and academic affairs, the writing center director looked to NEASC Standard 6.12 for guidance: "As appropriate, the institution supports opportunities for student leadership and participation in campus organization and governance" (p. 18). This single statement not only justifies the implementation of writing tutors as student leaders, but it also encourages the alignment of the writing center as a student-organized, student-developed, and student-focused entity that not only meets the needs of its clientele but offers advanced opportunities for the students working there, the tutors themselves. Therefore, by tapping into tutor concerns through meetings, email communication, suggestion boxes, and so on, the tutors become part of the administrative decision-making process. They become active participants in the writing center's management and governance.

Another way to increase tutor authority is to create classroom opportunities. In an effort to reduce the "boundaries" among the individual offices, the academic affairs dean has invited credentialed student services personnel to teach both regular three-credit and one-credit courses. These one-credit offerings are part of a unique Nichols four-year program, *Professional Development Seminar* (PDS). The first-year classes provide the faculty teaching them with teaching assistants (TAs), many of whom are writing center tutors. Therefore, individuals such as the director of student activities, the director of career services, and the vice-president for student affairs are paired with TAs who not only help teach the class, but who also engage students in activities and tutoring outside of class.

As it happens, the writing center is often a meeting place for PDS classes. Writing workshops and portfolio development sessions frequently occur in the center. For those PDS classes not assigned a TA who is also a writing tutor, a writing center tutor will, at the very least, visit the class and bring handouts, booklets about how to get good grades in college, and give-away prizes at different times during the semester. Consequently, when we ask, "How did you hear about the writing center?" on our end-of-semester surveys, the answer "PDS class" often receives the highest ranking.

The remaining three years of PDS require students to develop a professional portfolio to be used in their senior-year employment interviews. Once again, in conjunction with career services, the writing tutors are able to assist students with employment documents, like resumes and application letters, in addition to responding to reflection statements, essays, and research projects that are all required portfolio contents. However, for the writing tutors to be effective in their jobs, they need to have the PDS requirements and standards as established by the PDS coordinator. Therefore, conversations and training sessions are offered by career services to help prepare tutors and strengthen this communication pattern.

The impact of this relationship is that there is now an interesting synergy among the writing center, the PDS program, and the office of career services. This intercollegiate programming again encourages cross-campus initiatives to take place, starting with "ground-up" initiatives rather than with "top-down" administrative edicts, while addressing NEASC's concerns of student leadership and governance. Promoting writing tutors to accept visible roles helps increase their credibility with their peers as well as with the faculty, thus exceeding NEASC's objectives for student leadership.

The Office of the Dean of the Division of Graduate and Professional Studies (DGPS)

Another important relationship is that with the DGPS office. A letter from NEASC written in response to the Nichols College ten-year self-study report expressed a concern about the equality of support services provided the evening and on-line division of the college and the traditional day division. Therefore, increased attention has focused on building stronger links between day and evening divisions, especially with regard to services most often enjoyed by the day division, such as library services, career services, and the writing center. More specifically, NEASC Standards 6.7 and 6.8

address the need to ". . . identify the characteristics and learning needs of its student population and then . . . [make] . . . provision for responding to them [. . . and] in all cases, the institution provides academic support services appropriate to the student body . . ." (p. 18). In response, the writing center developed an on-line tutoring program. This on-line writing service allows non-traditional, evening, and on-line students to access the same writing tutors as the traditional day population. By training existing tutors and designing a usable interface with the aid of the information technology department, the writing center team began responding to students' inquiries through both the traditional face-to-face program as well as on-line. This latter approach now remains active twelve months a year as well as during the traditional day division holidays and breaks. It is available to our day division students, but the primary users are evening division and on-line students. Although one could argue that some of the benefits of traditional face-to-face communication are absent, on-line tutoring is likely to be as effective as traditional campus-centered writing center interactions because both approaches rely on the same leadership, training philosophies, and personnel.

Additionally, the writing center is offering services to a population who had very little contact with the writing center prior to this initiative. Consequently, with the new on-line tutoring program, the President's Council approved increased funding for additional tutors to help with the additional workload and summer hours. The writing center also received more computers that are available for other tutoring purposes when not being used for on-line tutoring, and, furthermore, the writing center has taken on administrative staff to help coordinate the logistics of operating an on-line environment. These benefits afforded to the overall writing center are a result of initiating and establishing meaningful relationships with other offices who, in turn, procured resources to benefit not only their own efforts but the overall writing center and its personnel. Ultimately, in 2006, funding was provided for an assistant director of the writing center. What made this position viable was the increased use of the writing center by evening students, undergraduate and graduate, for both on-line tutoring and traditional face-to-face meetings. The full-time assistant director helps oversee new professional staff and existing peer tutors. And, as might be imagined, the assistant director has taken on additional duties normally assumed by the director in order to keep up with the College's increasing enrollment goals.

CONCLUSION

In his landmark essay, "The Idea of a Writing Center," North (2001a) argues, "If writing centers are going to finally be accepted, surely they must be accepted on their own terms as places whose primary responsibility, whose only reason for being, is to talk to writers" (p. 78). Later, in "Revisiting 'The Idea of a Writing Center'," North (2001b) still pines for ". . . a situation in which the writing center's mission marches its resources and, to whatever extent possible, its image" (p. 89). Over ten years after "Revisiting," Ferruci and DeRosa (2006) still ask a central question to writing center relationships: "How do we develop and maintain sustainability in our writing centers, while moving forward with pedagogically and theoretically sound, progressive writing programs?" (p. 21). These landmark essays outline similar goals that appear and reappear over a thirty-year period and ask the same essential question: "How do we create and define a writing center that holds institutional influence?"

Part of the answer comes in the form of building these relationships that are mutually beneficial to the center and the overall institution. If writing centers wait for direction, they run the risk of being viewed as passive. If writing centers respond to upper administration's guidance for programs, they run the risk of trying to implement, generally poorly, programs that may not be feasible within their infrastructure. As mentioned in a previous publication, "If we [writing centers] are on the sidelines . . . then we lose our opportunity to contribute to curricula, to influence pedagogy, and to participate actively in the academic discourse of our own institutions (Bickford, 2007, p. 137). Regional accreditation guidelines and standards provide a common ground where writing center directors can tap into the larger concerns of the administrative offices who can help foster the center's growth. Likewise, directors are also placing themselves in positions of knowledgeable experts to whom institutional constituents look to for advice.

Within all of these concerns, the writing center at Nichols College has achieved both the ability to be accepted on its own terms, by offering programming consistent with its own financial and staffing abilities and limitations, and to be autonomous enough to create a self-sustaining mission statement. Perdue (1991) laments that members of administration ". . . rarely hear from our [writing center director's] teacherly or our scholarly side; neither do we invoke their teacherly or scholarly side" (p. 18). The use of the accreditation standards establishes a common playing field where "sides" are reduced or eliminated, and all parties are equal stakeholders in productive discussions. Writing centers have a grand opportunity to help place themselves in positions that do more than justify their worth through annual statistics and usage reports. They become authority figures in writing-across-the-curriculum efforts, curriculum changes, and administrative decision making.

Studying and applying the accreditation standards discussed in this chapter, such as those offered by NEASC and other regional agencies, helps to place the writing center in positions of both autonomy and collaboration within the institution. Writing centers and other campus operations that comprise a vital institution should examine themselves and their outcomes in relation to accreditation standards for two reasons: one, to find ways to better serve students; and two, to build strong relationships with other campus offices in order to further strengthen the institution's mission and goals.

REFERENCES

2007–2009 Nichols College catalog. (2007). *Mission.* Retrieved November 8, 2008, from http://www.nichols.edu/currentstudents/academicresources/collegecatalog/images/ Nichols_College_Rev10_07.pdf.

ARC Tutoring. (2008). *Purpose and goals.* Retrieved November 8, 2008, from http://www.nichols.edu/currentstudents/Academicresources/arctutoring/index.html.

Bickford, C. (2007). Inside looking out: Trading immediate autonomy for long-term centrality. In W. J. Macauley, Jr. & N. Mauriello (Eds.), *Marginal words, marginal work? Tutoring the academy in the work of writing centers* (pp. 135–150). Cresskill, NJ: Hampton Press.

Boquet, E. H., & Lerner, N. (2008). Reconsiderations: After "the idea of a writing center." *College English, 71*(2), 170–189.

Carino, P. (1995). Theorizing the writing center: An uneasy task. *Dialogue: A Journal for Writing Specialists, 2*(1), 23–27.

Ferruci, S., & DeRosa, S. (2006). Writing a sustainable history: Mapping writing center ethos. *The Writing Center director's resource book.* Mahwah, NJ: Lawrence Erlbaum Associates.

Fitzgerald, L., & Stephenson, D. (2006). Directors at the center: Relationships across campus. *The Writing Center director's resource book.* Mahwah, NJ: Lawrence Erlbaum Associates.

Gladstein, J. (2007). Quietly recreating an identity for a writing center. In W. J. Macauley, Jr. & N. Mauriello (Eds.), *Marginal words, marginal work? Tutoring the academy in the work of writing centers.* Cresskill, NJ: Hampton Press.

Harris, M. (1992). Collaboration is not collaboration is not collaboration: Writing center tutorials vs. peer-response groups. *College Composition and Communication, 43*(3), 369–383.

Heywood, J. (1977). *Assessment in higher education.* New York: Wiley Press.

Kinkead, J. (1996). The National Writing Centers Association as mooring: A personal history of the first decade. *The Writing Center Journal, 16*(2), 131–143.

Kuh, G., Kinzie, J., Schuh, J. H., & Whitt, E. J. (2005). *Student success in college: Creating conditions that matter.* San Francisco, CA: Jossey-Bass.

Lunsford, A. (1991). Collaboration, control, and the idea of a writing center. *Writing Center Journal, 12*(1), 3–10.

Marshall, M. J. (2001). Sites for (invisible) intellectual work. In J. Nelson & K. Evertz (Eds.), *The politics of writing centers* (pp. 74–84). Portsmouth: Heinemann.

New England Association of Schools and Colleges. (2005). *Standards for accreditation.* Retrieved April 6, 2006, from http://www.neasc.org/cihe.htm.

North, S. M. (2001a). The idea of a writing center. In R. W. Barnett & J. S. Blumner (Eds.), *The Allyn and Bacon guide to writing center theory and practice* (pp. 63–78). Boston: Allyn & Bacon.

North, S. M. (2001b). Revisiting "The idea of a writing center." In R.W. Barnett & J.S. Blumner (Eds.), *The Allyn and Bacon guide to writing center theory and practice* (pp. 79–91). Boston: Allyn & Bacon.

Perdue, V. (1991). Writing-center faculty in academia: Another look at our institutional status. *WPA: Writing Program Administration, 15*(1–2), 13–23.

Stay, B. (2006). Writing centers in small colleges. In B. Stay & C. Murphy (Eds.), *The Writing Center director's resource book* (pp. 147–152). Mahwah, NJ: Lawrence Erlbaum Associates.

INSIDER, OUTSIDER: REFLECTIONS ON WRITING CENTERS FROM A FACULTY ADVOCATE

Kelly L. Latchaw

Students come and students go, but faculty remain. The most present relationship for any writing center is with faculty, and yet, like an old marriage, it is a relationship that may be taken for granted. Over the past twenty years, as a faculty advocate for writing centers, I have increasingly supported writing center development in a variety of contexts; I have served as an interim writing center director, a writing center tutor, and a resource and tutor trainer for a variety of writing centers. From this experience, I believe I am in a unique position to comment on the various relationships and attitudes that faculty often develop toward writing centers. While it seems obvious and practical to develop ongoing and multivalent relationships between writing centers and faculty, I will be the first to admit that establishing such relationships can be like romancing a porcupine—faculty can be rather prickly—but I also believe that such relationships are possible and would be to our mutual benefit. While few faculty are hostile to writing centers, few are active advocates and collaborators. As one of those few advocates and collaborators, I hope to take this opportunity to present some observations about the relationship between faculty and writing centers from the faculty side, with the goal of enabling the development of more productive relationships on a broader scale.

Professional traits that we tend to share can make faculty challenging collaborators (Hrycaj & Russo, 2007; Jones, 2001), especially beyond our disciplinary boundaries. This is particularly troubling because collaboration is essential to the mission of a writing center and the pedagogy it employs. While Young (1992) has demonstrated the history and importance of collaboration as a particularly useful teaching tool in a writing center context, faculty, and particularly English department faculty, can disparage and diminish the role of writing centers and their directors, questioning everything from their pedagogy and efficacy to their institutional positioning (Grimm, 1996). This results in the hostile relationship described by Meagher (2000) as psychologically and professionally damaging.

The very traits that make faculty difficult to work with are the ones that have enabled our success to this point. As Readings (1996) observes, "few communities are more petty and vicious than University faculties" (p. 180). Most of us got where we are by being focused on our own field, confident in our own knowledge, capable of solving our own problems, and competitive and protective regarding our own programs. This often leads to territoriality. We do not want other people to do our work for us, and often we do not trust other people to assist us. As Speer and Ryan (1998) point out, faculty often have difficulties collaborating as teachers in practice even when they are highly motivated in theory to do so. Faculty often believe that the skills we work so hard for are uniquely our own.

Faculty are often unaware of the work done in other fields and how useful it could be. We often misuse resources such as writing centers and libraries because we have preconceived notions of their roles in the education process (Rabinowitz, 2000). Pulled in many directions by the sometimes conflicting responsibilities of teaching, research, and service, we become creatures of habit in many aspects of our professional lives for the sake of efficiency, and we are reluctant to disturb the status quo, often perceiving such changes as additions to our workload. This can cause us to expect instant and significant results from any change, particularly if it comes from outside, that is, from someone other than ourselves. When we do not see these immediate results, we regard the experiment as failed and we abandon it, becoming distrustful of any similar projects in the future. We are generally aware, whether we will admit it or not, that we do not know everything and that other people and other fields have skills and knowledge that we lack, but as a group that exists under constant scrutiny—particularly junior faculty, often those least bound by habit and most open to innovation—and the pressure of speaking always as authorities, we are loathe to allow anyone, least of all anyone outside our field, to witness our inadequacies.

Without formal training in rhetoric, composition, or pedagogy, most faculty, within and beyond English departments, do not separate content issues from the higher order concerns of writing, and so they do not always see either how a writing center is of use to us and our students, as we are responsible for content in our courses, or how individuated pedagogy as practiced in writing centers differs qualitatively from the classroom or laboratory pedagogy we practice. The first feature of our students' writing that we are consciously aware of, and for many of us the only one that we have the metalanguage to articulate, is "grammar," which leads to the desire for a "fix-it shop," a role that writing centers have actively resisted at least since North (1984). The faculty in many fields see writing as peripheral, forcing writing centers to collaborate with them subversively, effectively tricking them into acknowledging the value of writing (Gale, 2001).

All of these traits—our territoriality, our disciplinary isolation, and our professional and personal insecurities—can make us a difficult audience with which to communicate, especially on topics such as writing or research (Hrycaj & Russo, 2007; Zhu, 2004), which we use in our assessment of our students and ourselves but in which we may never have received overt training or theoretical knowledge. For writing center directors, an awareness of these traits can facilitate establishing a collaborative relationship. Knowing the tendencies of a faculty audience, its sensitivities, and background will better prepare writing center directors in crafting and delivering their message.

WELL, HOW DID WE GET HERE?

Faculty begin cultivating these traits in graduate school. I was a graduate assistant teaching first-year composition at a prominent research university and trying to prove that I belonged there. For my first year, I had the advantage of a mentoring program where I could discuss challenges with my peers and an experienced teacher. But the students of composition and rhetoric were segregated into their own mentoring groups, and so these were not the colleagues with whom I developed that trust relationship. We noncompositionists—linguists, literature scholars, and creative writers—defensively dismissed the field of rhetoric as esoterica largely because we had little contact with its practitioners. We had already begun the process, even within the same department, of dividing ourselves into Us and Them. Such a division inhibits collaboration and restricts communication. It reduces the probability of forming any productive relationship across those Us/Them divides.

There was an excellent and well equipped writing center at this university, and at the beginning of each semester, one of the tutors would visit our classrooms and our mentor group to remind us of its existence. These tutors were often perceived as somewhere between alien entities and infiltrators.

They spoke in a jargon the rest of us were not privy to about "higher and lower order concerns" and "communication triangles." In a display of a common sociolinguistic phenomenon of creating in-group cohesion and asserting dominance through the use of jargon and group-specific knowledge (van Dijk, 1997), they excluded us by their very language, and as a predictable result, we felt both inadequate and distrustful. Our general response to the former was to show no weakness, to never admit we needed their help to teach our own classes. Our response to the latter was to avoid contact and whenever possible denigrate their field as out of date or unrealistic. This relationship is perhaps the source of the sense of "shunning" described by Tassoni (2006), in which he describes the feeling of being unwelcome and unheard in his institution's writing center. I rarely sent my students to the writing center, gave them no special recognition if they went on their own initiative, and only set foot in the place twice myself in the six years I was there, and one of those visits was for a required meeting. Despite the fact that this well-established independent writing center was housed physically and administratively in the same English department where I was working, it was alien territory.

Many of the center's clients were either first-year writing students or students who had discovered the center in their first-year writing class and continued to use it. The English as a Second Language (ESL) student population, especially graduate students, also made some use of the center's resources, although saving face was a significant barrier for many of them. Bruce and Rafoth (2004) discuss the importance of directly addressing this issue in tutorials, but, at the time, even the writing center relied at best on the empathy of the tutors. When we began teaching at the sophomore level and above, my fellow graduate instructors and I primarily used the center, if we used it at all, to address lower order concerns. Higher order concerns, particularly for field specific writing, were generally perceived by the instructors as part of the course content, rather than a question of rhetoric and discourse. We felt that it was part of our job to teach the discursive structures of the field, and that we would be remiss if we foisted these duties off on the center. Besides, as many of us believed, the center wouldn't do it the way we wanted it done.

Because of a failure to communicate on both sides, we wasted a great resource. The professionalism, training, and resources the tutors brought to bear were great strengths in this writing center. The latest approaches to composition pedagogy were promptly integrated into the support materials in the center and the skill sets of the tutors. Technology was embraced and used innovatively. Everything was state-of-the-art. Unfortunately, these assets were largely self-contained. They rarely escaped the center. The professionalization described by Boquet and Lerner (2008) was certainly cultivated there, but it had the unfortunate effect of creating a kind of in-group mentality. The graduate students training there as future directors of composition programs and writing centers learned how complex the task could be, how broad a range of resources and approaches was available, how to utilize technology to facilitate organization and access to those resources—in short, how fully occupied one could be without ever venturing beyond the confines of the center. With such nifty toys at its disposal, it is easy to understand how the center could lose track of the broader context for its work and could forget that not everyone would see the intrinsic value of these tools.

Like most new teachers, I needed to expand my repertoire of techniques and not waste time reinventing already well developed wheels. I needed to know how to work with a wide range of students with multiple challenges ranging from learning disabilities to language differences. I needed to figure out how to prioritize my pedagogical goals. I needed to learn how to challenge advanced students even as I avoided discouraging those with less developed skills. And I needed to know that resources existed that could help me, that it wasn't my responsibility to fix all the problems by myself, and that I was not alone. Because of the gap that had been established between myself as a non-compositionist and the writing center, I dealt independently and inefficiently with most of these needs through a persistent system of trial and error and a determined autodidacticism for which I really didn't have time. It was the last two needs that I did not meet, at least not for many years after leaving that institution. Even today I find that resisting the modes for problem solving which were ingrained during my training period is a constant struggle.

In addition to my teaching needs, I also had needs as a student and scholar. I needed to shift to a more professional discourse and learn to express my ideas for diverse audiences. I needed to learn to approach language and communication in a variety of ways. I needed to master research and writing techniques that were not a part of my undergraduate training. These needs are not uncommon among graduate students in all fields, not just English. If anything, other fields do even less discipline specific professional style writing as undergraduates, and so they often flounder through their writing tasks. It was never suggested to me, or to my colleagues in other fields who sought me out "as an English major type" to help them with their writing, that we could find help with all of this at the writing center, and our perception of it as designed for assisting struggling first-year undergraduates with writing personal essays meant that we never considered the option on our own. It has taken many years for me to seek the advice and assistance of my colleagues in the field of rhetoric, and I know now that many of my colleagues as well as myself would have benefitted enormously from their perspective in our formative years. I did not seek out a relationship with the writing center because I perceived it as an admission of weakness and because I was unaware of the resources it could provide me as both a teacher and a writer.

Not only did I not seek out a relationship with the writing center, but I was resistant to attempts by the center to communicate with me. Its tendency to use both a jargon which I felt excluded me and the univalent, rather than dialogical, rhetorical strategies most commonly associated with announcements and advertising did not invite response or comment, did not express an interest in my needs, and seemed inflexible in its approach to writing, as if it already had all the answers and nothing I could say would make any impact on it. I felt that while the center wanted to have a voice in my classroom, it was not interested in giving me a voice in the center. Muriel Harris (2007) discusses this limitation and ways to begin overcoming it, to get past our disciplinary isolations and prejudices, by tailoring the appeal to the specific audience, and by listening to faculty in other disciplines regarding how writing is produced and used within their fields. The center's regular informational messages seemed more like commands or warnings than invitations, and certainly as a graduate teaching assistant I never received anything any more personal than these mass mailings. This one-way communication style likely caused the center to miss many opportunities to work actively with students and faculty at all levels, in a wide range of fields and discourses, on projects that would bridge the gap between the institution and the wider world. This failure then poses the threat of the center's perceived role slipping into fading or limited relevance beyond remediation, applicable primarily to lower level academic classroom work.

Opportunities for growth and development are missed on both sides of the relationship, and not just when we're graduate students. Barratt, Nielsen, Desmet, and Balthazor (2009) describe a joint analysis of library and composition instruction effects with an eye to improving both. Such a collaborative analysis, while it might benefit both the classroom instructor and the independent resource—in this case a library, but as easily a writing center—is impossible without open dialogue. Writing centers may lose opportunities to explore disciplinary discourse conventions and to develop new ways of engaging other fields in the project of communication. They can become isolated and unable to effectively define themselves as a resource for a broad audience and a site of knowledge which has relevance across the academic and professional world. Sadly, even as the graduate students in the center are learning to focus on their own work as an end in itself, graduate students not only in the other English concentrations but also across the university are often learning that a writing center is of little relevance to them. They are excluded from it and see no means of connecting to it. They can live without it, and so they do—not just while they are in graduate school, but often for the duration of their professional lives.

THE ADJUNCT EXPERIENCE

After graduate school, I began my career as an adjunct. Adjuncts often have the same prickly character traits as faculty, magnified by the tenuousness of their position. At many institutions, adjunct faculty are second class citizens, which tends to provoke a chip on their shoulder and something to prove. As if these weren't sufficient barriers to a relationship, many institutions also fail to fully integrate their adjuncts into the campus community, limiting their access to resources and colleagues at a time when many are most in need of such support. The high turn-over rate in adjunct pools also means that any institutional relationship with them is likely to be even more ephemeral than that with a student and even more one-sided in its benefits.

Adjuncts teach almost exclusively those courses which are, however mistakenly, most commonly associated with writing centers—basic writing and first-year composition. I was often assigned the less traditional classes which met in the evenings or at outreach campuses. The limited contact time made both the continuing feedback and focus on process, which are so useful in developing writing skills, logistically challenging. I also had no office space in which to meet with students outside of class, and I was not on the campus-wide mailing lists for receiving generally disseminated information. This was the case at all four of the institutions, seven campuses in toto, at which I adjuncted. Clearly, establishing a relationship with adjuncts like myself would be a challenge for any institutional entity, writing centers included. Just as students' likelihood to utilize the services of a writing center can be enhanced by a required visit (Gordon, 2008), so might adjuncts' use of the center be improved by a required face-to-face consultation at the time of hire. Remarkably little seems to have been written about this relationship, from either side, so I am forced to rely on my own observations and some analogical reasoning.

From 1995 to 1998, I worked as an instructor at a midsized regional state university with about 13,000 students where the average age of the undergraduates was 27, which is to say the school served a significant number of non-traditional students. In addition to baccalaureate, master's, and doctoral programs, the university had a number of associates and certification programs, filling the niche normally filled by community colleges. While there were relatively few ESL students at this institution, there was a greater than average number of students who were underprepared or out of practice academically. In response to the needs of this population, the university had set up an area adjacent to the student union for student support services. This space consisted of one large room with racks of instructional handouts, partitioned administrative areas, study tables, and small, separate study rooms for small group instruction or projects. The writing center was housed there, along with the Math Lab and the tutoring services for other, specific courses. The center's services were widely perceived as remedial, although being housed with other academic enhancement programs allowed the center cover from the stigma of remediation—while a student might be embarrassed to seek assistance with his writing, no one would look at getting help with Calculus or Organic Chemistry as remediation. This underscores the notion that many students and faculty do not regard writing as a learned and graduated skill in the way that they do math or science, a belief that is part of a long tradition in education of directly associating intelligence and verbal facility. That is, we have a deep conviction that smart people write well naturally. This belief in no way encourages upper level students or faculty to seek out the services of a writing center.

My first real contact and collaboration with the center came when the English department's linguist and I, after a conversation about our students' needs, approached the center's director with the proposal of conducting a series of seminars on the lower order concerns for the general campus community to be co-sponsored by the department and the center. The weekly seminars were announced in the school paper, and fliers were posted in all of the classroom buildings and the student union as well as the center. The seminars were well attended by a cross-section of the campus community, including staff and faculty, in addition to students. This demonstrated a broad need and desire for further discussion of these topics, but beyond repeating the seminars, no real changes were made.

The English department faculty in particular retained and transmitted to their students a more or less punitive view of the writing center similar to that described by Olson (1981), where students lacking lower order skills would be required to visit the center before submitting papers. Including discussions of lower order concerns in the first-year writing classes, let alone any higher level composition courses, continued to be perceived and talked about as "dumbing down the curriculum" by faculty inside the English department. The resulting attitude of restricting higher order concerns to the composition classroom and relegating lower order concerns to the writing center created a barrier to developing a useful relationship between the faculty and the center. This division of roles was passed along to the graduate students, most of whom were training to be high school or community college instructors. Its effect on the graduate students would predictably be to discourage future relationships with other writing centers in other contexts, as I have described in the prior section.

My adjuncting experience continued from 1998 to 2002, when I worked as an adjunct instructor at a community college. The community college had three branches—one urban, one rural, and one located in an industrial complex in a small town. I taught at all three and, having begun to see the potential use I could make of a writing center to improve the quality of my own classroom and my students' educational experiences, was pleased to find that all three had on-site centers. These were multi-purpose centers, with tutors and resources for multiple fields. But at each branch there was a part time director dedicated to the writing center and a handful of trained volunteer tutors drawn from the student body and faculty so that there was an actual person in the center whenever the college was open to offer guidance on the students' writing projects. Each center also served as the primary computer lab on the campus. These resource centers were heavily utilized by the students on all three campuses, and all of my first-year writing students were already aware of them by the second week of classes.

Each of these centers made an effort to expand its role beyond support for first-year writing courses. At the urban campus, ESL and GED tutoring were available and open to the community. At the rural campus, the center provided resources and assistance for students applying to four-year institutions. At the industrial park campus, the director of the center, who was also the only full time English faculty member at the site, conducted reading circles for the sophomore literature survey classes and initiated monthly poetry readings in the campus lounge. In each case, the strength of the center was its willingness to meet the goals of its constituents—the students, the faculty, and the community beyond the campus. Even adjunct faculty, including myself, were solicited to join in the programs offered by the centers. When there was a budget for it, adjuncts were offered hourly wages for their time.

The weakness of these centers lay in their lack of material resources. This they strove to make up for by reaching out for assistance to the full and part time faculty and to volunteers from the community. The relationship they established with the faculty was reciprocal. Faculty were not just propped up in a corner to serve out some of their office hours in a forum more public than their office—they were integrated into the running of the centers. Their suggestions were listened to, mutual resources were shared, and they were trusted to engage in the day-to-day management of the centers. The small faculty and diverse student body of the campuses gave the centers the opportunity to work closely with their constituents and to utilize their unique experiences as resources for other clients.

Being multi-purpose centers also created opportunities for cross-disciplinary cooperation. And being in heavily trafficked computer labs gave the centers the opportunity to create community on the campuses, whether through extracurricular activities or informal advising. These centers were not seen as having any limits on whom they could serve. The vision shared by all three of the centers was that these multipurpose learning support centers should be places of growth, exploration, opportunity, and cooperation for everyone involved with them, from students to administration to the community at large. They embraced the identity that Ellen G. Mohr refers to as "haven[s] for the hopeful" rather than "dumping ground[s] for the disenfranchised" (Pennington, 2009, p.134). These centers were dynamic and well known in their communities, despite limited resources. They assessed through dialogue the needs of their constituencies, both on and beyond the campus itself, and designed a limited number of programs that matched greatest needs to available resources.

At the same time that I was working with the community college, I was working at a small private liberal arts university with about 5,000 students. When I began teaching there, the English department had only recently eliminated both its graduate program and its first-year writing sequence. Students were required in their first semester to take a writing intensive first-year seminar. These were special topics classes taught by faculty from across the university, and they required at least fifteen pages of writing from the students in the course of the semester. Students were required to take one writing intensive course each year, and these were also distributed across the university. Many students, particularly in the sciences and social sciences, participated in undergraduate research projects which culminated in peer reviewed presentations and publications.

The writing center at this school was minimal. It consisted of two adjacent but not adjoining ten by twelve rooms housed among the English department faculty offices. In one room, there were a half dozen computers and two large work tables. In the other room were a conglomeration of chairs and couches and a set of book shelves stocked with the standard dictionaries and style manuals.

In the first few years of the first-year seminar program, faculty from outside the English department expressed frustration in both teaching and assessing the necessary writing for the course. In response, the center offered a series of workshops for the faculty on teaching and grading writing. This would have been a prime opportunity to initiate the kind of negotiations advocated by Fitzgerald and Stephenson (2006) as a starting point for broadening and deepening the relationship of the writing center with various constituencies, especially faculty. Unfortunately, these workshops were highly directed, reminiscent of the training I had received as a graduate teaching assistant. We could have taken this opportunity to engage in a dialogue, listening to each other's perspectives on writing and even sharing these with students (Petersen, 1995). But, rather than honoring the contributions the faculty from other disciplines could make to a working understanding of written communication, or respecting their desire to have students produce material in the discourse of their fields, the workshops held to a narrow model of academic writing and an ideological enforcement of writing as a process without discussion of its merits.

There was a reliance on the jargon of the field of composition and rhetoric which I suspect many of the faculty from beyond the English department found as alienating as I had when I was a graduate student. The focus of the workshops was on higher order concerns but without attention to discourse specific requirements. As Zhu (2004) notes, content area faculty use writing assignments primarily to assess content knowledge without necessarily being aware of the ways in which the critical thinking practices of a given discipline affect the expectations for presentation of that knowledge. The connection between disciplinary writing and disciplinary thinking remained obscure. The faculty generally expressed that this approach did not meet their needs, as for most of them it was the lower order concerns they had the greatest difficulty explaining to their students. The result was a sense of alienation between the center and the faculty. The center failed to establish what Byron Stay (2006) describes as "strategic alliances" (p. 147). Working to fill this void, the English department offered courses in Grammar and Usage, Etymology, Writing for the Sciences, and Writing for the Social Sciences. For these last two, the department worked in partnership with faculty in the disciplines who were directing undergraduate research projects expected to culminate in articles or conference papers. These courses consistently filled, indicating that there was in fact a desire on the part of the students for more overt instruction in language and composition.

This center relied on the assumption that if you build it they will come, providing little in the way of direct communication with either students or faculty. As Harris (2007) points out, this approach only reinforces the myths about writing centers being strictly remedial. The center provided the space and basic resources for its clients, but it waited for the clients to seek it out. The institution offered many opportunities for expanding the relationships of the center with both students and faculty, as evident in both the specialized English courses and the faculty's request for guidance. But these opportunities, when pursued, failed largely due to a habit—present too in many faculty—of leaping to conclusions about what the client really needs, rather than listening to them and negotiating best options with given resources. The greatest threat to this center was a general perception throughout the university community that it lacked relevance. The students did not need remediation; the faculty did not need to be taught basic teaching skills. This situation precisely reflected the one discussed by Devlin (1996), in which competent and advanced students recognize the value of honing their writing skills, but faculty persist in their conception of writing centers as remedial and focused on lower order concerns. What both groups required was more nuanced, in-depth discussion of the challenges they perceived and the resources available to meet them. But this would have required reconceiving the center as something other than remedial, and the habits of mind and past experiences of the faculty made this a challenge that was not being met.

At that stage of my professional development, I needed to know that as a teacher I could make use of a resource like a writing center in the design of my students' weekly assignments, to assist them in effectively breaking down the writing task even when I was not personally available to monitor and respond to each step. As a scholar at the beginning of my career, I also needed to know that there was somewhere I could go for feedback on my own writing and research skills. I needed active readers with whom I could engage in dialogue about my goals as a writer, my awareness of my audiences, and my use of available resources. I did not find these things at the institutions where I adjuncted, and I was too insecure professionally to actively seek them out. As addressed elsewhere in this volume, the writing center–adjunct faculty relationship has benefits not only for each other but for students as well. It is therefore worth the effort to build relationships with this most outside of constituencies.

LEARNING FIRSTHAND

When I finally secured a tenure track position, it was at a small Catholic university which had lost its writing center more than a decade earlier. Many of the students at the school came from rural districts with limited resources, and they were often underprepared for college level reading and writing tasks. Nearly 60 percent of incoming first-year students were placed in the pre-composition, basic writing course, based on their performance on an in-house placement exam which was assessed by the English faculty—all three of us. At the same time, the university was seeing a dramatic increase in their ESL population due to both increased immigration to the region, particularly from traditionally Catholic countries, and overseas recruiting of international students.

I got a small taste of how difficult it could be to establish relationships with faculty regarding writing on my first day, before I had even begun teaching. I had been assigned to teach a course in Business Writing, so I went to the faculty in the school of business and spoke to each of them individually regarding the skills they wanted me to help their students develop in the class. Each of them gave essentially the same response: "We want our students to be better writers." Even when I offered them specifics such as grammar, organization, audience and situation awareness, purpose, tone, etc., the response of the business faculty was, "Yes, all of those things." As a side note, three semesters after I began teaching the course, the school of Business began offering its own version of Business Writing because the course I designed in response to their stated needs was deemed "too demanding" for their students. I understood then their desire for a magic wand solution in which, by simply taking a class called Business Writing, their students would magically acquire writing skills without having to spend time understanding or practicing them. I suspect this is the expectation that many faculty have when their students visit a writing center—an instant transformation without effort. And when, as in my case, the change was neither instantaneous nor dramatic, the faculty lose faith in the project and resort to an ad hoc alternative which is more directly under their control and perhaps meets more precisely their needs, which I was unable to get the faculty to articulate but which they nonetheless certainly had a conception of for themselves.

I joined the majority of the faculty in advocating for a new writing center, and I kept track of the number of hours I spent tutoring students on their writing skills outside of my own classes, so that these figures could be added to the argument. Ultimately we prevailed, and a writing center was opened. A year later, a director was hired, and the facility is still actively utilized by the students and supported by the faculty. This support, however, while I was there, consisted primarily of resisting any administration attempts to cut the center's budget and regularly sending students of all levels to visit the center. Faculty rarely visited the center themselves or provided feedback to the center on their needs or its effectiveness. As someone actively involved at the center's inception, even before a director was hired, I remained in close contact with the center as long as I was at that institution. I regularly collaborated and shared resources with the center as the campus worked to develop ESL and distance learning curricula. The center was an invaluable resource for these projects.

During this initial period, I became aware of how many of the faculty viewed writing instruction as part of their teaching, regardless of discipline. It often took a great deal of persuasion to convince them that the center had no intention of encroaching on their territory, but that engaging experts with training and experience in teaching language and composition could allow the faculty to spend more of their efforts and class time on their own areas of interest and expertise. The writing center also provided a means of connecting across disciplines for presentations and campus conferences which drew together students and faculty from the different fields in collaborative and complementary projects to be shared with the campus community. For example, when the Master of Social Work program felt that they had talented students who lacked the academic preparation in writing to succeed in completing their course work and their theses, they came to the center and asked for a series of seminars specifically tailored for their incoming students. This kind of active collaboration makes for a more productive relationship between faculty and the writing center (Dobie, 1998).

I had had a significant role in setting up the writing center. I had a vested interest in it, which led me to assert a relationship with it that I had not so strongly pursued in my previous positions. Because, after many years of struggling with my own relationships with writing centers and some necessary intensive research on instituting writing centers, I had some idea of what a writing center could be and do within a campus community, I was active, even aggressive, in maintaining a relationship with the new center.

The center, being new and housed as it was within the library which was itself housed within the administration building, was not well positioned to initiate contact with faculty. In practice, I became a sort of liaison, bringing faculty concerns to the attention of the center and informing faculty of the center's services and functions. While the faculty attitudes and the constantly evolving writing center were factors which made the relationship between the two more dynamic than I had previously encountered, the importance of physical and temporal availability became clear to me here. If the center had had hours and a location independent of the administrative offices, there would have been more opportunity for contact and dialogue with the faculty. Yet even if the center was situated in an ideal location, it may not have been enough. Having been an interim director and an advocate, I now knew that direct contact with the faculty must be ongoing, would involve a lot of face time and leg work, and even then would still require a lot of persuasion.

A CENTER TO WORK WITH

I am now making my academic home at a midsized state university with about 7,500 students. My first year here as the English department linguist was also the first year for the campus to have a full-time writing center director and a writing center based on more than the volunteer hours put in by English department faculty. As I had already seen, starting up a writing center is a daunting task, and there are many ways for the director to define its role in the community. The director here has transformed a bare computer classroom in a Depression-era, CCC-built, stone cottage into a comfortable and inviting work space with large tables, state-of-the-art computers, and soft furniture. The center has developed programs and presentations tailored to the needs of Nursing, Business, Athletics, Geography, and Social Work. It has assisted the Computer Information Systems program in their professional accreditation, which, like many others, includes a component on teaching and assessing professional written communication skills. It has even engaged one of the local high school teachers who adjuncts at the university in developing a writing center for the high school. I have worked with the center on several of these projects, and as the English department linguist, I am available to train its tutors in the recognition of and response to lower order concerns.

In this case, the center's greatest strength is a director who is willing to listen to anyone from the Athletic Director to the Dean of Nursing to the adjunct writing instructor to find out how the center can help them reach student writing goals. He has what Mullin, Carino, Nelson, and Evertz (2006) might call the "intrapreneurial" spirit to design new programs in collaboration with area faculty and others, whose skill sets and interests are known to him through other projects, to reach those goals. The tutors themselves, coming from a variety of disciplines, serve as practical ambassadors for the center, not unlike the writing fellows in the program described by Severino and Knight (2007). The weakness here is that the resources of the center—its director, tutors, and budget—are stretched to their limit. This makes a necessity of virtue by requiring the additional time, energy, and skills brought by external collaborators, such as faculty, and the unremunerated outreach efforts of the tutors, to supplement the resources of the center and prevent or at least delay exhausting them. The director is continually identifying new opportunities for the center and its staff to work with individuals and groups at all levels of the campus and community. Word of mouth has identified him as collaborative and, therefore, valuable to a wide range of constituents. Shankle (2001) used interviews with faculty in order to identify the goals and expectations of writing in different fields, which in turn enabled her to transform a director-centered WAC program into a faculty-centered one. Similarly, the writing center director at my current institution uses regular face-to-face communication to assess the needs and expectations of faculty who use writing in their courses, thus keeping his center focused on his constituents.

I had the good fortune of being hired into my current position at the same time as the university's first writing center director. This meant that we met during our orientation and were able to establish a personal relationship which facilitated my relationship with the center itself. It is worth noting here that, while I have been talking about the relationships between writing centers and faculty in general or myself in particular, the fact is that the most productive and genuine relationships are between people, actual individual human beings with emotions and agendas, attributes and needs, who can sit across a table from one another—or across a computer link— and negotiate through dialogue for the most mutually satisfying course of action. I do not have a relationship with an institution; I have a relationship with the people who animate that institution—in this case, the center's tutors and its director.

Through our conversations, the director became aware of my interests and abilities, and he has called on me to work with the center on a number of projects which ideally suited my professional development while providing the center with additional resources in the way of training and project development. I have also felt more comfortable talking with center tutors not only about the specific goals I have for my students but also about my own research. I have made use of the tutors' skills in locating sources for individual projects and brainstorming different approaches to presenting information. This mutually beneficial relationship has been rewarding for me and has led me to regret not taking the initiative to attempt such relationships with other writing centers in my past. In my defense, I will say that writing centers often share a number of prickly traits with faculty, having gone through similar trials by fire and being at least as subject to institutional pressures as any faculty member. This, combined with the prejudices I developed during my graduate training, has powerfully inhibited the development of my own relationships with writing centers.

LESSONS LEARNED

While disciplinary isolation seems to be endemic to higher education, it should not create insurmountable barriers to developing successful relationships beyond our own arenas. A writing center is inherently a place of inter-disciplinarity and cross-disciplinary knowledge production, as literacy is requisite for all academic fields. Runciman (1996) approached this environment by posing a series of practical questions and role questions to both himself, as writing center director, and to faculty engaged in curriculum redesign. This strategy of constant re-examination can form the basis of a partnership between faculty and writing centers. The center is a place where scholars and their trained apprentices utilize their expertise in language manipulation and discourse management to facilitate the sharing and exploration of knowledge within and between content areas. The center is, by its very nature, not so much marginal as liminal.

Academics are often territorial by nature. To bridge the gaps—between students and services, between faculty and resources, between disciplines, and between the university itself and the surrounding community—requires extraordinary effort, open-mindedness, and responsiveness to need. These can be achieved even with very limited resources, although more resources will almost always make the job easier. What doesn't work is talking at rather than listening to the other in the relationship. None of us wants to be stuck at the party with the person who only talks about himself. All of the centers I have encountered directly have expended significant energy and resources on talking about what they do; few among them have actively sought to discover what their communities perceived as needs and the overlaps among their interests.

It is critical for writing centers to routinely re-examine the assumptions that affect their relationships with their stakeholders. It isn't only the evolving and competing epistemologies of writing center theory and practice which must, as Eric Hobson (2001) argues, be critically considered. In addition, the diverse discourses of the university community must be engaged. Tools for making this engagement, such as Critical Discourse Analysis (Fairclough, 1995) and Critical Language Awareness (Clark 1997), already exist. Many of these tools are informed by Paulo Freire's dialogic critical pedagogy, which engages students and colleagues in the discovery of relationships among the various ways of knowing practiced within the university. Not surprisingly, writing centers are ideally positioned to facilitate these discoveries. By their very nature, writing centers enhance the literacy skills of all constituents with which they have relationships. Literacy, as Abdul Janmohamed (1994) puts it, "implies a greater control of one's past and present. And that control, when combined with an understanding of the future as pure possibility, significantly enhances one's agency" (p. 251). This is the goal of both critical pedagogy and writing centers. Lawrence Grossberg (1994) echoes the idea that literacy enhances agency in his description of a praxical pedagogy, which "attempts to offer people the skills that would enable them to understand and intervene in their own history" (p. 17). Writing centers engage in this practice on a daily basis. For Henry Giroux (1994), developing agency takes the form of representational pedagogy, which will "give students the opportunity not simply to discover their hidden histories but to recover them" (p. 50). This is a central purpose of education, and it need not be limited to students, but can embrace everyone involved in the educational enterprise.

It is possible, albeit challenging, for a writing center to learn to regard faculty as collaborators rather than clients or competitors, just as it is possible for faculty to learn to trust the writing center and regard it as a resource. There are multiple benefits to creative collaboration open to cooperatively changing practices (Mahaffey, 2008), including increased efficiency, the ability to answer client needs faster, and the use of a common language. This positioning of the writing center is widely advocated but generally discussed in terms of the relationships within the center, particularly between the tutors and their clients (Bruffee, 2001; Eodice, 2003; Harris, 2001; Lunsford, 2001; Mullin, Reid, Enders, & Baldridge, 2008; Smith, 2001; Trimbur, 1997). The advice offered by Jennifer Brice (1998) regarding multicultural writing centers — "1) create a 'safe house'; 2) learn before you teach; 3) listen; 4) be polite; 5) negotiate" (p. 171) — might be productively followed in cross-disciplinary as well as cross-cultural encounters and by writing center directors working with faculty, as well as tutors working with clients. In this way, we might engage productively with what Carter (2009), following Chantal Mouffe, calls the "writing center paradox." wherein the tension between the plurality of voices and the conventions of the disciplines can be, if not resolved, then actively negotiated.

When I received the notes from the center as a graduate assistant, the message I got was, "Try not to inconvenience us." When the center was housed in a student space, such as the student union, contact with faculty became limited and one-directional; the center sent notes to the faculty member regarding student visits, but the center never heard from the faculty members and was necessarily at something of a loss to meet the community's specific needs. None of these conditions must be the norm. Even a community college, if it is listening to its constituents, can select a limited number of programs to make best use of its limited resources for the greatest benefit of its community. And even the students at an elite school recognize that they can benefit from improving their writing skills. The key is to resist the desire to say that the center knows what is best for the community and instead to let the community define the needs to be met. For administrators, faculty, or writing center directors to have a fixed vision of what a writing center is, can be, or should be prevents adaptation to the needs of the other in the relationship. The community will not come to the center, follow its vision, or adhere to its expectations. Rather, the center benefits from becoming a site of negotiation and adaptability. The center must persuade the community of its value, not assume that the value is inherent and universally perceived, and it will do this by paying attention to and appealing to the vested interests of its constituents, not its own agenda, as it builds those relationships that will make it recognized as an indispensible part of the university. It is my hope that the reflections offered here will allow both sides in the writing center–faculty relationship to more openly and productively approach one another, for our mutual benefit, for the benefit of our institutions, and for the benefit of our students.

REFERENCES

Barratt, C., Nielsen, K., Desmet, C., & Balthazor, R. (2009). Collaboration is key: Librarians and composition instructors analyze student research and writing. *Portal: Libraries and the Academy, 9*(1), 37–56.

Boquet, E., & Lerner, N. (2008). RECONSIDERATIONS: After "The Idea of a Writing Center." *College English, 71*(2), 170–189.

Brice, J. (1998). Northern literacies, northern realities: The writing center in "the contact zone." In T. Capossela (Ed.), *The Harcourt Brace guide to peer tutoring* (pp. 169–174). Fort Worth, TX: Harcourt Brace & Company.

Bruce, S., & Rafoth, B. (2004). *ESL writers: A guide for writing center tutors.* Portsmouth, NH: Boynton/Cook.

Bruffee, K. (2001). Peer tutoring and the "conversation of mankind." In R. Barnett & J. Blumner (Eds.), *The Allyn and Bacon guide to writing center theory and practice* (pp. 206–218). Boston, MA: Allyn & Bacon.

Carter, S. (2009). The writing center paradox: Talk about legitimacy and the problem of institutional change. *College Composition and Communication, 61*(1), 133–152.

Clark, R. (1997). *The politics of writing.* London: Routledge.

Devlin, F. (1996). The writing center and the good writer. *Writing Center Journal, 16*(2), 144–63.

Dobie, A. (1998, April 1–4). *Working together: WAC, the departments, and the writing center.* Paper presented at the meeting of the Conference on College Composition and Communication, Chicago, IL.

Eodice, M. (2003). Breathing lessons, or collaboration is. In M. Pemberton & J. Kinkead (Eds.), *The center will hold: Critical perspectives on writing center scholarship* (pp. 114–129). Logan, UT: Utah State University Press.

Fairclough, N. (1995). *Critical discourse analysis: The critical study of language.* New York: Longman.

Fitzgerald, L., & Stephenson, D. (2006). Directors at the center: Relationships across campus. In C. Murphy & B. Stay (Eds.), *The writing center director's resource book* (pp. 115–126). Mahwah, NJ: Lawrence Erlbaum Associates.

Gale, C. (2001, May 31–June 2). *Going it alone: Supporting writing across the curriculum (WAC) when there is no WAC program.* Paper presented at the meeting of the National Writing Across the Curriculum Conference, Bloomington, IN.

Giroux, H. (1994). Living dangerously: Identity politics and the new cultural racism. In H. Giroux & P. McLaren (Eds.), *Between borders: Pedagogy and the politics of cultural studies* (pp. 29–55). New York: Routledge.

Gordon, B. (2008). Requiring first-year writing classes to visit the writing center: Bad attitudes or positive results? *Teaching English in the Two-Year College, 36*(2), 154–163.

Grimm, N. (1996). Rearticulating the work of the writing center. *College Composition and Communication, 47*(4), 523–548.

Grossberg, L. (1994). Introduction: Bringin' it all back home—pedagogy and cultural studies. In H. Giroux & P. McLaren (Eds.), *Between borders: Pedagogy and the politics of cultural studies* (pp. 1–28). New York: Routledge.

Harris, M. (2001). Collaboration is not collaboration is not collaboration: Writing center tutorials vs. peer-response groups. In R. Barnett & J. Blumner (Eds.), *The Allyn and Bacon guide to writing center theory and practice* (pp. 272–287). Boston, MA: Allyn & Bacon.

Harris, M. (2007). Writing ourselves into writing instruction: Beyond sound bytes, tours, reports, orientations, and brochures. In W. Macauley & N. Mauriello (Eds.), *Marginal words, marginal work? Tutoring the academy in the work of writing centers* (pp. 75–84). Cresskill, NJ: Hampton Press.

Hobson, E. (2001). Maintaining our balance: Walking the tightrope of competing epistemologies. In R. Barnett & J. Blumner (Eds.), *The Allyn and Bacon guide to writing center theory and practice* (pp. 100–109). Boston, MA: Allyn & Bacon.

Hrycaj, P., & Russo, M. (2007). Reflections on surveys of faculty attitudes toward collaboration with librarians. *Journal of Academic Librarianship, 33*(6), 692–696.

Janmohamed, A. (1994). Some implications of Paulo Freire's border pedagogy. In H. Giroux & P. McLaren (Eds.), *Between borders: Pedagogy and the politics of cultural studies* (pp. 242–252). New York: Routledge.

Jones, C. (2001). The relationship between writing centers and improvement in writing ability: An assessment of the literature. *Education, 122*(1), 3–21.

Lunsford, A. (2001). Collaboration, control, and the idea of a writing center. In R. Barnett & J. Blumner (Eds.), *The Allyn and Bacon guide to writing center theory and practice* (pp. 92–99). Boston, MA: Allyn & Bacon.

Mahaffey, M. (2008). Exploring common ground: US Writing Center/Library Collaboration. *New Library World, 109*(3/4), 173–181.

Meagher, E. (2000, April 12–15). *The case for independent writing programs.* Paper presented at the meeting of the Conference on College Composition and Communication, Minneapolis, MN.

Mullin, J., Carino, P., Nelson, J., & Evertz, K. (2006). Administrative (chaos) theory: The politics and practices of writing center location. In C. Murphy & B. Stay (Eds.), *The writing center director's resource book* (pp. 225–236). Mahwah, NJ: Lawrence Erlbaum Associates.

Mullin, J., Reid, N., Enders, D., & Baldridge, J. (2008). Constructing each other: Collaborating across disciplines and roles. In C. Murphy & S. Sherwood (Eds.), *The St. Martin's sourcebook for writing tutors* (3rd ed., pp. 189–205). Boston, MA: Bedford/St. Martin's.

North, S. (1984). The idea of a writing center. *College English, 46*(5), 433–446.

Olson, G. (1981). Attitudinal problems and the writing center. *Liberal Education, 67*(4), 310–318.

Pennington, J. (2009). Review: *Inside the community college writing center: Ten guiding principles* by Ellen G. Mohr. *The Writing Center Journal, 29*(1), 131–134.

Petersen, L. (1995, September 27–30). *Engaging the faculty: A successful strategy.* Paper presented at the meeting of the International Writing Center Conference, St. Louis, MO.

Rabinowitz, C. (2000). Working in a vacuum: A study of the literature of student research and writing. *Research Strategies, 17*(4), 337–346.

Readings, B. (1996). *The University in Ruins.* Cambridge, MA: Harvard University Press.

Runciman, L. (1996, March 27–30). *When general education reforms include writing, what happens to the writing center?* Paper presented at the meeting of the Conference on College Composition and Communication, Milwaukee, WI.

Severino, C., & Knight, M. (2007). Exporting writing center pedagogy: Writing fellows programs as ambassadors for the writing center. In W. Macauley & N. Mauriello (Eds.), *Marginal words, marginal work? Tutoring the academy in the work of writing centers* (pp. 19–34). Cresskill, NJ: Hampton Press.

Shankle, N. (2001, May 31–June 2). *Creating a discourse community with writing-intensive instructors.* Paper presented at the meeting of the National Writing Across the Curriculum Conference, Bloomington, IN.

Smith, L. (2001). Independence and collaboration: Why we should decentralize writing centers. In R. Barnett & J. Blumner (Eds.), *The Allyn and Bacon guide to writing center theory and practice* (pp. 408–414). Boston, MA: Allyn & Bacon.

Speer, T., & Ryan, B. (1998). Collaborative teaching in the de-centered classroom. *Teaching English in the Two-Year College, 26*(1), 39–49.

Stay, B. (2006). Writing centers in the small college. In C. Murphy & B. Stay (Eds.), *The writing center director's resource book* (pp.147–152). Mahwah, NJ: Lawrence Erlbaum Associates.

Tassoni, J. (2006). Blundering border talk: An English faculty member discusses the writing center at his two-year campus. *Teaching English in the Two-Year College, 33*(3), 264–278.

Trimbur, J. (1997). Consensus and difference in collaborative learning. In V. Villanueva (Ed.), *Cross-talk in comp theory: A reader* (pp. 439–456). Urbana, IL: National Council of Teachers of English.

van Dijk, T. (1997). Discourse as interaction in society. In T. van Dijk (Ed.), *Discourse as social interaction* (pp. 1–37). London: Sage Publications.

Young, A. (1992). College culture and the challenge of collaboration. *Writing Center Journal, 13*(1), 3–15.

Zhu, W. (2004). Faculty views on the importance of writing, the nature of academic writing, and teaching and responding to writing in the disciplines. *Journal of Second Language Writing, 13*(1), 29–48.

REVISITING
"TALES TOO TERRIBLE TO TELL":
A SURVEY OF GRADUATE
COURSEWORK IN WRITING
PROGRAM AND WRITING CENTER
ADMINISTRATION

Michael A. Pemberton

In this collection and others, writing center scholars have discussed the ways in which institutional relationships are created and maintained, sometimes focusing on specific units in particular university settings (such as Litman, Munday, Dye and Modey in this collection), sometimes reflecting on the administrative and philosophical issues that can enable or interfere with effective collaborations (such as Doe, Whalen, Herb and Purdue in this collection). These discussions highlight how important institutional partnerships are to successful and sustainable writing centers, and they also show, implicitly, how thoroughly writing centers have managed to weave themselves into the fabric of the academic enterprise. Instead of seeing ourselves as marginalized or out of the mainstream, we are now thinking of ourselves as colleagues and contributors to larger institutional initiatives, to collaborations built to distribute our knowledge, training, and resources to others.

Still, as is our habit in the field of writing centers, we seem to have been swept up in a round of local concerns to the exclusion of questions that might be considered external to our immediate work, but that could nevertheless have a direct impact on the quality and scope of the local work we can do. One such question might be the role of professional organizations in encouraging high quality scholarship. Another could be our historical reluctance to network with administrators outside of writing centers, such as WPA conference participants. Yet, no question of this kind is more essential than the training that graduate programs are providing to prepare students for the real work of administering writing programs and centers. What we can do in, through, and with our writing programs and centers is a direct reflection of our ability to manage the multiple demands of those programs and centers, and managing those demands is much more difficult when a new WPA or WCA is unprepared for the actual work. If expectations for a new administrator are high going in and institutional relationships need to be forged from day one, there is virtually no time for that learning to occur on the job.

The matter of WPA/WCA training has concerned me for the better part of twenty years, partly—perhaps largely—because of my own experiences as a newly-minted assistant professor. In 1991, I was two years into a tenure line position and the director of a new writing center, already feeling pressure to publish the requisite number of peer-reviewed articles for tenure but constantly struggling just to keep up with the quotidian demands of administrative work. On one particularly frustrating day, while wrestling with a writing center schedule that seemed to change every five minutes and fielding calls from faculty who wanted me to give class presentations in ten minutes, it suddenly struck me that my graduate school training and coursework had completely failed to prepare me for the parts of my job that routinely demanded the most time and energy. While I had learned how to do research on the composing process, had taught first-year composition courses, and had presented at national conferences while a grad student—all in the interest of vita building and making myself look attractive to future prospective employers—I had not been taught anything about how to structure a writing program, how to run a writing center, how to train graduate students, how to schedule courses, how to work with budgets (and the administrators who determined those budgets), or how to act appropriately when supervising others. In short, I had been given no training and had accumulated virtually no knowledge of how to be an effective WPA or WCA.

A little research showed me that I was probably in good company. The early 1990s was a time of explosive growth in rhetoric and composition. While tenure track positions for PhDs in English Literature were scarce and getting scarcer, positions for rhetoric/composition scholars were abundant, with the demand far outweighing the supply. For those of us coming on the job market at the time, the prospects could hardly have been rosier: lots of interviews at the MLA conference, numerous campus visits, and, for many of us, multiple job offers to choose from. The dark side of the story, though, was that most of these new positions carried a heavy burden of administrative work, sometimes mentioned in job ads, but just as often not. My survey of two years' worth of MLA job announcements revealed that, of 177 listings for specialists in rhetoric and composition in 1990 and 1991, 87 (close to 50 percent) included WPA or other administrative duties as an integral part of the position. Beyond this, however, my own experiences in interviews seemed to indicate that even if administrative work wasn't mentioned specifically in a job ad, search committees often made it clear that candidates would be expected to assume WPA duties within a year or two of the time they accepted the job (Pemberton, 1993, p. 157). In effect, both statistical and anecdotal evidence substantiated Trudelle Thomas' (1991) observation that

> [c]andidates entering the job market with Ph.D.s in Composition and Rhetoric quickly discover that they, more than other new instructors, must assume administrative responsibilities early in their careers. Many are hired immediately into positions as writing program administrators; others are hired with an eye toward moving into such positions within a few years. (p. 41)

I reported these research findings in the first part of "Tales Too Terrible to Tell: Unstated Truths and Underpreparation in Graduate Composition Programs," a chapter in Fontaine and Hunter's *Writing Ourselves into the Story*, and went on to describe what I saw as the *real* problem: in spite of the "unstated truth" that rhetoric/composition scholars would almost certainly be expected to perform some WPA work in their new faculty positions, there were no courses in any of the writing studies programs I researched in 1991 that trained graduate students in how to fulfill those duties. A few programs offered one- or two-semester WPA apprenticeships to a limited number of students or had them spend time tutoring in the writing center, but it seemed that most graduate student TAs had to rely on departmental lore and occasional encounters with their faculty WPA or WCA to glean some sense of what went on behind the administrative curtain (Pemberton, 1993, pp. 159–162).

I concluded the chapter by speculating about some of the ideological, pragmatic, and political reasons why administrative coursework might not yet exist in these programs—they *were* relatively new, after all—and offered a hypothetical syllabus for such a course, ending with the (perhaps unsurprising) peroration:

> We need to prepare graduate students for the real-world situations they will find themselves in. If they are to take on positions of responsibility as the heads of writing programs, we should give them the same consideration we give our undergraduates, providing them with the training, experience, and guidance that will allow them to excel in the practical matters of administration as well as the more esoteric matters of research and scholarship. (p. 169)

ADMINISTRATIVE TRAINING
AND INSTITUTIONAL RELATIONSHIPS

Though most of my expressed concerns about WPA/WCA courses in 1993 had to do with graduate students' need to acquire essential job skills—a reflection, no doubt, of my own perceptions and frame of reference at the time—the fifteen years of experience I have garnered as a writing center administrator since then have only further convinced me that graduate-level coursework in writing program administration is an essential component of a rhetoric/composition degree. In addition to showing students how to grapple with such mundane matters as scheduling, budgets, and hiring, administrative courses can also play a critical role in teaching graduate students how to see themselves and their programs within larger institutional contexts and, correspondingly, how to foster strong cross-institutional relationships that will be indispensable to their future success.

Administrative training will, for example, help new WPAs and WCAs to work capably with other campus units whose missions may overlap the writing program's. First-year experience programs may ask the WPA/WCA to give presentations or writing workshops for new students. Librarians may want the WPA/WCA's help in designing new materials, tutoring students, or compiling resources. Directors of first-year composition programs may be asked to create special sections for honors students or chemistry majors or themed freshman interest groups, and writing center directors may be asked to arrange classroom visits or supervise writing fellows programs in first-year courses across the entire campus. Graduate coursework that familiarizes future administrators with the departmental structures they will encounter and the intradepartmental relationships they will be expected to cultivate will not only make them more attractive to future employers but make their first years on the job far more productive.

This sense of institutional familiarity, a developing awareness that WPA/WCA work serves a campus- rather than a department-wide mission, will also encourage innovation and open the door to new possibilities in curriculum and instruction. Administrative coursework can prepare graduate students to embrace the scholarship of writing program administration and to think of their future writing centers and/or writing programs as research sites, places where new ideas and pedagogies can be explored and assessed. Rather than seeing administrative work as mind-numbing labor, they will begin to see it as a vast network of opportunities with connections that reach, potentially, into every department and every classroom.

So, now, nearly twenty years after my initial survey, having watched the field grow exponentially in the number of conferences, journals, publications, graduate programs, and newly created faculty positions that are available to specialists in rhetoric and composition, I wondered whether, in the intervening years, there had been any significant movement to provide graduate students with the WPA or WCA coursework and training that had been so clearly absent in 1992.

My expectations were not particularly high, especially in light of Balester and McDonald's 1997–1998 (2001) survey of writing program and writing center directors, which noted that

> [g]iven the complexity of writing program administration, professionalization should, but usually does not, include training in non-curricular skills such as budgeting, management, and marketing. Respondents reported that institutions almost never offer anything more than mentoring and/or consultation to train WPAs. Since graduate programs in composition or related fields generally also neglect education in the management and administration of writing programs and writing centers, this represents a significant problem for professionalization efforts. (pp. 65–66)

On the other hand, I knew that in 2003, Rebecca Jackson, Carrie Leverenz, and Joe Law had identified a dozen graduate courses in writing program and writing center administration that had been taught in a variety of institutions since 1995, so I anticipated finding a number of these courses still on the books.

My research goals, then, were threefold: first, I wanted to determine the extent to which specific coursework in writing program administration and writing center administration were either now or recently available to graduate students; second, I wanted to know how those courses were designed and what comparisons could be made between those courses with a WPA emphasis and those with a WCA focus; and third, I wanted to investigate—in the case of generic WPA courses—how much attention was being paid to writing center administration as a specific component of WPA work. The following research questions, therefore, framed my research:

1. How many courses in Writing Program Administration have been offered since 1991? How frequently have they been taught, and at which graduate institutions have they been offered?
2. How many courses in Writing Center Administration have been offered since 1991? How frequently have they been taught, and at which graduate institutions have they been offered?
3. How stable are these courses? Do they have permanent listings in college or university catalogs, or are they "special topics" courses that are offered only periodically?
4. What is the *focus* of these WPA and WCA courses? How much class time is spent on institutional relations and the administrative contexts of other writing programs such as first-year com-

position, basic writing, writing centers, ESL, writing across the curriculum, and so on?

5. What do the results of this survey indicate about the current status of WPA and WCA courses in graduate rhetoric/composition programs?

Identifying Courses in Writing Center and Writing Program Administration

I began my research with a simple Web search, looking for course descriptions and syllabi posted online. I quickly found several examples, including "English 680W: Writing Program Administration" (http://web.ics.purdue. edu/~roses/680F05/680WPA2005syllabus.doc) taught by Shirley Rose (Purdue)[1] and "CCR 760: The WPA as Negotiator" (http://wrt-howard.syr. edu/Syllabi/760schedule.html) taught by Rebecca Moore Howard (Syracuse). The list of twelve courses and institutions earlier identified by Jackson, Leverenz, and Law provided me with further sites to investigate and course catalogues to examine. In addition, I posted requests on WCenter, WAC-L, and WPA-L in April 2008, asking whether anyone could supply me with information about current or past course offerings in writing program, writing center, or WAC administration. I made clear that I was interested specifically in graduate administration courses for future career professionals and not in courses that, for example, trained undergraduate peer tutors to do writing center work. Over the next few weeks, I compiled a list of sixteen courses and syllabi that colleagues were generously willing to share. They were:

- "English 680W: Writing Program Administration" (Shirley Rose, Purdue)
- "CCR 760: The WPA as Negotiator" (Rebecca Moore Howard, Syracuse)
- "English 904: Writing Program Administration" (Amy Devitt, University of Kansas)
- "Education 253D: Theory and Practice of Writing Program Administration" (Sue McLeod, UCSB)
- "English 531: Administering a Writing Program" (Diane Kelly-Riley, Washington State University)

---

[1] Rose has more than one WPA syllabus on the Web, so I have opted to include only the most recent document in this study. Her other syllabi are located at http://web. ics.purdue.edu/~roses/engl680/index.html, http://web.ics.purdue.edu/~roses/WPA 2000/6802000home.html, http://web.ics.purdue.edu/~roses/Engl680WPA2003/ 680WPA2003syllabus.htm

- "English 652: Advanced Composition Studies: Writing Program Administration" (Duane Roen, Arizona State University)
- "English 696e-003: Writing Program Administration" (Edward White, University of Arizona)
- "English 5933-04: Designing Writing" (Michael Neal, Florida State University)
- "English 656: Composition Theory, Pedagogy, and Administration" (Valerie Balester, Texas A&M University)
- "English 914: Writing Across the Curriculum and Writing Centers: History, Theory, and Practice" (Cinthia Gannett, University of New Hampshire)
- "English 680C: Writing Center Administration" (Linda Bergmann, Purdue)
- "English 5323.1610: Writing Center Administration" (Mary Stanley, Northeastern State University)
- "Literature 5131: Writing Center Theory and Administration" (Chloé Diepenbrock, University of Houston, Clear Lake)
- "English 5317: Writing Center Theory, Practice, and Administration" (Rebecca Jackson, Texas State University)
- "English 7/6550: Writing Centers: Theory, History, and Practice" (Trixie Smith, Middle Tennessee State University)
- "English 717-01: The Study of Writing: Writing Center Theory and Practice" (Joe Law, Wright State University)

I make no claim that this list is comprehensive or exhaustive; it represents only those courses taught by faculty who subscribed to one or more of the listservs I queried; who were listed in the 2003 Jackson, Leverenz, and Law article; who were willing to send their syllabi to me by email; or who had posted their syllabi online in a way that was relatively easy to find using a Web search engine. Other WPA and WCA courses no doubt exist. This list also includes only the most current version of the course(s) taught at each institution and/or the most current institution where a particular instructor teaches the course.[2]

This list of syllabi also does not reflect the many workshops, professional development sessions, or conference activities that are widely avail-

---

[2]For example, the English 531 course at WSU, described by Jackson, Leverenz, and Law (2003) as a course in "Administering a Writing Lab," has since been redesigned and renamed "Administering a Writing Program." That is the version of the course described here. Similarly, Rebecca Jackson's course in "Writing Centers: Theory, Practice, and Administration," taught in 2003 at New Mexico State University, moved with her to Texas State University. Because the course is no longer taught at NMSU, only the Texas State course is included here.

able to graduate students and new WPAs outside of a formal classroom environment. The Council of Writing Program Administrators, for example, has offered summer workshops to new and experienced WPAs for more than twenty years, and a great many WPAs and WCAs, individually, have given hundreds of presentations, workshops, and brown-bag seminars for students, faculty, and administrators on their own campuses. I should note, as well, that this brief list of syllabi fails to account for graduate courses in rhetoric/composition that address WPA and WCA issues implicitly, as a broad contextual framework for class discussions, rather than explicitly, as a named portion of course content. Seminars that prepare TAs to teach first-year composition, for instance, will almost always touch on administrative policies regarding plagiarism, grade complaints, sexual harassment, and the like, but because these matters are likely to arise circumstantially or be only a small part of the overall course content, they do not often appear in syllabi. Nevertheless, even given these provisos, I would argue that the sixteen courses represented here offer a reasonably comprehensive snapshot of WPA/WCA courses taught over the last ten years and as such provide a window into the extent to which graduate students are currently being trained, via formal coursework, for WPA and WCA positions.

THE FREQUENCY AND STABILITY OF WPA AND WCA COURSE OFFERINGS

It has to be acknowledged, right at the start, that given the complete absence of WPA/WCA courses in 1992, the existence of sixteen new courses today is a substantial improvement. Statistically, it's infinitely better. But before we celebrate this accomplishment too quickly, we should see that number in a larger context. Currently, the number of PhD programs in rhetoric and composition remains steady at about 65 (White, 2007, p. vii), the same number identified and studied by Gail Stygall in 1998 (2000, p. 380). This means that at best, only 28 percent of these programs offer WPA/WCA courses, a percentage that gets even smaller (15 percent) when we note that Purdue accounts for two of the sixteen and that five of the institutions which provided me with syllabi (Wright State, Middle Tennessee, UH Clear Lake, Texas State, and Northeastern State) grant only master's degrees, not PhDs, and were therefore not included in White's tally.

Also noteworthy is the fact that few of these WPA/WCA courses are stable offerings with permanent course numbers and descriptions in university catalogs. The vast majority, twelve of the sixteen, are offered through "selected topics" listings such as "Seminar in Teaching and Learning" (UCSB), "Studies in Rhetoric and Composition" (Univ. of Arizona), "Specializations in Rhetoric and Composition" (Texas State), and "Advanced Composition

Studies" (Arizona State). Only four of the courses I examined—at Texas A&M, Northeastern State, Washington State, and Middle Tennessee State—have separate listings with their own numbers and catalog descriptions.

Admittedly, the presence or absence of a distinct course number in a university catalogue is not the most reliable measure of a course's stability or how frequently it might be offered. For some institutions, offering a WPA/WCA course under a selected topics option may simply be a matter of convenience because (a) it's much harder to propose a permanent course than it is to propose a selected topics course; (b) if only one faculty member is qualified to teach the class (not unlikely if a department has only one WPA), then departmental politics may make a new permanent course difficult to justify; and (c) selected topics courses do not have to be offered as frequently as permanent courses, which, because they are permanent, must often be included in regular course rotations. But even so, some institutions may allow selected topics courses to appear as often as courses that have their own numbers.[3] Edward White's WPA course at Arizona, for example, was originally offered in 2000 as a special topic in "Studies in Rhetoric and Composition." He has since taught the same course with the same number several times, most recently in the spring 2007 semester. Shirley Rose, too, has taught her WPA course multiple times.

But even if there is some inherent flexibility in selected topics courses and, perhaps, some ambiguity about the overall frequency with which they can be offered, the relatively small number of permanent WPA/WCA courses does signify a certain degree of ambivalence about their perceived importance to graduate study in rhetoric and composition. As Catherine Latterell (2003) points out, WPAs now tend to fall into one of two "camps" regarding graduate students and administrative work (p. 23). One camp maintains that administrative coursework and/or apprenticeship is a crucial component of graduate student training. Given the virtual inevitability of administrative work for rhetoric/composition PhDs, say the members of this camp, writing programs are ethically and professionally obligated to prepare students for their future job responsibilities. In the introduction to her 2007 collection, *Untenured Faculty as Writing Program Administrators*, co-editor Alice Horning asserts this point of view strongly, saying that "such training is absolutely necessary and truly helpful" to graduate students (p. 6).

Members of the opposing camp question this emphasis on administrative apprenticeships and coursework, "suggesting the practice be seen as part of a larger problem with the push to professionalize graduate study" (Latterell, 2003, p. 23). There is a clear danger, they say, that graduate stu-

---

[3]The requirements for selected topics courses will vary depending on the institution. At my home institution, Georgia Southern, a course is only allowed to run twice as a selected topic. After that, the course must either be significantly modified or proposed as a permanent course.

dent WPA/WCA appointments may send the wrong message to others in the academy (i.e., "WPA/WCA work requires no special skills or intellectual grounding; it can be performed adequately by disciplinary apprentices"), but administrative "job training" courses may be equally dangerous because they imply that curricula can (and should) be determined by market forces, a slippery slope that very few academics will wish to start sliding down. This uneasiness, coupled with the already stringent demands on graduate students to take existing courses in composition theory and research, is probably another reason why WPA/WCA courses do not appear more often and why they are offered only as special topics sections when they do.

THE FOCUS OF WPA AND WCA COURSES

To get a clearer sense of the diverse approaches and topics that are covered in these sixteen administrative courses, please refer to the charts in Figures 16.1 and 16.2.

WRITING PROGRAM ADMIN	UNIV.	DEG.	SEL TOP	FYC WKS	WC WKS	WAC WKS	TOPICS
Devitt 1997 "Writing Program Administration"	Univ. of Kansas	PhD	Y	2	1	1	Professional role Social contexts Literacy Feminism, Assessment "Nuts and bolts"
Howard 2002 "The WPA as *Negotiator*"	Syracuse	PhD	Y				Professional role Assessment *Curriculum design* Scholarship Research methods Social & political issues Ethics Grammar (local context)
McLeod 2005 "Theory and Practice of Writing Program Administration"	UCSB	PhD	Y		1		Professional role Assessment Staffing TA training Promotion & tenure Curriculum design Finances, Legal issues History

WRITING PROGRAM ADMIN	UNIV.	DEG.	SEL TOP	FYC WKS	WC WKS	WAC WKS	TOPICS
Rose 2005 "Writing Program Administration: WPA's Ways of Knowing"	Purdue	PhD	Y				Professional role Experiential, communal, narrative, research-based, theoretical, and contextual knowledge
Kelly-Riley 2006 "Administering a Writing Program"	WSU	PhD	N	2	2	2	Professional role "supervised internship" Assessment Finances
Roen 2007 "Writing Program" Administration	ASU	PhD	Y	1	0.5	1	Professional role Curriculum design Promotion & tenure Assessment Legal issues & ethics Placement Staffing Technology Finances TA training
White 2007 "Writing Program Administration"	Univ. of Ariz.	PhD	Y	2	0.5	0.5	Professional role Finances Assessment Technology Scholarship Social & political issues
Balester 2007 "Composition Theory, Pedagogy, & Administration"	Texas A&M	PhD	N	1	2	1	Professional role Scholarship WID Composition theory Afr-Amer literacies Assessment
Neal 2008 "Designing Writing"	FSU	PhD.	Y	4	4	4	Program design Technology Placement Ethics TA training

FIGURE 16.1. Courses in Writing Program Administration

The division in these charts between writing program administration (WPA) and writing center administration (WCA) courses reflects the particular focus attributable to each course syllabus. (I received no syllabi for any courses in WAC administration in response to my request; only Gannett's course devotes class time explicitly to issues in WAC administration.) With two exceptions (Howard and Rose, which I discuss later), seven courses treat WPA as a professional career with multiple possible paths, including first-year composition (FYC), writing centers (WC), and writing across the curriculum (WAC).[4] Six of these courses identify themselves explicitly as "Writing Program Administration" classes, and Michael Neal's "Designing Writing" syllabus, approaching WPA work from multiple perspectives rather than a single programmatic point of view, seems to fit in this category as well. Columns five through seven detail the number of weeks each syllabus devotes explicitly to administrative issues in each of the three programs, but it's probably fair to say that these numbers do not reflect the actual amount of attention given to each program during the course of a semester with 100 percent accuracy. For example, though McLeod's syllabus does not indicate that any single week will be devoted to administrative issues in first-year composition, class meetings that discuss TA training, contingent faculty, and curriculum design will almost certainly approach these matters from the point of view of an FYC administrator.

Two of the WPA courses, Rebecca Howard's 2002 course, "The WPA as Negotiator," and Shirley Rose's 2005 course, "Writing Program Administration: WPA's Ways of Knowing," as I noted earlier, take a somewhat different approach to administrative training than the other WPA courses listed here. Rather than approaching the course as a kind of survey, in which students learn about several distinct administrative roles in university writing programs, Howard and Rose teach administration by immersion, getting students to think and act as if they were actual WPAs confronting a specific programmatic problem or issue.

The second set of syllabi, outlined in Figure 16.2, includes seven courses that focus primarily, or at least substantially, on writing center administration. Several of these courses identify themselves as purely "Writing Center Administration" courses, while others fold topics such as history, theory, and pedagogical practice into their titles. (Even the "pure" WCA courses, it should be noted, focus on topics other than administration, as can be seen from the chart.) Like their WPA counterparts, these WCA courses address administrative issues linked to FYC and WAC programs, but they

---

[4]From this point in the chapter onward, the term "WPA courses" will refer specifically to those courses that either identify themselves as "writing program administration" courses or explore writing program administration from multiple administrative perspectives.

do so from a somewhat different perspective. Rather than familiarizing students with the administrative matters that directors of FYC or WAC programs might need to confront, these courses attend more to the administrative connections and possible frictions that the writing center might need to confront.

WRITING CENTER ADMIN	UNIV.	DEG.	SEL TOP	FYC	WC	WAC	TOPICS
Bergmann 2006 "Writing Center Administration"	Purdue	PhD	Y	1	4	1	History Assessment Research methods Technology Cultural diversity Program design Tutor training Reporting lines Staffing
Gannett 1999 "Writing Across the Curriculum and Writing Centers: History, Theory, and Practice"	UNH	PhD	Y		2	4	History WC/WAC connections Research methods Curriculum WC/WAC theory Technology Local contexts Service learning Program development Assessment
Law 1998 "The Study of Writing: Writing Center Theory and Practice"	Wright State	MA	Y		1		History WC Theory Conceptualizing Administration
Smith 2005 "Writing Centers: Theory, History, and Practice"	MTSU	MA	N		3**	2	History Theory Tutoring strategies Ethics Cultural diversity Technology Reporting lines
Jackson 2007 "Writing Center Theory, Practice, and Administration"	TSU	MA	Y	1	2	1	History Theory Tutoring strategies Ethics

WRITING CENTER ADMIN	UNIV.	DEG.	SEL TOP	FYC	WC	WAC	TOPICS
Jackson 2007							Cultural diversity
							Assessment
							Technology
							Reporting lines
							Professional role
Stanley 2008 "Writing Center Administration"	NSU	MA	N		5	1	History
							Reporting lines
							WC theory
							Program design
							Tutor training
							Cultural diversity
							Technology
Diepenbrock 2008 (summer) "Writing Center Theory and Administration"	UHCL	MA	Y	0.5	5		History
							WC theory
							Staffing
							Reporting lines
							Assessment
							Finances
							Physical design
							Tutor training

FIGURE 16.2. Courses in Writing Center Administration

COMPARING WPA AND WCA COURSES

Even a quick perusal of the charts—particularly the "Topics" course content category—reveals that WPA and WCA courses have a lot in common. Because writing centers and first-year composition programs are generally situated in academic institutions, the directors of both programs will have to face similar problems, similar constraints, and similar institutional issues that affect their daily operations. All writing program administrators, for example, will have to deal with staffing—who to hire, how to hire, when to hire, how much to pay—so it's no surprise that nearly all of the syllabi in both categories address these issues to some extent. Most syllabi also recognize that program assessment is an important part of any WPA's or WCA's job, so a week or two is usually set aside for examining assessment research and data collection strategies. WPA and WCA courses both talk about finances, funding, and budgets; they study the effects that technology has had and will continue to have on writing programs (including hardware and software purchases, computer labs, and online writing centers); and they frequently wrestle with ethical concerns that will impact not only the decisions they make as program directors but their future relationships with students, faculty, and upper administration. Teacher training, too, is a shared concern in WPA and WCA syllabi, though WPA courses tend to focus on training graduate TAs to be first-year composition instructors and WCA courses focus on training undergraduate peer tutors to work in writing centers.

More revealing, though, are the *differences* between WPA and WCA courses. One topic that routinely appears in the first few weeks of nearly every WPA course, for example, is how to define and understand what it *means* to be a writing program administrator. In Sue McLeod's syllabus, the topic for the second week of class is, "Who are you as a WPA?"; in Diane Kelly-Riley's, the second and third weeks consider "The role of the WPA"; and in Ed White's, the question for the first week is, "What is a composition program and what is a WPA?" To some extent, the prominence (and prevalence) of this topic in WPA courses reflects the survey approach that many such courses take. There are several "flavors" of WPA, and it could be useful for graduate students as future job-seekers to understand, right at the start, how those flavors might appear in different institutions with different sizes, populations, missions, and funding levels. But it's equally likely that WPA courses want students to start thinking of themselves as future administrative professionals right away. The shift in perspective this entails—from student to faculty, from employee to employer, from novice to expert—will not be an easy thing for most graduate students to achieve partly because of their inexperience and partly because the critical dimensions of this new frame of reference are completely unfamiliar to them. Ed White (2002) observed this phenomenon the first time he taught his WPA course in 2000 (without first asking the "What is a WPA?" question):

> ... [the students'] total lack of experience led to much distortion of the material because the students—excellent advanced PhD students to be sure—had to construct the issues and problems we were dealing with from their reading, their imaginations, their slight sense of administration in their undergraduate colleges, and their graduate experience at the University of Arizona, hardly a typical academic environment. (p. 102)

As the chart shows, most WPA courses (including the updated version of White's course) now try to address this inexperience at the start of the term and get students to think seriously about the new contexts they will be entering in their future professional lives.

WCA courses, by contrast, do not generally ask students to re-envision themselves as administrative professionals or as members of a larger discourse community. No syllabi ask them, "Who are you as a WCA?", and only one syllabus (Stanley's) asks them to "Develop a Philosophy for Effective Operation" in the fifth week. While five of the seven WPA courses surveyed require students to lurk regularly on the professional listserv WPA-L, only one of the seven WCA courses asks students to join WCenter and familiarize themselves with the conversations, issues, and activities that take place within the discipline. The obvious question arises: why should this be so? Is it a discomforting oversight or, worse, do course instructors believe writing center administrators are less likely than other WPAs to *need* professional enculturation?

One reason for the omission may be purely pragmatic: there's too much material to cover in WCA courses and not enough time in the semester. As noted earlier, few courses in writing center administration focus on administrative concerns alone; writing center theory, history, pedagogy, and other areas of disciplinary study often make up a large part of course content, limiting what can be covered in the few weeks dedicated solely to administrative duties.

Another explanation—and one that's probably a bit closer to the truth—is that WCA courses use the study of writing center history to inculcate a sense of professional identity in graduate students. By tracing the origins, development, and evolution of writing centers from "skills laboratories" into their present process and post-process forms, instructors perhaps expect that students will begin to develop a sense of their own administrative and pedagogical identities both in relation to and in contrast with the theories and approaches that have come before.

A third and perhaps more provocative reason why WCA courses don't generally focus on the development of a professional "persona" is because many of the people taking these courses *already* think of themselves as writing center professionals. A quick glance at column three of the chart ("Deg.") reveals that while all seven of the courses in the WPA category are offered at institutions with composition programs that award PhDs, nearly all of the WCA courses (with two exceptions) are offered in graduate programs that offer only terminal master's degrees. This distinction makes a certain amount of sense. PhD students in composition are most often training to become academics, though they will probably not know, right up until the time they accept a position, where they will teach or what their administrative duties might be. For this reason, they will benefit most from a course that exposes them to all the administrative possibilities they will have to face.

For graduate students in MA programs, these circumstances—and these needs—may be quite different. Chloe Diepenbrock (2008), reflecting on her course at UHCL, remarks that "many of the students who took [her] course in writing center administration were new directors of writing centers at local community colleges or graduate students who had already held administrative positions in [her] writing center." They were not inexperienced administrators searching for personal management philosophies; they tended to be career teachers who had been in their school systems for many years, did not want to pursue graduate study past a master's degree, and were taking the course for professional development reasons, to learn how to do the jobs they already had more knowledgeably and effectively. The demographic in Diepenbrock's class is also consistent with Balester and McDonald's survey of WPA and WCA professionals, which found that 81 percent of the WPAs held PhDs, whereas only 53 percent of the WCAs had doctoral degrees (p. 63).[5]

Several other topics covered in WPA courses are absent from WCA syllabi as well. Curriculum design does not appear, no doubt because while WPAs are often responsible for planning, structuring, and mentoring teachers in first year composition programs, WCAs are rarely expected to design and oversee similar large-scale, multi-section courses to meet university writing and literacy requirements. WPA courses also allot class time to discussions of political, social, and legal issues that impact first-year and other writing programs, including (but not limited to) confidentiality, discrimination, gender, affirmative action, intellectual property, and academic honesty. WCA courses do not explicitly address most of these concerns in their syllabi, though it would be difficult to imagine a WCA course that did not include attention to topics such as confidentiality, gender, and ethnicity in a writing center setting.

A final set of topics common to many WPA courses but not found in WCA syllabi is career-focused: scholarship, promotion, and tenure. In keeping with the way most WPA courses begin—by asking students to think of themselves as WPA professionals—they often end by asking students to consider how their administrative activities will contribute to their scholarly output, their publication records, and eventually the cases they make to promotion and tenure committees about the scholarship of writing program administration.[6] WCA courses, on the other hand, do not typically ask stu-

---

[5]The Writing Center Research Project's 2005 survey of writing center directors indicates that the number of writing center directors with master's degrees may, in fact, be increasing. Only 49 percent of WCAs responding to their survey said they held PhDs, whereas 44 percent had master's degrees (Griffin, Keller, Pandey, Pedersen, & Skinner, 2005, Table 8).

[6]Richard Gebhardt (2007), interestingly, sees this as a hidden benefit of hiring untenured faculty to be WPAs. Because they will *have* to justify their administrative work in scholarly terms when applying for promotion and/or tenure, "their work— and their successful tenure reviews—can help challenge traditional ideas of faculty work and expand departmental understanding of rhetoric and composition and of writing program administration as a venue for teaching and scholarship" (p. 21).

dents to think about these professional concerns perhaps because a high proportion of writing center directors (58.6 percent according to the 2004
WCRP survey) will find themselves in non-tenure track positions (Griffin,
Keller, Pandey, Pedersen, & Skinner, 2005, Table 11), where research and
publication are not formal requirements for continuing employment.

Courses in writing center administration also address topics that are
overlooked or slighted in WPA courses. Disciplinary history, as mentioned
earlier, is one, providing students with a diachronic context for the scholarly, political, institutional, and professional milieu in which WCAs must
work. This focus on history, institutional placement, and professional status
in an academic hierarchy is frequently emphasized in other parts of WCA
courses as well. All WCA syllabi, for example, devote time to a consideration of reporting lines — where the writing center is placed in administrative
flow charts, how many different "masters" writing centers must often report
to (chairs, deans, provosts, faculty committees, etc.), and how to work har-
moniously with first-year writing programs, WAC programs, ESL programs, and the like. The ubiquitous presence of this topic in syllabi is almost
certainly linked to the study of writing center history earlier in the term, a
history replete with horror stories of poorly funded centers and capricious
administrators who have, without warning, eliminated writing centers with
a quick slash of the budget pen. Understanding reporting lines and honing
negotiation skills have become critical survival strategies for most WCAs.[7]

One other course topic that appears regularly in WCA syllabi, though
not, strictly speaking, an administrative issue, is cultural and linguistic diversity. WCA courses generally ask graduate students to consider how writing
centers and, by implication, the tutors who will be trained to work there
should deal with non-standard dialects, culturally inflected rhetorical strategies, and non-native speakers of English. In some ways, it's surprising that
none of the WPA courses considers the subject; the student populations that
frequent the writing center are certainly no different from the populations
that enroll in first-year writing classes or writing-intensive WAC courses.
Questions about standardization, discrimination, assessment, and "students'
right to their own language" are as central to FYC and WAC as they are to
writing centers. It's possible, though, that writing center administrators feel
compelled to attend to diversity issues more often and with more urgency
than other WPAs. Though writing centers have long tried to overcome the
stigma of being "remedial," it's nonetheless true that a great many students
who come to writing centers do so because their writing does not yet conform to the conventions of SAWE.

---

[7]Though WPAs, too, may benefit from these strategies, the typical WPA's status (faculty, tenure-track) and the sanctity of first-year writing and/or WAC programs (frequently part of the core curriculum or a university-wide requirement for graduation)
makes WPAs somewhat less vulnerable, professionally, than the typical WCA.

CONCLUSIONS AND REFLECTIONS

It's clear that the situation today, in terms of course offerings in writing program and writing center administration, is far better than it was in 1993. The sixteen courses reviewed here suggest that a growing number of programs believe these administrative courses fulfill a critical need in their students' curriculum, but they also suggest that that belief is only halfhearted. Only four of these sixteen courses have permanent places in a course catalogue; the rest are offered solely under "special topic" designations. Overall, more WPA courses (nine) have been offered than WCA courses (seven), and while all of the WPA courses were taught in PhD-granting institutions, a majority of the WCA courses (five of seven) were taught in universities with a terminal MA degree.

Despite the multiple differences I have catalogued here between WPA and WCA courses—differences that are, I believe, reflections of institutional demographics as well as the employment profiles of writing program and writing center directors—the syllabi in all these courses demonstrate that students are taught, to a greater or lesser degree, to see administrative work as a complex process that takes place within an intricate web of institutional relationships. WCAs and WPAs are responsible to and intimately connected with a host of other programs, units, departments, and people on their campuses; they must understand how these programs operate and know how to achieve their own goals through negotiation and an informed sense of diplomacy. The greater a WPA/WCA course's success at instilling this perspective and providing these skills, the better prepared and more successful the program's graduates are likely to be, whether they are hired to direct a large, well-established writing center in a Research One university or to create a new first-year writing curriculum in a small, private college.

Still, I have to admit, it's somewhat disappointing to find that today, more than fifteen years after sharing my original "Tale Too Terrible to Tell," courses in writing program administration (of whatever flavor) are still not treated as the vital parts of graduate curricula in rhetoric and composition that they should be. They are offered in only a small percentage of existing programs, usually as selected topics courses, and with questionable frequency. Though the tale has a somewhat happier ending now—I actually did find a few WPA and WCA courses this time—it's a bittersweet ending nonetheless. I had hoped to see far more progress and far more permanent courses appearing in far more rhetoric and composition programs by now. Still, optimist that I am, I'm looking forward to the time, fifteen years from today, when I can revisit this chapter once more and report that the "Terrible Tale" has finally become a tale with a happy ending.

REFERENCES

Balester, V., & McDonald, J. C. (2001, Spring). A view of status and working conditions: Relations between writing program and writing center directors. *WPA: Writing Program Administration, 24*(3), 58–82.

Diepenbrock, C. (2008, July 18). Personal interview.

Gebhardt, R. C. (2007). The importance of untenured writing administrators to composition and to English studies. In D. F. Dew & A. Horning (Eds.), *Untenured faculty as writing program administrators: Institutional practices and politics* (pp. 15–39). West Lafayette, IN: Parlor Press.

Griffin, J.A., Keller, D., Pandey, I., Pedersen, A., & Skinner, C. (2005). Table 8: Comparison of two surveys' reports of writing center director degree. *Writing centers research project.* Retrieved from http://coldfusion.louisville.edu/webs/a-s/wcrp/reports/analysis/WCRPSurvey03-04.html#Table_8:_

Griffin, J.A., Keller, D., Pandey, I., Pedersen, A, & Skinner, C. (2005). Table 11: Percentage of time in writing center and employment category. *Writing centers research project.* Retrieved from http://coldfusion.louisville.edu/webs/a-s/wcrp/reports/analysis/WCRPSurvey03-04.html#Table_11:

Horning, A. (2007). Introduction: What is wrong with THIS picture? In D. F. Dew & A. Horning (Eds.), *Untenured faculty as writing program administrators: Institutional practices and politics* (pp. 3–12). West Lafayette, IN: Parlor Press.

Jackson, R., Leverenz, C., & Law, J. (2003). (RE)shaping the profession: Graduate courses in writing center theory, practice, and administration. In M. A. Pemberton & J. Kinkead (Eds.), *The center will hold: Critical perspectives on writing center scholarship* (pp. 130–150). Logan: Utah State University Press.

Latterell, C. (Fall/Winter 2003). Defining roles for graduate students in writing program administration: Balancing pragmatic needs with a postmodern ethics of action. *WPA: Writing Program Administration, 27*(1/2), 23–39.

Pemberton, M. A. (1993). Tales too terrible to tell: Unstated truths and underpreparation in graduate composition programs. In S. I. Fontaine & S. Hunter (Eds.), *Writing ourselves into the story: Unheard voices from composition studies* (pp. 154–173). Carbondale: Southern Illinois University Press.

Stygall, G. (2000). At the century's end: The job market in rhetoric and composition. *Rhetoric Review, 18*(2), 375–389.

Thomas, T. (1991, Spring). The graduate student as apprentice WPA: Experiencing the future. *Writing Program Administration, 14*(3), 41–51.

White, E. M. (2002). Teaching a graduate course in writing program administration. In S. C. Brown & T. Enos (Eds.), *The writing program administrator's resource: A guide to reflective institutional practice* (pp. 101–112). Mahwah, NJ: Lawrence Erlbaum Associates.

White, E. M. (2007). Preface. In D. F. Dew & A. Horning (Eds.), *Untenured faculty as writing program administrators: Institutional practices and politics* (pp. viii–ix). West Lafayette, IN: Parlor Press.

AUTHOR INDEX

SUBJECT INDEX

CPSIA information can be obtained at www.ICGtesting.com
Printed in the USA
BVOW02s1550150813

328382BV00002B/73/P